Asian Nationalism
in the Twentieth Century

By the same author

A HISTORY OF MALAYA

Asian Nationalism
in the
Twentieth Century

J. KENNEDY, M.A.

Principal Lecturer
and Head of the Department of History
Madeley College of Education, Staffordshire

MACMILLAN
London · Melbourne · Toronto
ST MARTIN'S PRESS
New York
1968

Published by
MACMILLAN & CO LTD
Little Essex Street London W C2
and also at Bombay Calcutta and Madras
Macmillan South Africa (Publishers) Pty Ltd Johannesburg
The Macmillan Company of Australia Pty Ltd Melbourne
The Macmillan Company of Canada Ltd Toronto
St Martin's Press Inc New York

Library of Congress catalog card no. 68–19079

Printed in Great Britain by
ROBERT MACLEHOSE AND CO LTD
The University Press, Glasgow

Contents

Plates

Preface

This book attempts within a concise framework to survey, analyse and illustrate the growth and nature of twentieth-century nationalism in Asia.

Asia is a wide and varied continent and, even in selective treatment, it is not easily captured within the covers of one book. Regions which are fundamental to a study of Asian nationalism are, however, all at least touched upon here and, for this purpose, the Arab, Jewish and Turkish areas are defined as western Asia. The author's own particular interests give a little extra weighting to the Indian subcontinent and South-East Asia, but China and Japan are also treated in their own right.

The Source Readings have been chosen in the main from the writings and speeches of Asian leaders or from the impressions of contemporary observers. They relate closely to the general survey but specific cross-references have not been thought necessary since there is a manageable breakdown into regional groupings. Footnotes have also been avoided but it is hoped that the suggestions for Further Reading will offer, as a sample, an indication of the kinds of printed material available in English on this wide-ranging and important topic.

J. K.

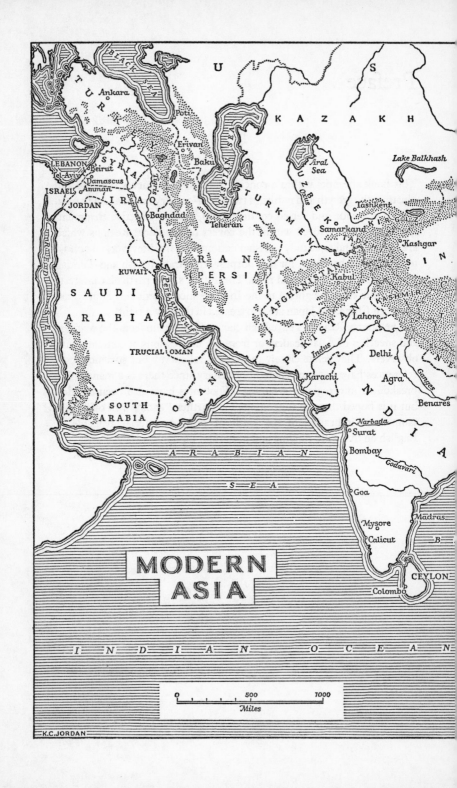

MODERN
ASIA

K.C.JORDAN

| | 500 | 1000 |
Miles

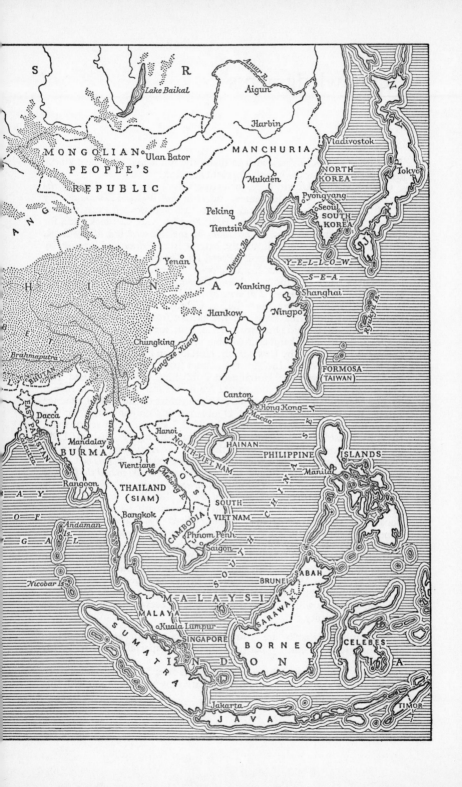

Acknowledgments

The author and publishers wish to thank the following, who have kindly given permission for the use of copyright material:

George Allen & Unwin Ltd., for extracts from *The Rise and Fall of the Japanese Empire*, by D. H. James, and *Asia and Western Dominance*, by K. M. Pannikar; George Allen & Unwin Ltd. and Beacon Press, for the extract from *Mahatma Gandhi*, by B. R. Nanda; A. & C. Black Ltd., for the extract from *The Invasion of China by the Western World*, by E. R. Hughes; Curtis Brown Ltd., for the extract from *Prince and Premier*, by H. Miller; Cambridge University Press, for *The Boxer Uprising 1900*, by V. Purcell, and the extract from *Colonial Policy and Practice*, by J. S. Furnivall; Chatto & Windus Ltd. and Frederick A. Praeger Inc., for the extract from *The Changing Patterns of the Middle East, 1919–1957*, by P. Rondot, translated by Mary Dilke; Chatto & Windus Ltd. and the University of California Press, for the extract from *Divide and Quit*, by Penderel Moon; Gerald Duckworth & Co. Ltd., for the extract from *Japan in China*, by W. H. Chamberlin; Robert Hale Ltd., for the extract from *Land of the Dragonfly*, by Lewis Bush; Hutchinson Publishing Group Ltd. and E. P. Dutton & Co. Inc., for the extract from *Japan and Her Destiny*, by Mamoru Shigemitsu; Hutchinson Publishing Group Ltd. and The Macmillan Company, for the extract from *Admiral Togo*, by G. Blond, © The Macmillan Company, 1960; the Executors of the T. E. Lawrence Estate, Jonathan Cape Ltd. and Doubleday & Company Inc., for the extract from *Seven Pillars of Wisdom*, by T. E. Lawrence, Copyright 1926, 1935, by Doubleday & Company Inc.; John Murray (Publishers) Ltd., for extracts from *Jinnah*, by H. Bolitho, and *The Awakening of Japan*, by Okakura-Kakuzo; Oxford University Press, for extracts from *The Chinese View of their Place in the World*, by C. P. Fitzgerald, *Mao and the Chinese Revolution*, by Jerome Ch'en, and *Nehru: A Political Biography*, by Michael Brecher; Oxford University Press, Bombay, for the extract from *A Nation in the Making*, by Sir Surendranath Banerjea; Premier Books, for the extract from *Vietnam*, edited by Marvin Gettleman; Simon & Schuster Inc., for the extract from *Ten Years in Japan*, by Joseph C. Grew, Copyright 1944 by Joseph C. Grew; The Society of Authors as the literary representative of Mr Christopher Dawson, for the extract from *The Revolt of Asia*; and *The Times*, for the extract from 'A Statement of Protestant Missionary Societies', from *The Times*, 24 August 1900.

In a few cases the publishers have been unable to trace the copyright-holders, but they will be pleased to make the necessary arrangements at the first opportunity.

The author's thanks are also due to the patient and considerate attention given to him by his publishers and especially by Mr T. M. Farmiloe.

Miss L. Timmis typed the manuscript with care.

The author's wife and family have endured his preoccupation with this work with great forbearance.   J. K.

Part One

Survey

1 Patterns of Nationalism

NATIONALISM IN THE WEST

NATIONALISM has been one of the great motivating factors of the
modern world yet it defies any precise definition. It is a concept in which
the loyalty and allegiance of the individual are held to be due primarily
to the nation-state. Put another way, it can be described as the desire of
a people to be united as a sovereign nation. Many writers on nationalism
have emphasised that it exists in the form of a state of mind or a general
will. Throughout history men have been moved by an attachment to
their native soil and to local traditions and conventions, but the nation-
state as we know it today is essentially a product of the modern era. Its
earliest developments may be traced in Western Europe from the
sixteenth and seventeenth centuries onwards, and especially from
the late eighteenth century. Subsequently, nationalism has spread,
sometimes gradually, sometimes quickly, through the five continents
of the world. It has been immensely significant in twentieth-century
Asia.

The painful evolution of an early nation-state was witnessed in
seventeenth-century England through a process of civil war, dictatorship
and constitutional monarchy. Among those who theorised on matters of
politics, John Locke (1632–1704) was pre-eminent in stressing the idea
of trust as between government and governed against a background of
individual liberties and responsibilities of citizenship. Although Locke
wrote only in the context of English politics, his ideas had a universality
and a breadth of interpretation which led them to influence European
political thought for several generations.

The beginnings of what may be called liberal and middle-class
English nationalism are thus evident in the early eighteenth century,
and the movement attracted the interest and enthusiasm of French
thinkers, notably Voltaire, who visited England between 1726 and 1729.
That England was somewhat idealised in French liberal writing at this
time does not detract from the importance of the spread of ideas in

which State and citizen became variously identified. Indeed, the cultural and intellectual leadership of France in eighteenth-century Europe ensured the wide dissemination of French versions of the desirable political society.

France awaited the upheavals of the Revolution of 1789 and its after-math before seriously establishing the new nationalism, but already by this time a new nation had come into being on the west side of the Atlantic. The creation of the United States of America in 1775 was made possible by the political legacies of seventeenth-century England and the political aspirations of eighteenth-century France. It was also in part due to the increasing identity of interests among the new Americans themselves. The fact that America became a modern nation by means of revolution against the 'mother country' has been closely connected with the growth of an anti-colonial attitude in America towards other empires. This was not, however, strong enough to prevent an imperialist element in America's own history. Conversely, the American Revolution and its consequences quickened the development of a Canadian nation and inspired the opponents of the *ancien régime* in France. The American Constitution became effective in the same year as the French Revolution.

In France, the liberalism of Voltaire was followed by the political idealism of Rousseau, whose *Social Contract* (1762) envisaged a com-munity capable of giving expression to a 'general will'. To many French minds the young American nation embodied the sense of community and many of the simple virtues which Rousseau idealised. In the event the new nationalism of France was to have an extremely complex and stormy infancy. Administrative measures helped to centralise the machinery of government, and particularisms in church and society were severely attacked. Citizenship was much invoked, the classical languages were rated of less value than French, there were patriotic songs and speeches, and papal enclaves within France chose, by plebiscite, to become parts of France. The fatherland became, officially, the symbol for the aspirations and sacrifices of the French people. The new nationalism ushered in a comprehensive system of national educa-tion with patriotic citizenship as one of its major aims; national festivals were planned and the first national museum was established in the Louvre in Paris.

In all these dynamic activities the course of later nationalisms in other countries and other parts of the world was foreshadowed. Before the end of the eighteenth century, French nationalism had become both intolerant and aggressive; the earlier despotism of kings had given way to the despotism of virtuous men, the true citizens of the fatherland. This development was greatly accelerated as the new French nation faced insurrections on the home front and invading armies on the frontiers. The army became the defender of the nation and, through the army, France came to have the personal dictatorship of a Napoleon.

Napoleon was hardly a nationalist but in his hey-day the collective power of the nation-state was demonstrated. French institutions were unified further and some of the French progress, notably in the spheres of law and administration, was passed on to conquered territories. The spirit of France which reached Germany, Italy, the Low Countries, Spain and Russia, was more one of efficient organisation and power politics than of liberal nationalism but new political horizons became just visible in these countries. French patriotic nationalism had its opposing counterparts in the Peninsular War, in the Russia of 1812, at Leipzig and at Waterloo.

Yet for most of Europe the end of the Napoleonic era was not followed by the creation of new nation-states. The Congress of Vienna did not take national self-determination as its guiding principle, though a few interesting experiments were made. An autonomous kingdom of Poland was revived, the former Austrian Netherlands (Belgium) joined Holland to become the Kingdom of the Netherlands, a new federal Germany was created and Norway was disengaged from Denmark and linked to Sweden but under its own national constitution. There was little here, however, to satisfy nationalist inspirations in Western Europe as a whole. Conservative monarchies remained the main feature of the political landscape and Prince Metternich, the Austrian Chancellor, symbolised the spirit of order rather than that of change, while the German federation remained more theoretical than real. Italy was as politically divided as ever and the French had their own political adjustments to make in relation to the new order.

For several years after 1815 continental nationalism in Europe was centred mainly in minority groups of mixed backgrounds. Many of the nationalists were young men, many were intellectuals; some were poets, some were dreamers, others were born revolutionaries. In most countries such nationalist groupings were considered by the authorities to be subversive and this resulted in their becoming, in effect, secret societies, biding their time and taking a sympathetic interest in similar organisations in countries other than their own. Revolution rather than diplomacy seemed to offer them the means of success. Political exile or imprisonment in his own country was a feature in the career of the typical nineteenth-century European nationalist, and this pattern was to be repeated in the story of twentieth-century nationalism in Asia.

A number of dates stand out significantly in the European setting of nationalism in the first half of the nineteenth century. In 1821, the Greeks organised a successful rising against Turkish rule. This was a movement which evoked considerable liberal sympathy in Western Europe and for many people modern Greece was identified with classical Greece. The Greek cause was one for which the English Lord Byron could give his support and his life, and Greek independence was won by means of substantial foreign aid. The Greeks in rebelling against a foreign yoke for their own national identity gave a political lesson which was not lost upon other nationalist elements in Europe, and particularly those who formed minority groupings within the Turkish and Austrian empires. Meanwhile, South American nationalism, again with foreign aid, had been busily overthrowing the rule of Spain.

In 1830, a series of political revolutions swept across Europe in a chain reaction. Two of these met with success. In Belgium, the uprising resulted in the separation of Belgium from Holland and the recognition of Belgian independence by the European powers. In France, the Bourbon monarchy was overthrown and a constitutional king (or citizen-king) Louis-Philippe was proclaimed. In other parts of Europe, however, including Italy, Poland and Germany, the risings were quickly suppressed and Switzerland and England became places of refuge for political rebels in exile. Among these exiles, Giuseppe Mazzini (1805-72) had a significance which went well beyond his own Italian boundaries. He appealed emotionally to the glories of Italian history and the place of Rome in Europe. He called for support from the young and asked for sacrifices in the interest of a united Italian nation. His Young Italy movement served as a model for similar organisations in other European countries, and the 'Young' description was used later in nationalist circles as widespread as Turkey, India and China.

In 1848 Europe experienced a second phase of revolutionary risings. Once again, France, or more particularly Paris, overthrew a king and established a republican government. Northern Italians from Milan and Venice rebelled against Austrian rule. A revolution in Berlin aspired to establish a constitutional monarchy for Prussia and to bring the German lands into close association with each other. In central Europe, the Magyars of Hungary initiated a strong nationalist movement in defiance of the Habsburg Empire and there were other nationalist stirrings among Poles and Ukranians, Czechs, Croats, and Rumanians. The existing political order was thus widely challenged in mid-nineteenth-century Europe and poets, journalists and teachers helped to create the nationalist climate of the new era. National languages and literature were recalled or re-created, historical or pseudo-historical traditions and political boundaries were proclaimed and fierce passions aroused. Lajos Kossuth (1802–94), Magyar leader in Hungary was, significantly, a newspaper editor and his professional career provides a good example of the part played by the Press in a nationalist cause.

There was much idealism among the European rebels and nationalists in 1848, which was also the year of the *Communist Manifesto*. Kossuth was not untypical of the nationalists who lived under alien rule and demanded constitutional reform, political liberties and national independence. The revolutionary movements, however, quickly died out or were overthrown. Their leadership did not always match their patriotism; the professional soldiers and statesmen of the old regimes reacted with considerable skill once the first impact was over.

Foreign aid, from Russia for example, in the case of the Austrian Empire, was sometimes called upon to repress rebellion. So far as nationalism was concerned the most significant factor was the great hostility of the new nationalities towards each other. The attempt by the Magyars, for instance, to represent a new Hungary was bitterly resented by Slovaks, Croats, Serbs and others, while German and Polish viewpoints came into collision over territorial boundaries between the two national identities. The failure of the new movements of 1848 in eastern and central Europe was in no small part due to severe conflict between the very nationalities which had inspired them.

Though there was much publicity about liberties and constitutions the new nationalisms had an intolerant and aggressive aspect which tended to increase as soon as some measure of power or success was gained. Violence and highly emotional patriotisms came to suppress the more liberal springs of rebellion and to place a new emphasis on power politics in the nationalist cause. To some extent this was true even in France where the new republic was overthrown by popular support for a new emperor who carried the name of Napoleon.

European nationalism in the second half of the nineteenth century is less a story of popular or spontaneous movements than one of government diplomacy and war. The drama centred more on the courts and the generals than on the popular following, and political theories tended to support the case for the powerful state. Even the romantic episode of

Garibaldi and his Red Shirts in southern Italy was capped by the diplomacy of a Cavour who then proceeded to hold plebiscites to justify the cause of Italian unification. There were signs already that nationalism had passed from the 'folk' stage to that of the nation-state and was launched into a third phase of expansionism.

In Germany, the influence of the rationalist philosopher, Georg Hegel (1770–1831) was highly significant to the growth of the idea of a German nation. For Hegel, the State was 'the Divine Idea as it exists on Earth' and true morality was based upon fulfilling one's duties towards it. Later German historians found evidence to support Hegel's concept of the all-demanding State in the pattern of events as Bismarck's Prussia transformed itself by war and diplomacy into the nucleus of the new Germany. Power, prestige and resources were the symbols of the enlarged national outlook. While Bismarck was not attracted by extreme theories of pan-Germanism, the annexation of Alsace-Lorraine from France in 1871 was based, in part, on the idea of bringing Germans back into their natural political homeland, and it took little account of the views of the population concerned. Conversely, it had the effect of arousing the strongest nationalist passions in France for the recovery of the lost territories.

As the process of unification proceeded in Germany and Italy, the Russian Empire was steadily expanding, often at the expense of other national claims. Poles and Ukrainians, Baltic Germans and Finns all felt the pressures of Russian policies which had little sympathy with ideas of self-determination on the part of the peoples within Greater Russia. Polish nationalism was remarkable for its spread through society and its persistence in the face of political domination, accompanied often by cultural oppression. One direction of Russian expansion was towards the Danube lands of the Turkish Ottoman Empire, and a Russian occupation of two principalities in this region was one of the causes of the Crimean War (1853–6) in which France and Britain supported Turkey against Russia. As a delayed outcome of the war, and to a large degree through French influence, the Turkish principalities of Moldavia and Wallachia became first united in 1859 and they were eventually internationally recognised in 1878 as the independent kingdom of Rumania.

The decade between 1860 and 1870 was a crucial period for the evolution in Europe of a new Italy and a new Germany; it was also the age of the American Civil War. The eighteenth-century revolution which had created the federation of the United States of America from the thirteen early colonies was fundamentally challenged by the deep division between north and south. The rights of self-determination and the liberties of individual states were claimed in the south, in opposition to the demand by the north for the essential unity of the federal republic. Different social and economic patterns in the American states caused loyalties to be sharply divided and led to four years of bitter and costly warfare after which the wounds to national unity were healed only very slowly.

In a brief outline it is not possible even to touch on all aspects of modern nationalism in the West before the twentieth century. Scattered national groupings which overlapped political boundaries were sometimes made the subject of wide ethnic-type nationalism. Italian nationalists who sought union with their fellows in non-Italian territories spoke of *terra irredenta*, or land waiting to be redeemed in the nationalist cause. Although pan-Germanism never got out of hand while Bismarck was in control, it flourished after his day, demanding *Lebensraum*, and colonies and, ultimately, union with Austrian and Sudeten Germans. Pan-Slavism was another of the wider movements, highly emotional at times, extremely complex and frequently divided within itself.

Biological nationalism is a term which has been applied to ideas associated with ties of 'blood' and 'purity' of race. Its firmest roots were struck in Germany well before the end of the nineteenth century, but its outright application awaited the coming of a Hitler. The hypothesis of a superior Nordic race implied the existence of inferior races, different in kind, and European Jews became the main scapegoats and victims of this mode of thought, not only, though most terribly, in Germany. Resentment against the minority which is in any way 'different' has often been a basic cause of the more chauvinistic forms of nationalism. A sense of identity among European Jews, on the other hand, aided at times by forms of oppression and persecution, led, in 1897, to the formation of an international Zionist organisation which demanded a national homeland for Jews in Palestine.

Britain had resistance problems to contend with in the Union with Scotland and its aftermath in the eighteenth century, and in the relationships with Ireland through much of the nineteenth century. The student of modern Irish nationalism can gain a remarkable insight into the whole topic of independence movements. Among the Irish nationalists there were men of diplomacy, liberals working within a constitutional pattern, and out-and-out revolutionaries seeking quick results by violent means. Poets, novelists and playwrights contributed to a cultural renaissance, linguists sought to restore the Gaelic language, while others formed an association to revive the national games. The encouragement of local industries and proposed boycotting of foreign goods were rooted in Ireland before they were effectively proclaimed in India.

John Stuart Mill (1806–73) was one of the main intellectual protagonists of liberalism in nineteenth-century England, and his essay, *On Liberty* (1859) stressed the high importance which he attached to freedom of thought and expression. In this context he offered, in due course, much to inspire those who felt themselves to be politically oppressed, yet it is interesting to note that he also saw the illiberal side of nationalism and deplored the sentiment of nationality where it outweighed the love of liberty. In a sense, Britain had an outlet for her nationalism in empire-building. In the hey-day of British imperialism, towards the end of the nineteenth century, a strong sense of the mission of the British race was detectable, with Joseph Chamberlain one of its leading advocates. Britain's imperial obligations were linked with a national or racial fitness to meet them and the running of an empire was both a duty and a source of pride. Chamberlain did not, of course, speak for all Englishmen and the opposite view of eschewing overseas responsibilities was voiced by a school whom he regarded as 'Little Englanders'. Nationalism in the Dominions showed itself later.

The urge to extend the British Empire was by no means always a conscious one and evidence for the impact of nationalism on imperialism might be a little more readily seen in the case of France after the Franco-Prussian War of 1870–1. In this war, France had been deeply humiliated and territories had been taken from her. The French had already developed commercial and political interests in mainland South-East Asia but the attention given to this area (parts of the modern Vietnam, Cambodia and Laos, then known as French Indo-China) increased remarkably after 1871. The build-up of a French colonial empire in the East did much to restore French prestige at home, and French military successes in this sphere were compensations for the debacle of Sedan.

The Congress of Vienna in 1815 had made only minor concessions to nationalism, but the peace treaties after the First World War gave considerable priority to the right of political self-determination among the peoples of Europe. The 1914–18 war had been preceded by Balkan Wars (1912–13) which were in part nationalist seccession movements from the European sector of the Ottoman Turkish Empire and in part power struggles among the emerging Balkan States themselves. The immediate occasion for the outbreak of the major war was the mounting friction between Serbia and the Austrian Empire, and the assassination of an Austrian Archduke while on a visit to territories which nationalist Serbs regarded as 'unredeemed'.

Among the political arrangements made at the Conference of Paris (1919–20) the new states of central and south-eastern Europe emerged as a sign of the times. Their existence or expansion was in some measure due to a 'spoils of victory' programme and a version of the European balance of power concept, but it also responded to some of the demands for national status. New national boundaries were thus drawn in Europe in an age which witnessed the first experimental machinery for world order through the League of Nations. An enlarged Serbian and Croatian State became Yugoslavia; Poland and Rumania were further extended and Czechoslovakia was created for Czechs and Slovaks out of some of the provinces of the old Austrian Empire.

The new European States had plenty of problems to face. Where they had gained territory and populations at the expense of other countries they naturally appeared as possible sources of political grievance and resentment. More significantly still, within their own boundaries, were elements of plural societies which would need careful and sympathetic integration and perhaps a generation or two in time for this to be accomplished. In the event, only twenty years were to pass before military solutions were again attempted in Europe and elsewhere, and within this period new nationalisms based on ideology, power politics and military strength were prominent features of the European scene. Pan-Germanism was revived in a new and extremely aggressive form in National Socialist Germany, and Mussolini's Fascist regime in Italy proclaimed the coming of a third Rome in world affairs. The Union of Soviet Socialist Republics made concessions at first to the several nationalities which it encompassed, but increasingly pursued a Russian policy of centralisation and uniformity in a communist State. For at least three major European countries the supremacy of the State had become paramount in a way described by a new word, totalitarianism.

Meanwhile, Spain, one of the first nationally-unified territories of Europe, which had, however, always carried strong regional traditions, was the victim not only of a civil war but also of the ideologically-rooted interventions of other States. Nazi Germany regained the mandated Saar territory and proceeded to a union with Austria and an invasion of Czechoslovakia, the latter begun in the alleged interests of the Sudeten German minority. New republics set up in the Baltic area, and civil war in Ireland added, in the post-1919 years, to the ever-changing kaleidoscope of national politics in Europe. Tariff barriers and military defence zones helped to intensify the character of national interests on the European side of the Atlantic, while isolation from European issues became an underlying principle of American politics.

Long before the unfolding of these latter events in the West, the stirrings of modern nationalism were clearly evident in the lands of the East and especially in the regions of the older civilisations. There are very many links and many similarities between the nationalism of the West and the nationalism of Asia but it would be misleading to carry these comparisons too far. Asian nationalism needs to be studied in its own setting and in its own right and it is to the Asian scene that we now turn our attention.

ASIAN NATIONALISM AT THE TURN OF THE CENTURY

Nationalism has been a remarkable phenomenon of modern Asia. Its origins have varied from country to country and, in many cases, they go back at least several generations. It would be wrong to suppose that modern Asian nationalism is entirely a product of the twentieth century, since in many ways it was evident in the second half of the nineteenth century or earlier. Its main developments, however, have occurred since about the turn of the century.

Modern nationalism in Asia was, as in Europe, at first the concern only of individuals or small groups. Among these were poets, philosophers, journalists, lawyers and schoolteachers who, in the main, stood apart from the large mass of peasant peoples for whom they acted as unofficial spokesmen. The typical Asian villager was by tradition inclined to regard government as some mysterious and distant power outside his control, and his political horizons tended to be bounded by the small community within which he lived. The affairs of government were often more readily witnessed in the towns, especially in the larger ones, and this fact, together with the greater concentration in towns of the small but growing middle class of civil servants, merchants and professional men, gave an urban setting to many of the early nationalist organisations. Literacy, too, advanced more quickly in the towns than the countryside as educational facilities were more urban than rural, especially in the politically significant field of higher education.

Many writers have treated the growth of nationalism in Asia in terms of an Asian revolt against a West which, in the nineteenth century, had often shown itself to be superior in skills of political and commercial organisation, technical achievement and military and naval warfare. That there was such a revolt, that it helped to characterise movements which aimed to halt the further advance of Western control in some parts of Asia and, eventually, to remove it from others, cannot be denied. Yet the 'revolt' conception does not adequately cover the nature of Asian nationalism, for this was also a rediscovery or renaissance era in which Asians in various countries sought to find for themselves a new ethos, a new soul. Many nationalist speakers and writers appealed to historical episodes which antedated the impact of Europeans on Asia, and worked for a revival of the traditional virtues and accomplishments of an Asian society untarnished by the insidious effects of the West. Even this traditional or revivalist type of nationalism had its revolutionary aspects, however, for the new national Utopia was not envisaged as an exact replica of the old monarchical State and society. Gandhi's revival of the village textile industries in India, to take one example, had a very traditional look about it in the 1920s and 1930s, but his attempts to weaken the caste barriers of Hindu society and to share the grievances of Muslim Indians were, by the standards of Hindu orthodoxy, revolutionary in the extreme.

Asian nationalism both past and present can be seen to be full of complexities and paradoxes. A broad outline drawn on a regional basis will show something of the scope of the topic but must inevitably tend to fragment it. Events both within Asia and outside it produced nationalist responses which had, at times, the pattern of a chain reaction and, as in Europe, there could be organisational and emotional links between nationalists from different countries. Nor was Asia the only setting for the growth of Asian nationalism; major European centres including Paris, London and Moscow provided some of the background scenes. Japan, China and the Indian subcontinent are three major areas for a study of Asian nationalism, while South-East Asia and western Asia each provide both regional and localised characteristics. One interesting feature of the growth of nationalism was the concept of Asia itself from the standpoint of Asians. By the mid-twentieth century, the term 'we Asians' was commonplace; few would have thought of using it quite so readily fifty years earlier.

At the turn of the century there were early signs of a resurgence of Asia, the most dramatic of which was the victory by Japan over Russia in the Russo-Japanese War of 1904–5. Here, for all Asia to witness, was evidence enough that a process of modernisation efficiently carried out could enable an Asian country to meet and defeat a Western power in military and naval terms. China was already restless in a climate of Western concessions, treaty ports, judicial rights and evangelical activity. In 1899, the Boxer Rising occurred, an anti-Western, anti-Christian demonstration of great violence and emotion. Though the rising was suppressed, it was a clear pointer to the Western powers to act more circumspectly in China and it brought to an end any possible speculations about the division of China into a series of Western protectorates.

For India, too, the end of the nineteenth and beginning of the twentieth century was a formative period in the nationalist story. The Indian National Congress was established in 1885 but it had only very moderate growth in its early years. The Viceroyalty of Lord Curzon in British India (1899–1905), with its striking changes and reforms administered from 'the top', gave the Congress some very pointed issues to fight for, and promises by Britain of constitutional reform in India provided a further stimulus for party organisation and tactics. At the same time, the activities of the largely Hindu Congress brought to the fore the fears of Indian Muslims, some of whom felt there was a need for a political organisation which would specifically define and defend Muslim interests. Thus, in 1906, was born the All-India Muslim League and, from this date, followed a long and complex political evolution which led eventually to India and Pakistan.

Most of South-East Asia was under some form of Western political control before 1900. In mainland South-East Asia, the British had conquered and annexed Burma in a series of three nineteenth-century wars and the French had, by a combination of diplomacy and force, established colony and protectorate relationships in what was loosely known as French Indo-China. Malaya consisted of the British Straits Settlements of Penang, Malacca and Singapore, the Federated Malay States, subject to a large measure of British control, and the so-called Unfederated States with more autonomy, but linked by treaties to Britain. Only in the case of Siam was an independent South-East Asian State discernible, and only great diplomatic skill and restraint on the part of the Siamese had made this possible. Wedged between British Burma and French Indo-China, Siam lost some traditional territory but kept sovereign her central territories based on the Menam valley.

French territories in the region were mainly protectorates, governed, in theory, indirectly, but in practice very much on centralised lines in accordance with French colonial policy. When the impact of French nationalism on nineteenth-century Europe is recalled it is not difficult to envisage the response to French ideas and traditions which might be aroused in highly intelligent people like the Vietnamese. Among the Vietnamese was a middle class whose economic roots were in rice-plantations and money-lending, and political aspirations were likely to arise in this society. The influence of China from the north-east was also of great significance in the story of Vietnamese nationalism. The anti-Western tone of the Boxer Rising, and the Chinese Revolution of 1911 with its attempts to produce radical internal changes in the Chinese regime, were both lessons which were not wasted on Vietnam.

Two quite different responses to Western pressures in the nineteenth century can be seen in Burma and Siam. The Burmese monarchy had, in general, defied the penetration of the West through trade and other channels: Siamese kings and governments proved to be both more tolerant and more realistic. A reformed monarchy and a gradual intro-duction of Western institutions brought Siam fairly painlessly into the modern age and kept the country free from colonial rule. Meanwhile, the Burmese monarchy had been deposed and Burma was treated mainly as a further province of India. Burmese nationalism needed a generation or so in which to recover from the drastic political changes of the nineteenth century.

There were British spheres of interest in island South-East Asia, notably in the territories of Sarawak, Brunei and North Borneo on the island of Borneo, but the most widespread colonial empire was that of the Dutch. The Dutch had been established in the area for three centuries. It would be easy and wrong to exaggerate the importance of the Dutch impact in the earlier periods, but throughout the nineteenth century their political and economic control of the Malay archipelago was steadily increasing. In the late years of the century, Dutch military forces were engaged in a long struggle for the conquest of the Achinese of northern Sumatra, one of the many spirited groups of Malay peoples who did not take kindly to alien rule. At the turn of the century, the Netherlands East Indies was a vast island area, directly and indirectly controlled, stretching from northern Sumatra to western New Guinea. In Java, the political centre of the East Indies, Western-educated Javanese officials formed a political association in 1908 to train its members for social and educational leadership.

Meanwhile, in another part of the island world of South-East Asia, there had just been a change in colonial rule. In 1898 war broke out

between Spain and the United States and within a few months the
Spanish fleet had been destroyed in Manila Bay and American forces
had occupied Manila itself. By a treaty of 1899, the Spanish Philippines
were surrendered by Spain to the United States, which thus became a
South-East Asian power. Filipino nationalists had taken part in the
war against Spain, and the United States was to find nationalism a
problem which she also had to face, immediately, in the same area.

Portents for the future were also at hand in western Asia. As elsewhere, the first nationalist symptoms were displayed much earlier than
the twentieth century, and the Ottoman Turkish Empire, with territories both in Europe and in Asia, was gradually losing hold of its
western provinces. The victory of Japan over Russia had its repercussions
in Turkey, where two officers wrote a five-volume history of the Russo-
Japanese War, and in Persia, where, in 1906, the Shah was forced by a
revolutionary movement to agree to a new, liberal constitution. Two
years later, revolutionary officers in the Young Turk movement forced
the Sultan of Turkey to renew a parliamentary type of constitution which
had been introduced in 1876 and then quickly suppressed when it had
proved too active.

The Arab peoples had always maintained a strong sense of separate
identity, but as Muslim subjects of a Muslim (Turkish) Empire they
were less disposed to popular revolution than, say, the Christian Serbs
and Greeks in the same position. Some intellectuals among the Arabs
called for an Arab renaissance, but, in the main, the Arabs remained
faithful to the Ottoman Empire until it was defeated. As Turkish
nationalism began to be concerned more with Turks as such and less
with the Ottoman Empire or with Islam, Arab national feeling began
to grow among those who were Muslim but not Ottoman. Syrians were
prominent among those who called first for a separate Arab state with
an Arab ruler, and this type of political Arabism can be dated to about
the beginning of the twentieth century.

The early years of this new century can thus be seen as a time of
transition in Asia. The old political and social order was coming under
pressure in many countries from forces both within and outside their
boundaries. Japan had proved that modernisation and military strength
could pay rich dividends. China was in the last decade of three centuries
of Manchu emperors. In India, two major political organisations had
been created (not as yet with any great popular appeal) and the demand
of Congress was for self-government. The transfer of the Philippines to
the United States marked a time of adjustment in Filipino nationalism.

Among the Javanese new political associations were taking shape. Young Burmans, still children, were to be the nationalist leaders of the 1920s and 1930s, and among their contemporaries were young Vietnamese who were to see Europe in the First World War and return home with new aspirations for their own country.

Viewed from a later age, the signs of the new Asia were apparent in many places at the turn of the century. Where the old monarchies had not already been challenged or suppressed from outside, they came under increasingly critical scrutiny from within. Where alien rule prevailed, it could be seen here and there that this was not necessarily an inevitable or permanent state of affairs. Nationalism, it is true, was not yet based on large, popular organisations, and the era of the new-style independent Asian States was, for the most part, not immediately realisable. In the event, two World Wars had much to do with the pace of change. Yet enough signposts to the future in Asia could be discerned around 1900 to suggest that here is a point of departure from which to follow the main trends of nationalism until recent times.

2 The Course of Asian Nationalism: Japan, China and the Indian Subcontinent

JAPAN

IN the course of only fifty years, the Japanese had progressed from staring with wonder and curiosity at the famous 'black ships' of the American Commodore Perry in Tokyo Bay (1853) to the sinking of much of the Russian Baltic fleet by Admiral Togo at the Battle of Tsushima (1905). The significance of this change was grasped elsewhere in Asia and, not unnaturally, it provoked a great feeling of pride among the Japanese themselves. The earlier Anglo-Japanese Alliance of 1902 was emotionally as well as politically important to Japan since it arose from mutual needs, and symbolised a parity with an advanced Western State in sharp contrast to some of the previous 'unequal' treaties which Japan had signed with Western countries. Thus, by 1905, Japan had an international status and prestige without parallel among other Asian countries. In Europe, the Japanese were regarded as a force to be reckoned with, and were generally recognised as an advanced and civilised people with many admirable qualities. On Asia, the impact of new emergent Japan was nothing less than dramatic; it was seen that an Asian country sufficiently modernised and industrialised could successfully challenge the domination of the West.

The Japanese government did not, however, at this time pose as a leader of Asia nor did it directly seek to promote pan-Asian feelings. Officially, Japan was concerned with a world position rather than an Asian one, but there were nationalist groups in Japan who were more Asian-conscious than the official circles. The great modernising changes in Japan in the second half of the nineteenth century did not ensure the abolition of the anti-foreignism which had traditionally characterised earlier Japanese relations with the West. Indeed, in some ways, increased political and economic contacts with Western countries helped to stir up resentment among groups of Japanese who felt that their country was making too many concessions or being subjected to too many humiliations.

One situation which caused widespread indignation in Japan was the modification of the peace treaty between Japan and China in 1895, following a Sino-Japanese war fought largely in Korea and Manchuria. One Japanese gain from this war was the island of Formosa (Taiwan). Combined pressure by Russia, France and Germany forced Japan, however, to give up Port Arthur and the Liaotung peninsula in south Manchuria at a time when China had little option but to sign these away. Another source of grievance which only began to be settled about the same time lay in the special extraterritorial rights and privileges of Westerners resident in Japan. By implication, Japanese laws and institutions were held inferior to those of the West. At government level, policy was directed to the revision of the Japanese criminal and civil legal codes, and diplomatic activity to secure the revision of treaties in which foreigners had been given special legal rights in Japan. Extreme nationalist groups had no sympathy for these official tactics and formed societies whose aims included the expansion of Japan's interest in Asia and the rejection of foreign ideas. At times these societies took direct action which included the planned assassination of government leaders.

Among these 'ultra-nationalists', as they have been called, was Toyama Mitsuru, founder of the *Genyosha* society and organiser of several political murders. This society, was responsible, among other incidents, for a bomb attack in 1889 on Okuma Shingenobu who was the Japanese Foreign Minister and engaged in treaty negotiations with foreign powers. In the period following the Russo-Japanese War, Toyama's home in Tokyo became a focal centre for rebels and would-be rebels from China, India, Annam and the Philippines. Of these visitors, the Chinese who were plotting to overthrow the Manchu dynasty in Peking were the most significant; in this way, a link was forged between ultra-nationalism in Japan and revolutionary nationalism in China.

An interesting clash of ideas is evident in the contemporary careers of two great Japanese statesmen who bridged the nineteenth and twentieth centuries. These were Ito Hirobumi and Yamagata Aritomo. Both were keen supporters of the role of the emperor and both were in favour of Japanese national expansion. Yamagata was the founder of Japan's modern army and for him the power of the army was of paramount importance in the new Japan. Ito supervised the preparation of the written constitution which was introduced in 1889. This included a Diet, characterised by some borrowings from Germany and consisting of two Houses, meeting normally for three months out of twelve. Ito's constitution was authoritarian but civilian. For its date and against a background of Japanese tradition, it was a start in parliamentary government which could have been more liberalised as time went on. During a later premiership of Yamagata in 1900, it was decreed by imperial ordinance that only generals or lieutenant-generals on the active list could be appointed Minister of War in the Japanese cabinet; similarly, only admirals or vice-admirals on the active list could be Navy Minister. The effect of this ruling was to equate the armed services with the cabinet and to leave open the possibility of military dominance in Japanese politics.

Japanese government at the turn of the century was oligarchical and its leaders came from two or three of the western clan groupings. Political parties existed in Japan from the 1870s but they ebbed and flowed round particular leaders rather than maintaining an identity of their own; party interests came to focus on cabinets. Until 1925 the electorate remained small and, in any case, the House of Representatives which it returned had only equal powers with the House of Peers which was very largely nominated. Cabinet ministers were not responsible, in the ordinary political usage of the word, to either House, and the emperor could still issue special ordinances which he sometimes did on the advice of a prime minister. For the student of the growth of modern Japanese nationalism until the end of the Second World War, two main themes emerge and they are interrelated. One is the growth of imperialism culminating in a wartime empire of vast extent; the other is the victory of ultra-nationalism over liberalism in domestic politics during the years between the two World Wars. The economic background of a major industrial revolution from the late nineteenth century onwards needs to be borne in mind.

The years immediately following the Russo-Japanese War witnessed Japan's increasing hold upon Korea. First, Japanese advisers were introduced into the country, then a Japanese Resident-General, followed, in 1907, by Japanese demands which would make a mockery of Korean sovereignty. Ito and Yamagata were both imperialistic in relation to Korea, but Ito favoured a more diplomatic approach to Japanese control, whereas Yamagata stood for annexation. In the event, the assassination of Ito by a Korean shortly after he had resigned office as Japanese Resident-General added further impetus to the policy of Yamagata and his supporters. By a treaty of 1910, the Korean king became a pensioner and his country became, in effect, a Japanese colony for the next thirty-five years. Japanese rule brought some benefits to Korea, especially in the material sphere, but there were no major concessions to Korean nationalism or to the desire on the part of Koreans for greater independence.

During the same period and into the years of the First World War, Japanese interests in China were increasing. First, former Russian rights in southern Manchuria were secured, then strong financial interests were built up in iron-mines and ironworks in central China. The outbreak of the 1914–18 war gave Japan, as an ally of Britain, the opportunity to attack and seize German holdings in China, and to establish control in Shantung. This success encouraged the Japanese to initiate a fierce diplomatic offensive against the Chinese President, Yuan Shih-kai, who had been nationalising the iron-mines, much to Japan's chagrin.

Japan's terms to China were embodied, in 1915, in the much written-about Twenty-One Demands. These demands were both extremely opportunist and wide-ranging and they have been variously described as 'notorious', from a Chinese standpoint, and 'unfortunate' or 'blundering', from a commentator generally sympathetic to Japan. They included the transfer of German leaseholds in Shantung to Japan, the extension of Japanese interests in Manchuria, and they had much also to do with Japanese advisers to China and the placing on the Chinese economy of controls advantageous to Japan. Under temporary stress, the Chinese government yielded by treaty to some of these demands and, though Japan dropped some of the more extreme claims, many of the Twenty-One Demands were sanctioned at the Versailles peace conference, despite Chinese protests and American reluctance. One important postscript to this situation was a deterioration in American-Japanese relations; another was a great hardening of feeling against Japan on the part of Chinese nationalists. To the patriotic Chinese, the imperialism of Japan was no more acceptable than that of the West.

Japan's position as a world power was recognised in the League of Nations and her status as a naval power was acknowledged at the Washington Conference in 1921–2. The agreement reached at Washington on the ratios of naval shipping (5:5:3) as between the United States, Britain and Japan did not meet all that the Japanese representatives wanted but it gave Japan the basis for naval supremacy in what the British regarded as the Far East. This situation was reinforced by further agreements which left the nearest American and British naval bases to Japan situated in Hawaii and Singapore respectively, with the Singapore base still, in fact, to be built.

By the early 1920s, whatever blunders Japan had committed or whatever disappointments the Japanese government had resigned itself to accept, there was much on record to give cause for national pride. Japan was in control of Korea, had extensive commitments in China and also, as a result of Versailles, had responsibilities in former German islands in the Pacific, north of the Equator. A more conciliatory line was taken with China and, in talks at Washington (1922) between Japanese and Chinese delegates, the Japanese agreed to restore to China most of the interests they had acquired in Shantung. Japan's position seemed secure yet a price had been paid for all that had been achieved. Britain, influenced in part by America, decided not to renew the Anglo-Japanese Alliance which had been a key feature of Japanese foreign policy since 1902. America became increasingly suspicious of Japanese motives and policies; south Manchuria and other Japanese interests in China were regarded as *terra irredenta* by Chinese nationalists.

The decade between the Washington Conference and the Manchuria Incident of 1931 witnessed, first, a liberalising of the Japanese nationalist outlook, then the emergence of ultra-nationalist views under strong military and economic pressures. 'Big Business' became at first linked with the support of political parties keen to reduce armaments, to treat China in a brotherly way and to undertake liberal reforms at home. All males above the age of twenty-five were given a vote and the electorate was expanded from three million voters to well over twelve million. Japan was moving slowly but surely towards liberal parliamentarianism, yet there was always an element of authority and control in the background. Socialism and Communism had very limited scope since organisations which adopted left-wing ideas often came under close government scrutiny and action. The nature of the constitution itself made difficult, if not impossible, the working of a well co-ordinated cabinet and both the House of Peers and the army saw as signs of weakness the conciliatory measures abroad and the liberal reforms at home.

A combination of factors brought the militarists and ultra-nationalists to the fore. A banking crisis in 1927 followed by the effects of world depression from 1930 combined to discredit the marriage between the big business concerns and politics. The prevalence of bribery and corruption in the Lower House brought the regime into further disrepute. Army and political assassinations by fanatics became features of the times, and there were too few influential statesmen who would speak out strongly against the dangerous turn which Japanese affairs were taking.

Meanwhile, in China, Chiang Kai-shek and his Kuomintang regime

Japanese attack on Pearl Harbor, 1941

The signing of the Japanese surrender in Tokyo Bay, 1945

Chiang Kai-shek,
in 1938

Mao Tse-tung

were extending their control northwards and making it quite clear that their ultimate objective was to reclaim the whole of the former Chinese Empire including Japanese Manchuria. Chinese nationalism provoked a strong counter-attitude in the Japanese army, as friction between Nationalist China and Japan arose over several Manchurian issues. After many signs and portents, and, in particular, the hardening of official Japanese policy towards China, the Japanese army in Manchuria embarked, in September 1931, on the conquest of the whole region. This was a direct army action, out of the hands of the home government, but a change of cabinet supported the army's move. Thus, in 1931, Japan took the long road of militarism and warfare which led to an all-out attack on China and eventually to Pearl Harbor and the conquest and occupation of South-East Asia in the Second World War.

The rising nationalism in China can be seen as a factor in the triumph of military nationalism in Japan in the 1930s. Japanese nationalism, in its turn, provoked a variety of nationalist responses in South-East Asia during the occupation years, 1942–5, and these are perhaps best seen from the South-East Asian setting. The Japanese concept of a New Order in South-East Asia, which followed an earlier concept of a New Order in east Asia, under Japanese leadership, and the slogan 'Asia for the Asians', which was much publicised, did a great deal to damage Western prestige, but Japanese military administrations did not succeed in gaining widespread support for the new post-war vision held by Japan.

The surrender of Japan to the Allies in August 1945 created the greatest soul-searching situation in the history of the Japanese nation. The fifty years from the time of Perry's ships to the Russo-Japanese War was now matched by a further period of forty years to humiliating defeat and foreign occupation; the emperor told his people that they must endure the unendurable and suffer the unsufferable. The essential unity of Japan and the authority of the emperor were never more manifest than in the general Japanese compliance with the Imperial command to surrender.

The American occupation of Japan lasted seven years. The monarchy was retained but it became truly constitutional and indeed, informal. Japan was demilitarised and, from the American point of view, politically re-educated. The atomic bombs which had been dropped on the towns of Hiroshima and Nagasaki had created their own horror of war and violence among the Japanese people, and some twenty-five former Japanese leaders, including two former Prime Ministers, were sentenced to death or various terms of imprisonment by an international war crimes tribunal.

Japan became an independent state again in 1952 with a new constitution in which American influence was evident, and a security pact signed with the United States. The overseas empire had been lost and the land of islands had to face many problems at home and abroad. On every hand there was an enormous amount of work to be done to restore and improve living standards and to rebuild national prestige. By the 1960s both these aims had been achieved to a remarkable degree. Japan was extremely active in international trade and diplomacy. The soul of the new Japan, though fascinating as ever, was still extremely complex. Militarism had received the most severe shock imaginable and Japanese politics tended to follow a Liberal-Democrat line, challenged by various shades of Socialism.

From 1910 to 1945, Korea was a Japanese colony and it is convenient here to note the main trends of Korean nationalism during this period. It was customary for the Japanese regime to be headed by a serving general or admiral and, in the early period, the nature of government was harsh and oppressive; some Koreans showed their resistance by joining armed guerilla bands in the mountainous regions.

The funeral of the former King of Korea in March 1919 provided a focal point for the *Mansei* movement which had been gaining ground for two or three years. President Wilson's doctrine of self-determination for peoples had reached intellectual circles in Korea and inspired Korean exiles and students overseas. A Declaration of Independence which stated Korean grievances was signed by thirty-three Korean leaders in Seoul and presented to the Japanese Governor-General. The thirty-three included Christian clergymen, officials of Chondogyo (a modern indigenous religion, the 'Heavenly Way') and Buddhist monks. The popular slogan which accompanied this peaceful revolt was 'May Korea be free for ten thousand years', abbreviated conveniently to the last word which was *Mansei*. Generally pacifist in intent and method, the movement did spark off some violence against the Japanese, particularly as a result of the harsh Japanese reaction to it.

Greater liberalism in Japan in the 1920s was reflected in a more diplomatic approach to the problems of Korean administration. The Japanese Admiral Saito set the tone for a more liberal atmosphere during his governorship. Cultural movements were encouraged, the Press was given more freedom and the police became a civilian rather than a military force. A small Korean Communist Party attempted to lead a nationalist demonstration in 1926 on the lines of the earlier *Mansei* movement, but the police suppressed this at the planning stage. Communism did not make any very wide appeal and its supporters were carefully watched by the authorities. A more liberal atmosphere without any real concessions to Korean political consciousness was bound to provoke sporadic demonstrations, and there were anti-Japanese student riots in 1928 and 1929; two years later there were further riots directed against the small Chinese trading minority in Korea, arising from anti-Korean incidents in Manchuria. On the eve of the Japanese invasion of Manchuria, the authorities in Korea were not inclined to discourage anti-Chinese feelings.

The occupation of Manchuria by the Japanese marked the triumph of militarism and a tightening of military control in Korea. In the next few years Korea came to serve as a staging point for the war in China which broke out on a full scale in 1937. In matters economic, Korea made great progress under Japanese rule, but increasingly in the 1930s the political orientation was towards Japan. Korean schools, for instance, were required to use Japanese as the main language of instruction, and government educational policy supported an emphasis in the curriculum on Japanese history and literature with a strong nationalistic bias. By the time the war years were over, there were Korean nationalist groups ready to return from exile but with no experience in political authority and divided among themselves. In Korea itself there was no sufficiently well-organised or well-led movement to speak for the country as a whole. For purposes of Japanese disarmament and repatriation the country was artificially divided by the Allies along the 38th parallel, with Russians to the north and Americans to the south; beyond this piece of expediency there was no clear plan. In the event, the government in the south soon became American in appearance and power while the government in the North had a Korean appearance but strong Russian and communist backing. The agreement to withdraw Russian and American forces in 1949 was paralleled by political and diplomatic moves to effect a solution for Korea in which cross-purposes were involved. By this time, and even more so with the military attack by the North in June 1950, Korea was very much an international problem. Two years of war in which Chinese forces helped the North and American and United Nations' forces the South ended on an uneasy truce-line.

CHINA

At many points, the course of Chinese nationalism in the twentieth century was linked with that of Japan. This was evident, as we have seen, in the Sino-Japanese War of 1894–5 in which Japan imitated the imperialism of the West in order to secure interests of her own in Korea, a land regarded by the Chinese as a tributary of China. The two nationalisms were evident then and later in Japanese gains in Formosa and Manchuria, in the harbouring by Japan of Chinese revolutionaries before 1911, in the Twenty-One Demands of 1915, the relationships with China in the 1920s and, finally, in the Manchuria Incident of 1931 and the euphemistically-named 'China Incident' which signified the invasion of China by Japan from 1937 onwards.

One irony of China's defeat at the hands of Japan in 1895 was that, culturally, Japan was very much in China's debt. The legacies of both Confucianism and Buddhism had passed from China to Japan and ancient Japanese cities were modelled on Chinese examples. Another irony was that China was very large and Japan relatively small. The very size of China, however, was an obstacle to its modernisation and a decadent Manchu dynasty together with a history of internal rebellions and foreign encroachments had, by the end of the nineteenth century, greatly fragmented and weakened the Chinese Empire. It seemed quite possible that the ancient Chinese Empire might disintegrate completely into a series of separate, alien protectorates.

That this did not happen was in some measure due to the event known as the Boxer Rising. The Boxers were a secret society, worshipping the traditional Chinese Taoist and Buddhist gods and practising ritual 'boxing' exercises in order to achieve long life. They exploited Chinese economic grievances and dislike of foreigners and created a widespread and popular movement. At first, they were anti-Manchu, but after a defeat at the hands of government troops, they concentrated on their anti-foreign policy, attacking foreign institutions, including those connected with missionary bodies and any Chinese associated with them. The foreign powers became alarmed at the extent of Boxer violence which culminated in the siege by Boxer forces of the foreign legations in Peking in the summer of 1900. An international relief force representing Britain, France, Russia, Germany, Japan, Austria-Hungary, Italy and the United States freed the legations, suppressed the Boxer movement and forced on China the payment of a large indemnity. This was all deeply humiliating to China, but the rising had demonstrated to the foreign powers the strength of certain Chinese feelings and the dangers and difficulties which would be involved in any partition of the Empire.

In the first decade or so of the twentieth century, Chinese intellectuals were turning increasingly to the West for the secrets of modernisation. This was a realistic appraisal of what might be done to save China from decadence and to match the old spirit to the new times. One obstacle to this renewal was the Manchu government. The Manchu dynasty had never been universally acceptable in China and anti-dynastic rebellions from the south in particular had been a marked feature of Chinese history in the nineteenth century. After the Boxer Rising, the dynasty lived on uneasily for a decade in the face of increasing revolutionary threats raised by leaders who were mainly living in the Treaty Ports or abroad in exile. In an attempt to hold back revolution, the Manchus promised to introduce a constitution modelled on that of Japan, but real power lay with the armed forces whose main purpose was to preserve the regime. When revolution came, one section of the army, led by a mandarin, Yuan Shih-kai, was to reap the spoils of victory in a manner reminiscent of dynastic changes in ancient China during troubled periods.

The main name associated with the revolution of 1911 was that of Dr Sun Yat-sen. Like many other revolutionaries, Sun Yat-sen had spent many years in other countries, including Japan, the United States and Europe. His first revolutionary society was formed among Chinese students in Tokyo in 1905 and its aims included the overthrow of the Manchus, the recovery of China for the Chinese, the establishment of a republic and the nationalisation of the land. Western-educated and Christian, Dr Sun proclaimed for China the Three Principles of the People: the Principle of Nationalism, the Principle of Democracy, and the Principle of the People's Livelihood. These principles were amended and expanded later as the basis for Nationalist China under the Kuomintang regime. Sun Yat-sen's influence was very considerable and his name is revered in present-day China but he was not primarily a man of action, and, though elected Provisional President of the Republic of China which was declared to have come into being in January 1912, he yielded place to 'strong man' Yuan in return for promises which Yuan failed to keep. Yuan, in fact, began to work for a revival of the empire with a new dynasty of his own making. He did not succeed in this project but died in 1916, leaving the realities of political and military power in China divided among provincial war-lords.

Though the revolution of 1911 did not work out as Sun would have had it, he did contribute very fully to the building up of the political party which was to attempt to re-unify China in the 1920s and 1930s; this was the Kuomintang (K.M.T.). Earlier in his revolutionary career, Sun Yat-sen had looked to Western countries for aid and encouragement; by 1923 he was ready and willing to take help and advice from Communist Russia. The Kuomintang was formed in 1912 as an outgrowth of Dr Sun's earlier 'Revolutionary League' (Tung Meng Hui) and its strength lay in south China and especially in the Canton area where Sun had his base. The reorganisation of the party with Russian help enabled it to work more efficiently and to spread its appeal further afield. One symbol of the widening horizons of the party was the holding of a first National Congress in Canton in 1924, and among those present were two zealous supporters of Marxism, Mao Tse-tung and Li Ta-chao.

The Chinese Communist Party dates from a very small gathering of intellectuals, including Mao Tse-tung, held in Shanghai in 1921 and quickly linked with Moscow. By 1923, the party, working in student and labour circles, had decided to enter the Kuomintang and to co-operate with it in a common front for the recovery of a united Chinese Republic from the war-lords. The immediate objective was to initiate a military campaign in the direction of central and north China. At its 1924 Congress, the Kuomintang showed itself ready to accept help and advice from Soviet Russia and from Chinese communists. One consequence of Soviet help was the establishment, in the same year, of the Whampoa Military Academy near Canton for the training of army officers. Its first head was Chiang Kai-shek, a professional soldier and committed revolutionary and an early member of Sun Yat-sen's Revolutionary League. Significantly Whampoa was also given a political department, the first head of which was Chou En-lai who had helped to found a Chinese Communist Party among students in Paris in 1921.

Sun Yat-sen lived only long enough to see the beginnings of the Kuomintang revival. He died in 1925, leaving a signed political testament which was read publicly for many years in schools and government offices as part of K.M.T. policy. Dr Sun's natural successor as leader of the Kuomintang was Chiang Kai-shek, who had been a close political friend and adviser of the party leader for many years. The party now had a dead hero who provided the ideological inspiration, and an active and able soldier at its head to lead the coming campaigns. Chiang, though he had been to Moscow as Sun's representative in 1923, was extremely wary about Russian help and communist co-operation. Politically, he was on the right wing of the Kuomintang and his nationalism was more in line with Confucian traditions of order, authority and a revival of the traditional Chinese virtues.

The upshot was that the alliance between Chinese communists and the K.M.T. was an uneasy one from the time of Chiang's leadership; fundamentally, they were fighting for different political ends. The Northern Expedition of Chiang's armies was remarkably successful at first, meeting little resistance in the southern and central provinces. The cause of anti-foreignism which the K.M.T. was propagating obviously met with widespread popularity, and more radical groups attacked foreigners and foreign property in towns like Hankow and Nanking. Though the campaigns in the more conservative north were harder, Chiang was in control of Peking by 1928. By this time, however, a show-down had taken place with the communists. The more revolutionary nature of communist plans became clear, during the advance, through labour organisations, strike committees and the extremely vigorous pursuit of anti-foreign, anti-capitalist and anti-landlord activities. Chiang's new National Government of the Republic of China, set up at Nanking in 1928, represented a China more unified than it had been for fifteen years or more, but it was virtually at war with Chinese communism which proved extremely tenacious wherever it got a foothold. A purge against communists began in 1927 and relationships with Russia were broken off. Communist leaders who survived the purge attempted to set up and hold limited areas of control.

One group of communist leaders established their first experimental Socialist state in the province of Kiangsi. By 1931, this was called the Chinese Soviet Republic and had Mao Tse-tung as its chairman and Chu Teh as commander of its armed forces. Chiang was well aware of the dangers of this kind of development to his Nationalist China and he campaigned against it both on military and socio-political fronts. Several expeditions were sent to crush the Kiangsi regime, while a New Life Movement appealing both to Confucian ethics and to the spirit of Christianity was combined with some modest economic developments into a constructive programme to win support for the government. The pressures on the communist leaders in Kiangsi and other bases became so great that, in 1934, they decided to undertake the epic 'Long March' of some 6,000 miles to Yenan in the mountainous province of Shensi in north-west China. Some 20,000 survived this extremely hard and hazardous journey to establish a new socialist regime in a much safer, more remote part of China and to plan for future victories.

For the time being, the Kuomintang was generally in charge of China and it secured a number of agreements with foreign powers for the limitation or abandonment of foreign rights and concessions. It also publicised the idea that Chinese people were always Chinese and, should they adopt another nationality when living overseas, they would acquire dual nationality, it being held impossible for them to give up their Chinese identity. This nationality concept was widely circulated by K.M.T. organisations among the Chinese in South-East Asia, and education policies were based on it. Not unnaturally, it led to situations where other nationalisms were aroused in opposition to that of the Chinese.

Despite some divisions within itself and uncertainties about the support of certain former war-lords, the Kuomintang party seemed, by the early 1930s, to be establishing the new China. The communist challenge was diminished though not suppressed. The next danger, however, came from Japan. The conquest by the Japanese of the whole of Manchuria (1931–2) was followed by the setting up there of a puppet state of Manchukuo with Pu-yi, ex-emperor of Manchu China, as its 'emperor'. Anti-Japanese feeling became very strong in China and a boycott was placed on Japanese goods, banks and steamers; the Japanese retaliated by attacking Shanghai and Nanking. Chinese students demonstrated for action against Japan but Chiang was cautious in the face of Japanese military and naval superiority and preferred to adopt time-gaining tactics, or, as some might say, a policy of appeasement. In 1936, in a curious and dramatic incident, Chiang was kidnapped by one of his own military commanders (a former war-lord from Manchuria) while inspecting troops engaged in anti-communist drives in western China. This was a military *coup* to force Chiang to stop the civil war against Chinese communists and call for a united anti-Japanese front. The immediate prospect – as Chiang was held prisoner and a Nanking general prepared a large expedition for his release – seemed to be a much greater civil war in China. But, after many face-saving activities on both sides, Chiang made an uneasy truce with the communist leaders and this persisted throughout the Japanese War which began in 1937.

Between 1937 and 1945, Chinese nationalism was further fashioned in the hard furnace of a bitter war with Japan in which large areas of eastern and southern China became enemy-occupied territories. The Chinese people endured incredible suffering and hardship. There existed two Chinese governments in addition to a Japanese-sponsored Nanking regime; that of the Kuomintang in Chunking, west of the Japanese advance, and that of the communists in Yenan; real co-operation between them proved impossible. On the military side, the Nationalists bore the main brunt of the Japanese advance and were responsible for much larger territories; the communists, working within more limited boundaries, concentrated on guerilla warfare, and on the build-up of their own organisation and membership. The presence of American forces in China was a further complicating factor.

The merging of the war in China with the wider war which broke out in Europe in 1939 and in the Pacific in 1941 brought help to and further recognition of Chiang Kai-shek but, as the war progressed, the Nationalists were weakened by the strain of the war itself, by inflation and loss of revenues and by increasing corruption within the party. The Kuomintang became more committed to the conservative landlords of west China while the communists directed their attention to winning large-scale peasant support. One happy development for the Nationalists was the surrender, in 1943, by Britain and the United States of extra-territorial rights in China, though this could not be immediately effective as they were in Japanese-held areas.

The Japanese aim was to sponsor a Chinese government which would be subservient to Japan and by this means to exercise control over China as over Manchukuo. In 1940, a puppet government was set up at Nanking, composed of what the Japanese regarded as true elements of the K.M.T. Within this framework Japan was also ready to give up concessions and rights to China and this example was followed by Italy and Vichy France. In these rather oblique ways, the path was being cleared for Chinese sovereignty once the Japanese had been defeated, but there remained the very vital question of whether the K.M.T. and the communists would work together and, if so, under what form of agreement. Despite negotiations and various attempts at mediation, especially on the part of the United States, the two parties bidding to represent and rule post-war China became involved in bitter civil war within months of the Japanese surrender. Mao Tse-tung had concentrated as much as possible on preparing the countryside for pro-communist revolutionary activities and this was put to the test in the years between 1945 and 1949. Although they possessed apparent advantages in the earlier phases, Chiang Kai-shek's forces were gradually defeated or they went over to the enemy until, by 1950, the remnants withdrew with the Generalissimo to make a government centre and stronghold on the island of Formosa (Taiwan). Meanwhile, on 1 October 1949, the People's Republic of China was proclaimed with Mao Tse-tung as Chairman and Chou En-lai as Minister of Foreign Affairs.

The achievement of a new China, strong and independent, was to be under communist leadership but this did not rule out the normal patterns of nationalism. The new regime became much concerned with territories and frontiers which might once have been subject to forms of control by the old Chinese Empire. Tibet, invaded in 1950, was one case in point; the Indian frontier was another. From the point of view of Communist China, Chiang's Formosa could only be regarded from the mainland as *terra irredenta*, while, of course, for Chiang's Nationalist government, the exact reverse was the case. Small adjacent foreign territories, once Chinese, like Hong Kong and Macao, could also expect to be viewed as 'unredeemed' though practical considerations or matters of timing might condition the attention given to them.

The dynamic nationalism of Communist China could not fail to have some influence among Chinese overseas and especially those in South-East Asia. China's increasing prestige and status was a source of pride to many Chinese who were not necessarily communists or communist sympathisers. Governments in South-East Asia were closely concerned about China's intentions as they always had been at times in history when China was strong. The new Chinese Republic faced vast economic tasks with great energy and resolution. In accordance with Chinese tradition, a corpus of written ideas and principles was a desirable accompaniment to the new order, and by the 1960s this was provided on a massive popular scale by the dissemination of selected quotations from the works of Mao Tse-tung. By this time, too, China had claimed pre-eminence in the cause of communist revolution and broken with Russia, whose leaders were regarded as 'revisionists' and betrayers of the revolution. China's own leaders still included some of those who had endured the Long March and the Yenan period but for this generation time was running out. Great efforts were made to pass on the revolutionary spirit to the young, with results which are still difficult to predict.

The dangers of 'revisionism' in China itself frequently attracted the attention of the communist leaders and especially of Mao Tse-tung. Intensive campaigns of indoctrination were a normal part of government policy following a brief and ill-fated period in 1957, when a measure of intellectual freedom was permitted in a 'Hundred Flowers' movement. Increasingly, the portraits and the writings and speeches of Mao himself became the hall-marks of the new orthodoxy of national conformity and the build-up of the personality cult of Mao stood in marked contrast to the contemporary official denunciation of this type of practice in the Soviet Union. By 1962 Mao was moving towards still more radical campaigns against what he saw as encroaching bourgeois and other non-revolutionary tendencies in China; it remained to be seen how far he could carry both the Party and the army along with him.

In the autumn of 1965 Mao launched a new anti-revisionist struggle, known as the 'cultural revolution'. Directed in the first place towards intellectual elements, this movement was extended into all fields of life and all areas of social and economic activity. A massive 'Red Guard' organisation of young Chinese from primary-school age upwards was created to revitalise the revolutionary tradition, and, within a year or so, China became convulsed in a mixture of ideological and power struggles between 'pro-Maoist' and 'anti-Maoist' factions to a degree sufficient for some outside observers to pose a civil war situation. A complexity of disturbances in which regional as well as social and economic factors played a part was, however, more reminiscent of a 'time of troubles' than of anything so clear-cut as a civil war in the western tradition.

The internal struggles of the cultural revolution seemed only to intensify Chinese hatred towards those foreigners who were either 'revisionists' or 'imperialists'. Relationships with Soviet Russia were near to breaking-point as the Soviet Embassy in Peking became the focus of a series of very hostile incidents and demonstrations. Embassy and Legation buildings and personnel in Peking became convenient targets for the expression of a revived form of Chinese xenophobia. The attack on the British Legation (burned down in August, 1967) was linked with very considerable pressures on the British position in Hong Kong, where the challenges of anti-British and pro-communist elements were being firmly met.

With foreign Legations in Peking in the limelight once more, events in China appeared to have touched again a chord heard at the very beginning of the century; the general circumstances, however, could hardly have been more different. Only so far as the events of 1967 and of 1900–1 could be judged as portents for the years to come could a common element of enigma be traced in the views of contemporary observers.

THE INDIAN SUBCONTINENT

One paramount power, Britain, presided over Indian politics at the dawn of the twentieth century. About three-fifths of India, divided into provinces, was under British rule and about two-fifths, divided into very many states, both large and small, was ruled by Indian princes who accepted a general British paramountcy and, often, British advice. The two areas, which were somewhat intermingled especially in central and southern India, were technically known as British India and the Princely States. This was, however, only one of very many divisions in India. India was a continent of many cultures and traditions, and national unity was only to be achieved if many barriers could be broken down and many gaps bridged.

The first major political association for the promotion of Indian interests was formed in 1885 with the title of Indian National Congress. It was sponsored by retired British members of the Indian Civil Service and tacitly approved by the Governor-General of the time as a mouthpiece for educated and liberal Indian opinion. The founder membership totalled about seventy, mostly university graduates who had become lawyers, journalists and schoolmasters. The National Congress in its early years was anything but national or representative in character; it moved in small circles of Western-educated middle-class Indians. In dress, manner and procedure many of its members could hardly have seemed more British. Yet some of the causes for which it spoke were truly Indian. Prominent among these were the cause of government reforms to provide more Indian representation in central and provincial councils and the plea for improved opportunities for Indians in the civil service and the armed forces. The Congress also directed attention to the fundamental problems of Indian poverty; only a government of India by Indians, it was argued, would be able to attempt the amelioration of human miseries so evident in the country.

Congress soon developed an organisation of local branches, general committee, working committee, annual conference and annual president. The presidential address and the resolutions passed at the annual conference embodied the main aims and hopes of the movement, not without considerable repetition over the years. Although the party was open to all Indians it was clearly of an elite character in its early years, appealing only to certain classes; one British administrator described it as a 'microscopic minority'. Those who joined Congress were mainly Hindus; Indian Muslims of similar social status, with some important exceptions, remained aloof as they felt that the separateness of the Muslim identity might be lost in a combined movement where Hindus could be expected to outnumber Muslims by four to one.

English liberalism and a touch of Italian nationalist idealism were among the sources of inspiration of the early Congress. The second president, Dadhabai Naoroji, was for some years a Liberal M.P. in the British Parliament but there was another nationalist current in the movement, less Western and more traditional in outlook. B. G. Tilak, editor of the Marathi newspaper, *Kesari*, became the leader of the more traditional, yet radical wing of the party, while his contemporary, G. K. Gokhale, led the moderate or liberal elements. Gokhale saw Indian political advancement in terms of gradual constitutional reforms and he looked forward to parliamentary rule for India in a liberal framework. Tilak looked back to the glories of Hindu India and took as his hero Sivaji, one of the warrior princes who had fought against Muslim supremacy. Tilak sought a revival of Hindu traditions and culture and opposed the rapid spread of Western influences; he was anxious to broaden the appeal of Congress to the ordinary people of India along these lines. Tilak's approach was both revivalist and revolutionary and his writings and speeches tended to incite to violence. Congress split into two camps of 'moderates' and 'extremists' in 1907, and in the following year Tilak was sentenced to six years' imprisonment, served in Burma, on charges of inciting to violence.

The British were prepared to make political concessions, from time to time, to meet the Indian case for greater representation in government circles. An Indian Councils Act of 1861 was an early measure in this direction and another Act of the same name, passed in 1892, brought more Indian opinion and advice into the central and provincial councils. During the first decade of the twentieth century, a further instalment of political advance for Indians was being discussed during a period in which sharp Congress reaction was shown to Lord Curzon's measures to reform Indian universities and to partition the large and important province of Bengal for its better administration. Curzon, Viceroy 1899–1905, offended the professional middle-class Congressmen by what they saw as his unfair interference with universities with which they and their families were associated. By his partition of Bengal, he aroused a Hindu reaction against the weakening of a historically important province, which was predominantly Hindu in overall population but which had a largely Muslim community in its eastern sector. This sector now formed the nucleus of a separate province.

The agitation over Bengal and the prospect of further constitutional reforms stirred Indian Muslims to form a political organisation of their own and to state and defend the case for Muslim rights wherever these were seen to exist. Thus, in 1906, the All-India Muslim League was born. Leading Muslims were conscious that their community had made less response to the Western challenge than the Hindus, especially, for instance, in education, including the use of English. One nineteenth-century Muslim leader, Sayyid Ahmad Khan (1817–98), a judge from Delhi, was convinced that Indian Muslims must come to terms with the West, both politically and culturally, otherwise they would be out-distanced in the race for government favour. He was one, among others, to put forward the view that Western knowledge need not be incompatible with the tenets of Islam and he was largely responsible for the opening of the Anglo-Oriental College at Aligarh in 1875, an institution which had both British and Indian members of staff and a curriculum which included both Islamic and Western learning.

Congress did not welcome the emergence of the All-India Muslim League, especially as it encouraged Muslims to join its own ranks. From the Congress point of view, a divided nationalist movement gave Britain the opportunity to play off one party against another and hold on to the essentials of political power indefinitely. In the year which witnessed the birth of the League, Congress adopted the aim of self-government for India.

The 1909 Indian Councils Act, often referred to as the Morley-Minto Reforms, advanced the Indian position considerably but in doing so took account of the separate interests of the Muslim community. Indian members were now to be appointed to the Viceroy's Executive Council, to the provincial Executive Councils of Bombay and Madras, and to the Council of the Secretary of State for India in London. The role played by elected Indians in legislative councils was still, however, mainly an advisory one; provision was made for separate community electorates, where appropriate. A magnificently-staged visit by King George V and Queen Mary to India in 1911 was accompanied by further gestures to Indian opinion. These included the repeal of the partition of Bengal, the announcement of new universities, an enquiry into the role of Indians in the civil service and the potential award of the Victoria Cross to Indian soldiers.

Generally, the years just before the First World War were marked by an all-round improvement in relationships between Britain and India. The more moderate leaders were dominant in Congress as Tilak served his prison sentence. Even at this period, however, another element in Indian nationalism occurred from time to time; this was terrorism, the use of the bomb and the gun against government officials and others. Political agitation in Bengal had earlier produced outbursts of terrorism, and similar incidents in the Punjab were due mainly to social and economic grievances. Even in the comparative calm of 1912 there was an attempt to assassinate the Viceroy in New Delhi.

The First World War had a marked effect on Indian nationalism. Indian pride was stirred by the great contributions which the country made to the war effort, and Indian soldiers won five V.C.s. The war brought its strains, too, and these included shortages, high prices and a flu epidemic in 1918 which killed five million people. British prestige suffered with the long duration of the war and with reverses such as those of Kut-al-Amara in Iraq, and Gallipoli. Indian Muslims had mixed feelings about the British Empire's war with Turkey, for the Sultan of Turkey was also the Khalifa or chief political figure of the Muslim world.

Gokhale died in 1915, leaving a vacuum in the leadership of the Congress 'moderates'. In the following year, Tilak emerged from 'retirement' to become a leading Congress figure again and he helped to persuade the Muslim League to join a pact at Lucknow (1916) for the achievement of Home Rule. Congress agreed to recognise separate electorates. Among Indian Muslims a movement known as the 'Khalifate' developed which was opposed to any post-war dismemberment of the domains of the Turkish Sultan. Tilak, though not so militant as earlier, brought a new note of urgency to Home Rule, and the Khalifate movement contained threats of violence.

From the British side came what may have seemed to the more ardent Indian nationalists the usual mixture of promises of constitutional reforms accompanied by further measures of repression. New legislation was promised in 1917 to 'increase the association of Indians in every branch of the administration and the gradual development of self-governing institutions, with a view to the progressive realisation of responsible government in India as an integral part of the Empire'. In the same year, however, a committee under Mr Justice Rowlatt considered how the law could be strengthened to deal with subversive activities. The Rowlatt Bills became law in 1919 and they represented an extension of wartime restrictions into the post-war period; political cases could be heard without a jury and provincial councils were endowed with powers of internment.

The immediate post-1914–18 years were critically important in the evolution of Indian nationalism. There was great unrest due to the usual problems of economic hardships and returning soldiers, in addition to the feelings of Khalifate Muslims and the resentment felt especially by nationalists towards repressive legislation. Moreover, the spirit of the Versailles peace settlement was strongly in favour of the right of self-determination for peoples under alien rule, at least so far as the European setting was concerned.

Tilak, the old Congress warrior, died in 1920 and M. K. Gandhi, a Gujerati lawyer, emerged as a popular leader, stimulating meetings in protest against the Rowlatt Acts. Gandhi, with his mixture of ordinary humanity, saintliness and political acumen was soon to become known as 'Mahatma', or the 'Great Soul'. The authorities, especially in the Punjab, became nervous about demonstrations and at a prohibited meeting in an enclosed square at Amritsar in 1919 troops under the command of a British general opened fire and killed about four hundred people with more than a thousand wounded. Martial law and other punitive and humiliating measures followed. Indian nationalism now had its martyrs (however unintentionally) on a large scale, and Gandhi was to quote Amritsar and the Rowlatt Acts among the factors which turned him towards a policy of non-cooperation in 1920.

The new Government of India Act of 1919 thus appeared against an unhappy background. Although it was a further substantial advance along the road to self-government, the new constitution was not accepted by Congress. Some Congressmen chose, however, to work it in order to achieve further reforms from within, while others followed Gandhi's lead in a boycott of schools, colleges, law courts, elections, councils and British goods, the whole movement to be non-violent in accordance with Gandhi's spiritual principle of *satyagraha*. It was virtually impossible to keep violence completely out of any widespread non-cooperation movement and, in 1922, Gandhi was arrested on charges of inciting to violence, tried and sentenced to six years' imprisonment. At this stage, the non-cooperation movement lost much of its force; the case of the Khalifate Muslims also ended when the Turkish Sultan was deposed by a revolution in his own country in 1923. By the mid-1920s, the Congress Party was using constitutional tactics again and was well represented in the elected councils and assemblies. The arrival in India of a very sympathetic Viceroy, Lord Irwin (1926–1931) prepared the way for further political discussion. Gandhi, released from prison in 1924 on the grounds of ill-health, remained outside the mainstream of Indian politics for the time being, devoting his energies to the problems of the 'untouchables' and the peasant economy.

The new Viceroy helped to bring forward the date of a commission of enquiry into the working of the constitutional reforms of 1919 and this commission, under the chairmanship of Lord Simon, visited India

Mahatma Gandhi in London, 1931

Jawaharlal Nehru

M. A. Jinnah

in 1928 and issued its report two years later. There was much outcry about the absence of Indian members from the appointed commission, and Congress boycotted its activities and took part in organised demonstrations against it. As a counter-measure, Congress took the lead in convening a committee under the elder Nehru to frame its own constitutional proposals. Included in this Nehru Report was a timely demand for Dominion status which was connected with contemporary developments between Britain and the 'older' Dominions. Some younger Congressmen, including the younger Nehru, held that all this was not enough and that Indians should press for a complete break with Britain and complete independence. The Muslim League was divided on the issue of the Simon Commission and was drifting further away from Congress on the question of constitutional reform.

By about 1930, therefore, political India was ripe for another period of disturbances, terrorism, non-cooperation and repression. The home-made bomb made its appearance in the Punjab, Congress passed the younger Nehru's Independence resolution and Gandhi prepared himself to lead another non-cooperation movement, this time more aptly described as civil disobedience. Despite considerable diplomacy on the part of Lord Irwin, the civil disobedience movement got off to a good start in February 1930 when Gandhi undertook his dramatic western march to the sea and symbolically made illegal salt (a taxable item) on the sea-shore. The attack on the salt tax (not in itself a very oppressive item) was repeated elsewhere, together with other activities such as the picketing of liquor shops and the boycotting of foreign cloth. The government replied in due course by arresting Gandhi, outlawing branches and committees of Congress and introducing Press controls. In 1931, however, Gandhi was freed in order that he could attend a Round Table Conference which had been called in London to try to find a solution for the Indian problem.

It proved impossible to reconcile all points of view at the Conference and Gandhi's return to India was followed by further upheavals. His special role as the representative of Congress was challenged by other Indians, including some of the minority groups. The British government proceeded via White Paper proposals and a Joint Committee of both Houses to the drafting of a very complex piece of legislation which eventually became the Government of India Act of 1935. This offered self-government at provincial level but delayed the offer of the same status centrally until a federation had been formed which would include the provinces and at least half (by population) of the Princely States.

D

The franchise was extended to a total of about thirty million voters and arrangements were made for communal representation.

Congress was opposed to much of the 1935 Act, especially the lack of responsible government at the centre and the involvement of the princes who were regarded as conservative if not reactionary. The Muslim League had similar misgivings but was favourably disposed towards a federal principle which would allow strong provincial autonomy; it was also keen to apply itself to the details of communal representation. By these means, it was hoped, Muslim Indians would be able to retain a separate identity. Mohammed Ali Jinnah came to the fore in these circumstances as the energetic leader of a revived Muslim League with a programme of separatism which was eventually to lead to the creation of Pakistan.

Despite much disparagement of the Act, Congress, under Gandhi's influence, did enter the elections of 1937 and form governments and ministries in the provinces where it was strongest. The Princely States, for their part, showed no urgency to join a new federation and India was in this transitional situation politically when the Second World War began. It was a matter of intense irritation to Indian nationalists that India entered the war only through an announcement made by the Viceroy, and the Congress ministries resigned in protest. Though there was an early and widespread feeling that it was not India's war, loyalty and co-operation were not lacking. At what was for Britain a dark period in the war, after the fall of Singapore to the Japanese, Sir Stafford Cripps, leader of the House of Commons, was sent to India (March 1942) with a special offer to the Indian leaders. This offer included Commonwealth status for India after the war and the draft details of a Constituent Assembly which would prepare the transfer of power.

Congress leaders, including Gandhi, rejected the 'Cripps Offer' and embarked on a 'Quit India' campaign towards the British which was not quite so drastic in intent as it sounded. The upshot was that the whole Working Committee of Congress was interned for the rest of the war and the party itself was outlawed. The Muslim League stood outside these troubles and gained greatly in strength and organisation during the war years. Another party which grew at this time was the Indian Communist Party which had its beginnings with Russian help in the 1920s and was active in labour movements in the years before the war. Opposed to the war effort at first, the Indian Communist Party changed its policy, as happened with communist parties elsewhere, when the Germans invaded Russia in June 1941.

By 1940, the Muslim League had more or less moved to a policy which demanded a separate State or States for Indian Muslims, but this was by no means a solution which Congress would willingly accept. When Gandhi was released from gaol in 1944 (through ill-health brought on by fasting) he tried to negotiate with Jinnah to prepare a common front for national independence. The critical difference in the two viewpoints at this stage was that Jinnah made partition a prerequisite of independence whereas, for Gandhi, partition could only be regarded as a last resort, if other solutions failed, after independence. Jinnah gained in prestige as a result of this approach made by Gandhi.

The ending of the war in Europe and the expectancy of a long struggle still against Japan gave India a special strategic role for the massive counter-offensive in the East. In this situation it was politic to gain maximum Indian co-operation, and the Congress leaders were released in June 1945. Lord Wavell (Viceroy since 1943) called a conference of Indian leaders at Simla, but this broke up on disagreement between League and Congress. Within its own supporting ranks Congress felt tensions at this time through communism at one extreme and right-wing Hinduism at the other.

The sudden ending of the war with Japan gave further urgency to a settlement for India. At elections held in 1945 the Muslim League received overwhelming support in Muslim areas and largely proved its case to be the one political mouthpiece for Muslims. A cabinet mission which included Sir Stafford Cripps was sent to India by the Labour government of Britain in April 1946. It produced an ingenious three-tier plan for a federal union with provinces and unions within it, and suggested an interim coalition government under the Viceroy. While all this was being discussed and debated, increasing tension between Hindus and Muslims flared up into communal violence in Bengal. By the end of the year talks had been moved to London, and in February 1947 the British Prime Minister, Clement Attlee, announced his government's intention to transfer power into responsible Indian hands not later than June 1948. It was by no means clear to whom exactly power would be transferred. Lord Wavell was replaced as Viceroy by Admiral Mountbatten who now had special responsibility for preparing and supervising the transfer.

From August 1946, Jinnah had called for 'direct action' to bring about Pakistan, and as communal violence spread to the Punjab the new Viceroy judged that a united India could not be imposed except at the cost of a major civil war. Thus was born the plan for partition which

League and Congress came to accept in principle and the date for transfer of power was brought forward to 15 August 1947. Boundaries for the two new dominions of India and Pakistan remained to be worked out, together with the question of accession of the India of the princes to one or other of the new States. In the event, the Princely States came to terms with the new situation and, apart from three notable exceptions, they made their accessions without much difficulty. Kashmir proved to be the most significant of the exceptions and was subsequently to prove a very real bone of contention between India and Pakistan. A large number of lesser states were joined into six big unions.

What was apparently not entirely foreseen by anyone was the massive human upheaval which followed the partition of the Indian subcontinent. The massacres of Muslims by Hindus and Hindus by Muslims were on a terrifying scale; perhaps half a million people died in the aftermath of the partition and about twelve million people trekked from their homes. Pakistan alone took in upwards of five million refugees.

The main party leaders became active heads of their respective States, Mohammed Ali Jinnah in Pakistan and Jawaharlal Nehru in India. Pakistan was rather uncomfortably divided into West and East with roughly a thousand miles between them. Within India, and indeed within Congress, decentralising forces were soon to be at work. The bloodshed of 1947 was a very unhappy legacy bequeathed to the relationships between the two new States. By a bitter irony of history the revered old prophet of non-violence, Mahatma Gandhi, was assassinated in 1948 by a Hindu fanatic who felt that the Mahatma had betrayed Hindu orthodoxy.

By mid-century, India and Pakistan were attempting to shape their new constitutions. Nehru's India represented an experiment in both parliamentary democracy and in the principle of secularism for the State. Jinnah died in 1948 about a year after independence. His own leadership had been somewhat autocratic and this tendency was to continue in the internal politics of Pakistan. Both countries had enormous social and economic problems and there were also instances of 'unredeemed' lands. Small French territories were transferred to India but Portuguese Goa was a reminder to nationalist India of the colonial past and was to be forcibly occupied. Both India and Pakistan raised claims to and went to war for a short period over Kashmir. Nation-making was not to prove a short-term project for either India or Pakistan separately and they had to find the means of sharing the subcontinent amicably with each other.

The theme of Indian nationalism is such a big one that there is little scope in a brief survey of this kind to do justice to the pattern of nationalist developments in the island of Ceylon. It would be easy to repeat a once commonly held view that Ceylon was a model colony which had made a gradual and peaceful transition to national sovereignty, despite the multi-racial and multi-cultural character of its population, but to do so would be to underestimate the importance of communal and sectarian movements and tensions. Political consciousness in the modern sense developed first among the small Westernised middle class, but a more broadly-based Ceylon National Congress, influenced by the Indian example, was formed in 1919.

British policy, as in India, included the granting of periodical consti-tutional reforms, each of which provided for greater Asian representa-tion in the councils of government. The Donoughmore Commission of 1927–8 was Ceylon's counterpart of the Simon Commission for India, and the resulting Donoughmore Constitution of 1931 provided a useful training ground for future leaders. Naturally, it fell short of nationalist aims and it also offended minorities who saw more power going to the majority people, the Sinhalese, and, among the Sinhalese, to those of the Goyigama caste. Among the minorities were Ceylon Tamils, descended from immigrants from south India, Indian Tamils of more recent arrival and Muslims of Indian and other racial communities. The roots of Sinhalese culture were Buddhist and any evidence of strong Buddhist revivalism was likely to be watched with apprehension by Hindu, Muslim and other cultural groupings.

In the Second World War, Ceylon remained well outside the area of Japanese occupation and the island became the headquarters of Admiral Mountbatten's South-East Asia Command. A commission headed by Lord Soulbury visited Ceylon in 1944 and the eventual outcome was a self-governing constitution for Ceylon which, with the Indian and Pakistan examples so close at hand, was quickly replaced in February 1948 by complete independence within the British Commonwealth. The United National Party (U.N.P.), founded by D. S. Senanayake, dominated the political scene until 1956, with Mr Senanayake in the office of Prime Minister until his death in 1952. What began as a splinter group became Mr Bandaranaike's Peoples United Front which won the election of 1956. A tendency may be noted here, in passing, to the tenure of high political office by a few well-established and aristocratic family groupings.

The real, and often tragically violent, challenges latent in a plural society seemed to emerge in Ceylon after 1956. The first wave of nationalism, though including some Muslim-Buddhist riots in 1915, had, in the main, led gradually and unviolently to independence. A similar moderate atmosphere seemed to mark the first eight years of the new nation, but power struggles, assassinations and fierce communalism came into the open from the mid-1950s. It was as though, not having had to fight (in the literal sense) for independence from the British, the peoples of Ceylon had, in their own society, left many serious gaps yet to be bridged on the road to national unity.

3 The Course of Asian Nationalism: South-East Asia, Western Asia

SOUTH-EAST ASIA

THE course of nationalism in South-East Asia was clearly affected by nationalist developments elsewhere in Asia. The growth of political parties in India, the emergence of Japan as a major power, and the Chinese revolution of 1911; all had their repercussions in the very largely dependent countries of South-East Asia. In the case of overseas Indians and Chinese, the effect of events in their countries of origin was often to divert nationalist thoughts and aspirations towards the country of origin and thus away from the country of adoption. In so far as this process helped to delay the integration of minorities in South-East Asian countries, its long-term effect could be to promote indigenous nationalisms in response to those of India and China; it could in certain circumstances direct nationalist politics into communal groupings.

The First World War and the subsequent peace treaties encouraged South-East Asian nationalists to feel that what was good for Europe by way of self-determination should also be good for Asian countries. Nor, in the case of colonial territories, did the West appear to be entirely unsympathetic to these views, but there was the usual gradual and cautious approach on the one side, matched at times by mounting impatience and irritation on the other. Where and when nationalists took to violent means, the tendency was for the colonial power to put the brake on further concessions and resort to restrictive measures.

The influence of the Japanese in conquering and occupying the whole of the region during the Second World War was dynamic in many ways. Western prestige received a blow from which it would never fully recover, and by a combined policy of humiliating Europeans and promoting Asian consciousness the Japanese drove the lesson home fully. The enormous suffering and hardship of the war years gave South-East Asian peoples an awareness of race and country far more vividly than anything that had happened to them before. The deliberate sponsoring by the Japanese of some of the nationalist elements in the region did not result, as they intended, in a 'Co-prosperity Sphere' under Japanese leadership, but it was still immensely significant for nationalist developments after the war. Yet the Japanese era must not be seen as accounting for all that came afterwards. Although it undoubtedly heightened and quickened nationalist hopes and activities in South-East Asia, the impact of Japan did not in itself create nationalism. Rather, it hastened the growth of a plant whose roots were already well established.

In the Philippines, two nationalist groupings were active in the late years of Spanish rule. One, the Young Filipino Party, was intellectual in character and, at first, moderate and constitutional in approach. The failure of the Spanish authorities to work harmoniously with this party allowed the initiative to go to a revolutionary group, the Katipunan. The armed revolution against Spanish rule coincided with the war between America and Spain, and the Americans deliberately encouraged, helped and transported Filipino revolutionaries, some of whom had been in exile in Hong Kong and elsewhere. The revolutionary movement did not take kindly to American rule and guerilla resistance lasted until 1901.

The American government in the Philippines was soon energetically occupied in schemes of public works and social reform. Nationalism gradually channelled itself into a constitutional pattern, especially through a Nationalist Party bent on gaining influence in the elected legislative assembly which dated from 1907. As elsewhere, the First World War encouraged the right of self-determination in the Philippines, and the United States gave Filipinos greater autonomy, promising to recognise political independence as soon as a stable government could be established. The American response to Filipino nationalism varied with the party in power at Washington. In general, the Democrats were sympathetic and forward-looking, the Republicans cautious and less inclined to see the case for an early change.

Curiously enough, the economic effects of the great depression of 1929–32 caused American farmers, labour unions and other groups to argue the case for Filipino independence on the grounds that this would put an end to the free trade with the United States which the Philippines enjoyed. A decisive step was taken early in the presidency of Franklin Roosevelt. The Tydings–McDuffie Act, approved in 1934, provided for a ten-year period of self-government under a new constitution, to be followed by full independence. Economic safeguards in terms of trade quotas were written into the agreements in order to allow the economy of the Philippines to adjust itself gradually to the loss of free trade with the United States. The new Nationalist government came into being in the Philippines with Manuel Quezon as the first President.

No other colonial territory in South-East Asia was given a target date for complete independence at any time before the Second World War. In this context, the Filipino experience was a happy one but there were still struggles to come. The new regime was oligarchical; the American market was virtually indispensable to the economy of the islands and, before the promised date could arrive, the Philippines underwent the trials and hardships of a Japanese wartime occupation. The Japanese installed a puppet government in the Philippines and promised independence. Filipino nationalists ran, in some cases, the risk of being labelled collaborators with the enemy in the event of an American victory. In general, however, American sentiment was sympathetic to the nationalists' dilemma and, after resuming control, the Americans granted independence in July 1946. The question of economic dependence upon the United States was still a very vital one. It has been argued that throughout the American period, Filipino political organisations, and especially the Nationalist Party, represented family and regional groupings rather than anything truly nationalist. The internal issues after 1946 were to be concerned with land and class and the emergence of new parties; the personalities of individual leaders greatly influenced the course of the new nation-making.

The story of Indonesian nationalism has been at times so complex that a short summary can do no more than hint at some of the subtleties. The first organised society was the Budi Utomo or 'Glorious Endeavour' which arose from a Young Java Congress in 1908. Many of its members were Western-educated government officials and intellectuals and the movement made no mass appeal. Its early concern was for social improvement among Javanese people, notably through education. There were many shades of opinion within the movement on the extent to which the ways of the West should be adopted, but, in general, the society aimed at gradual social and political progress in co-operation with the Dutch. A wider appeal came from the Sarekat Islam association, founded in 1911–12 on the inspiration of an Islamic revival among Sumatrans and Javanese. Its immediate purpose was to protect Indonesian traders in the village textile industries against the control of the Chinese middleman. By the emphasis on race and the contact with villagers Sarekat Islam stirred up a more popular and dynamic nationalism than Budi Utomo. By 1916, it had eighty branch organisations with a total membership of 360,000 and was demanding self-government on the basis of union with the Netherlands.

In the main, these new organisations were not intrinsically anti-Dutch in their outlook, though an 'Indische' party founded at Bandung in 1912 claimed that Indonesia belonged to those who had been born there, irrespective of their racial origin. The Dutch authorities felt that this was too dangerous a creed and exiled the party's early leaders. The Dutch had for some time been conducting an 'ethical' policy which included the sponsoring of local government at village level and the benevolent use of indirect rule through Indonesian rulers, subject to Dutch guidance. A People's Council (Volksraad) was introduced in 1916 to the Netherlands Indies by an Act of the Dutch Parliament and it held its first meeting two years later. This was not a respresentative assembly and its function was to be essentially advisory, yet it was seen by the Dutch authorities as a training arena for the growth of Indonesian political maturity.

The 1914–18 war, however, stepped up the pace of nationalism in Indonesia, as elsewhere. The Russian revolution of 1917 and the greater militancy of the Indian nationalist movement influenced Indonesian nationalism, while Western-educated Indonesian students returned from Dutch universities in the early post-war years to add their measure of discontent and feelings of injustice. In the 1920s greater numbers of Dutchmen came out to Indonesia, either as administrators and technicians on long-service terms or as settlers for indefinite periods. To the Indonesian nationalist, especially in Java, it must have seemed that the Dutch promises based on the old 'ethical' policy were being counter-balanced by a deliberate plan of greater Dutch control and exploitation. The Sarekat Islam Party gained further strength against all this background but also faced a sharp internal conflict which ended in the expulsion, by 1923, of communists who had already founded their own 'Perserikatan Komunist Indie', or P.K.I., the Indonesian Communist Party. In Sarekat Islam and the P.K.I., Indonesia had a loose contemporary counterpart to the situation of the K.M.T. and the Chinese Communist Party in China, but the political patterns were never identical and were to be woven differently with the passage of time. Other political parties emerged in Indonesia in the 1920s and 1930s, some being offshoots of parties in Holland and others representing communal interests, such as those of the Chinese.

The communists proved extremely active in promoting labour unrest and strikes and, with some rather unrealistic hopes of support from Russia, they initiated an armed rising in parts of Sumatra and Java in 1926–7. The Dutch put down this movement rigorously and arrested a large number of P.K.I. members, many of whom were deported to New Guinea. The effect of this unsuccessful *coup* was to discredit, in Dutch eyes, the nationalist movement as a whole. Communism was not entirely suppressed but Sarekat Islam was left clearly as the main nationalist organisation. Not surprisingly, its aims and activities failed to satisfy the more radically-minded, and in 1927 a new party, 'Partai Nasional Indonesia' (P.N.I.), came into being with the object of uniting existing nationalist organisations into a common front with a non-co-operation policy. Among the leaders of the new party was a young engineer and popular public speaker, Achmed Sukarno. By the end of 1929 he was in prison for revolutionary activities.

A cautionary attitude towards Indonesian nationalism was maintained by the Dutch authorities throughout the 1930s. A greater recognition of the interests and needs of the East Indies was apparent during and after the depression years of the early thirties; Indonesian trade and industry were encouraged and a sense of partnership was fostered. The development of higher education was slow, however, and government-sponsored education had such an air of control about it that nationalists established 'wild' schools in virtual opposition to official policy. Those who schemed and worked for nothing less than complete independence sooner or later came under suspicion and arrest. Sukarno was arrested for a second time in 1933 and exiled from Java to Flores; two other nationalists, Mohammed Hatta and Soetan Sjahrir, both recently back from university in Holland, were sent, in 1934, to a concentration camp in New Guinea and later moved to the Moluccas. All three men remained in prison until the Japanese invasion of 1942. An air of suppressed nationalism was noted in Indonesia in 1936.

Self-government for Indonesia still seemed, in the official Dutch view, a distant goal at the outbreak of the Second World War. A possible change of heart was, however, evident after the German conquest of Holland and the establishment of a Dutch government in exile in London; in July 1941, a conference on self-government was promised for immediately after the war. In less than a year the Japanese were in control and the leading nationalists released from prison. During the Japanese period, Sukarno and Hatta worked above ground, negotiating with the Japanese, while Sjahrir and others formed underground resistance movements. All aimed at the eventual independence of

Indonesia, first through the collapse of the Japanese position and then through the establishment of a *de facto* government which would resist the return of the Dutch. In the later period of occupation, the Japanese fostered these aspirations by sponsoring an Indonesian army which soon became thoroughly alive to nationalist ideas. In a speech in June 1945, Sukarno proclaimed for Indonesia the 'five principles' of nationalism, humanitarianism, representative government, social justice and belief in God.

The Japanese made promises of independence to Indonesia as early as 1943, but these had little significance. At the time of the Japanese surrender, Indonesian independence was proclaimed but it had yet to be effective. The new Indonesian republic named by Sukarno and his colleagues was at first mainly Java-centred though it was intended to embrace the whole of the former Netherlands East Indies. British troops, landing in Java, gave a measure of recognition to the republican situation, but Dutch policy for the next two or three years alternated between negotiation and military action in what was an extremely complex and emotional environment. Eventually through the spirit of Indonesian nationalism and the influence on the Dutch of the U.S.A., Britain and the United Nations, full sovereignty over the former Netherlands East Indies (excluding New Guinea and adjacent islands) was transferred to the Indonesian republic in September, 1949. Sukarno was the first President and Hatta the first Prime Minister. The break with the Dutch had been a bitter one on both sides and there was further conflict to come until the Dutch gave up their interests in western New Guinea (West Irian). Within Indonesia there were problems enough. The leading nationalists had rejected a federal scheme of government in favour of a unitary one, and here lay the crux of tensions and troubles between a central government in Java and the separatism of some of the other island regions. Nationalist and communist organisations and the army itself were all to press their claims to speak for Indonesia, and political stability was to centre on some form of internal balance of power under a recognised head of state, a position skilfully held for many years by Sukarno. Despite its own difficulties and uncertainties, the new Indonesia did not hesitate to proclaim its new nationalism to the world and to point the dangers of colonialism in a new guise. At Bandung in Java, in 1955, a conference of Afro-Asian states met to discuss some of the political and economic issues which faced new and developing nations. In the years which followed, Indonesia appeared frequently on the international scene and, notably, through the 'confrontation' with Malaysia (1963–6) and the internal *coup* and counter-revolution which led to the abandonment of this policy and fall of Sukarno himself (1966–7).

The British conquest of Burma was only fully completed in the late years of the nineteenth century and the deep-rooted feelings of identity among the Burmese took some time to recover from the shock of the resultant changes. Constitutional developments from the first decade of the twentieth century generally followed the pattern of gradual progress towards self-government which was being worked out in India. The Montagu–Chelmsford Report of 1917, however, recommended that Burma should be treated as a separate case from that of the provinces of British India itself, and this idea of separation aroused strong national sentiment in Burma at the time. Eventually, in 1923, the system of 'diarchy', whereby certain departments of government were transferred to the care of Asian Ministers responsible to the legislature, was extended to Burma and a new Legislative Council was set up with a large electoral element based upon householders.

The years immediately following the 1914–18 War were very significant in the story of nationalism in Burma. The constitutional changes stimulated the growth of political parties while the establishment of the University of Rangoon in 1920 provided a focal point for a lively agitation on the nature and control of higher education. While party leadership and loyalties were worked out in the Legislative Council, the university in time produced some of the graduates who were to be Burma's future leaders.

The 'Opposition' in the Council was strongly nationalist and could usually outvote the government. Moderate nationalism was represented in the People's Party led by U Ba Pe but there was also extreme nationalism under the leadership of U Chit Hliaing, President of the Grand Council of Buddhist Associations; these latter boycotted the Council. The main nationalist demands were for improved education and entry prospects into the government service for Burmese, for economic developments which would improve the lot of the Burmese people, and for the curtailment of foreign exploitation. The extension of British control over Burma had been accompanied by substantial Indian immigration into the country and Indians predominated in many sectors of the public services and played a highly significant role in the economic life as traders, moneylenders and, through loans and mortgages, controllers of important rice-growing lands, especially in the Irrawaddy delta. The Burmese nationalist saw his country as being economically exploited both by Europeans and by Indians. But the population of Burma was still more divided by the existence of well-defined minority groups like the Shans and the Karens, whose own race-consciousness and nationalisms were stiffened in response to the emergence of strong nationalist feelings on the part of the Burmese.

For many nationally-minded Burmese, political separation from India appeared in the 1920s to be a necessary landmark on the road to independence, yet when the Simon Commission, investigating the working of the reforms of 1923, came to recommend separation, Burmese opinion began to veer the other way. (The Burmese have sometimes been called the 'Irish of South-East Asia'.) Separation became increasingly viewed as the sinister offspring of imperial government and Big Business, and an Anti-Separation League advocated that Burma should join the Indian federation which the Simon Report recommended, but retain the option of secession. When Britain made it clear that Burma would not be able to contract out of the new Indian government at will, the Anti-Separationists changed their views, and eventually the Government of India Act of 1935 provided for the separation of Burma by April 1937.

Two leaders dominated Burmese politics in the 1930s: Dr Ba Maw, European-educated and a member of the Legislative Council from 1932, founded the *Sinyetha* or Poor Man's policy with a political programme based on peasant needs. Under the new constitution of 1937, Ba Maw became the first Burmese Prime Minister in a largely self-governing Burma which still fell far short of a nationalists' dream of political fulfilment. During the Japanese period, Ba Maw became head of the puppet regime. U Saw, who was Ba Maw's rival, was less tied to politics or programmes and was even more of an opportunist. He edited at one period an anti-British and pro-Japanese newspaper, and he visited Britain in 1941, seeking an unqualified pledge of post-war dominion status for Burma. While on his return journey, U Saw was detained in Ethiopia on charges of communicating with the Japanese, and his subsequent political career was dramatic but short. Arriving in Burma in 1946, he hired assassins in the following year to kill the Burmese Prime Minister, Aung San, and six of his Cabinet colleagues; he was subsequently arrested, tried and executed.

Aung San had risen to prominence during the Japanese period as head of the Japanese-sponsored Burma National Army (B.N.A.). In the late 1930s, he was the more revolutionary type of young nationalist, one of a group of 'Thakins' (or 'sahibs') who addressed each other by this title to indicate their intention of replacing their European masters. The Thakin movement emerged as an aftermath of a students' strike at the University of Rangoon in 1935; by the time of the Japanese invasion of Burma in 1942 some of its members had prepared themselves for collaboration with the Japanese. The shifts of strategy and tactics among Burmese nationalists during the Japanese occupation were scarcely less complex than those in Indonesia. Resistance movements, some of them communist-led, existed from the beginning. By 1943, the Thakins themselves were fostering one while the Japanese were proclaiming 'independence' for Burma. Disillusioned with Japanese promises and noting the mounting successes of the British and Indian counter-offensive in Burma, the Nationalist army defected to the Allies in mid-1945. At the end of the war, two fundamental questions hung over Burma. How would Britain come to terms with Burmese nationalism as represented in particular by Aung San and his party, now known as the Anti-Fascist Peoples Freedom League, the A.F.P.F.L? How would Burmese nationalism affect the attitudes and aspirations of the non-Burmese minorities in Burma?

British policy for Burma was to grant Dominion status after a short transitional period of direct British rule in co-operation with the Burmese. Aung San and his followers wanted nothing less than complete independence. Gradually Aung San won greater confidence from the British government, and agreed elections held in April 1947 put the A.F.P.F.L. in a commanding position. The assassination of Aung San left to his successor, Thakin Nu (to be known later as U Nu – a plainer title), the main burden of planning and negotiation which ended in Burma's independence on 4 January 1948. The new State was republican and chose to remain outside the Commonwealth. Independence was followed by a series of rebellions, all pulling in different directions, some communist-led, others based on minority fears and grievances. U Nu survived these upheavals with remarkable success and with the aid of a small Cabinet he succeeded, by 1950, in restoring confidence.

The very difficult problem of nation-making in Burma continued throughout the 1950s. There was an uneasy balance of forces for several years. Nu's Buddhism stood opposed to the Marxism of the socialists and the treatment of minority groups called at all times for great sensitivity. Eventually an army *coup* of 1962 dissolved Parliament and set up a Revolutionary Council under General Ne Win, who had held the effective leadership in an earlier emergency period (1958–60). The importance of an army role in nationalist politics was by no means only a Burmese phenomenon; in different ways, for example, the army played a part in the widely-differing countries of Turkey, Japan and Indonesia.

What was known in its colonial setting as French Indo-China consisted technically of the French colony of Cochin-China and the French protectorates of Annam, Cambodia, Laos and Tongking. Asian monarchies and officials continued to exist in Annam, Cambodia and Laos, but a strong French administration permeated this façade, and cultural and political assimilation were the twin prongs of French colonial policy. The nationalist response came from the Annamites or Vietnamese who represented about three-fourths of the population of Indo-China and among whom there was a middle-class element with an economic basis of rice-planting and money-lending. Culturally, the Vietnamese owed a great deal to China and it is not surprising that events in China at and after the time of the Boxer Rising influenced the growth of Vietnamese nationalism. As in many other countries, the movement was at first of an elite and intellectual character, marking a mild revolt on the part of a proud and intelligent people against the paternalism of French colonial policy. At the same time, where, as in Cochin-China and Tongking, French rule had been established by conquest, there were frequent anti-government conspiracies and acts of banditry.

Moderate nationalists pressed in Indo-China, as elsewhere, for better educational facilities, and the University of Hanoi was opened in 1907, only to be closed again the following year on account of the nationalistic attitudes of its students; it was not reopened for a decade. Although there were men of liberal outlook in the French administration, notably General Albert Sarraut, Governor-General 1911–14 and 1917–19, the French authorities on the whole failed to come to a working partnership with the more moderate and liberal elements in Vietnamese nationalism, and this helped to turn the movement into more revolutionary channels.

The First World War was a turning point. Some 100,000 Vietnamese were recruited for war service as soldiers and workers in Europe; many of these returned home full of new and, from the French standpoint, subversive ideas. At the same time, the intellectuals noted that self-determination in the Versailles context meant one thing for Europe but another for Asia. The growth of the Chinese Kuomintang and communist parties in the early 1920s gave a significant impetus to Vietnamese nationalism, for southern China was a close neighbour and there

Ho Chi Minh

Dr Achmed Sukarno, in 1949

U Nu

Aung San

were movements of ideas and revolutionaries across the frontier. More distant, but also inspiring in its way, was the Indian example of a more militant and popular Congress movement pressing for self-government. Thus during the twenties, the first political parties emerged in Indo-China. Bui Quang-chieu and Pham Quynh led separate parties both with a programme of constitutional reform along democratic lines. Had the French government warmly recognised and encouraged parties such as these, some of the revolutionary movements might have gained less ground, but the failure of the moderates to achieve practical gains left the way open for more extreme tacticians.

The Revolutionary Party of Young Annam was founded in 1925 and it organised a series of strikes which invited close supervision and repression by the government; it was also weakened by internal differences among its leaders. A Nationalist Annamite party in Tongking came into being about 1927, based very much on the left wing of the Chinese Kuomintang. It used terrorism as a political weapon and tried to subvert Vietnamese units in the army. By 1930 it was launching an ill-timed and ill-prepared rebellion which the French put down with great severity. Revolutionary leaders who escaped arrest did so only by going underground or leaving the country; among those who escaped was Nguyen-Ai-Quoc, better known as Ho Chi Minh.

Ho had joined the Communist Party in France before the First World War. He had subsequently studied revolutionary technique in Russia and lived among left-wing revolutionaries in Canton. In his own programme, Ho put the cause of Vietnamese independence first with communism to be brought in later; he urged the reduction of taxation, redistribution of land and the abolition of conscription among Vietnamese for service abroad. After the failure of the 1930 rebellion, Ho fled to Hong Kong where he served a prison sentence, but his communist organisation held together and in 1939 it provided the nucleus for his new Viet Minh party, or League for the Independence of Vietnam. At the outbreak of the Second World War, Vietnamese nationalism appeared to have achieved little and independence seemed a very distant goal. In retrospect, Ho can be seen as a leader of great skill and strength of will, and during the Japanese occupation the Viet Minh became the main force for nationalism and independence.

The Japanese used the fall of France in 1940 and their alliance with Hitler Germany as a lever to gain, first, military and air bases in Indo-China, then to occupy the whole area. The 'Vichy French' administration continued under Japanese control. The course of the war by March

E

1945 led the Japanese to declare the end of French colonial status for Indo-China and to encourage the Emperor of Annam, Bao Dai, and the Kings of Cambodia and Laos to declare their independence. Ho Chi Minh had meanwhile carefully built up the Viet Minh and, at the Japanese surrender, his following was strong enough to seize both Hanoi and Saigon and declare a republic of Vietnam. Bao Dai abdicated and was thereupon made Supreme Councillor of State in the new regime. Naturally, the situation did not end there. First, the Allies had agreed at Potsdam just how to handle the immediate take-over of Indo-China by the use of Chinese troops to the north of the sixteenth parallel of latitude and British troops to the south of it. Secondly, the French were anxious to maintain the principle that, ultimately, the future of Indo-China was the concern of France. The outcome was that Ho Chi Minh, with Chinese support, refused initially to admit French forces into the north and that, despite negotiations and the offer by France of associate status to Vietnam, Laos and Cambodia within a French Union, the Viet Minh continued to stand for full independence for Vietnam. In March 1947, Ho was quoting the example of the United States in the Philippines and Britain in India, but this was a path which the French were reluctant to follow.

Ho's communism made him generally unacceptable to the French but he was perhaps first a nationalist relying on much nationalist and non-communist support. The Vietnamese situation developed into full scale war between the communist-held north and the non-communist south which, in time, had a civil war of its own linked with the bigger conflict. An international agreement on partition for Vietnam was reached at Geneva in 1954; Cambodia by this time was recognised as independent; Laos, too, was theoretically independent, but had violent right-wing and left-wing troubles of its own. Vietnam became increasingly a matter of international concern and America took on the role of France in supporting non-communist regimes in both Vietnam and Laos.

Siam had retained political sovereignty in the age of Western imperialism in South-East Asia, but her national survival was due in part to a process of adaptation of the ways of the West and this had helped to increase national awareness. Siamese (or Thai) nationalism did not need to take the form of an independence movement against an alien dominant power; instead it turned to internal issues, notably the nature of Thai monarchy and government and the status and activities of the Chinese minority in the country.

The Thai monarchy had led the way to the Westernisation and modernisation which helped to maintain national sovereignty from the late nineteenth century onwards, but the pattern was one of benevolent despotism and little was done to broaden the basis of government. A combination of middle-class social and political discontent with the grievances of army officers led, in the aftermath of economic depression in 1932, to a bloodless revolution against the power of the monarchy. The leader of the revolution, known best by the name Pridi, was a Paris-trained lawyer and Professor of Law at the Chulalongkorn University. He drafted a constitution which included a Council of Ministers and a People's Assembly and this the king accepted. The new government was oligarchical and represented the group who had gained power through the revolution rather than wider national interests. A conservative reaction centred round the king brought about a more restricted version of the constitution and Pridi and his close followers were branded communistic for their plans for the national economy. For a time (1933–4), Pridi was forced into exile but he returned as a popular figure and was cleared of charges of communism.

Meanwhile an army revolt in 1933 was suppressed, and prominent in the work of suppression was a right-wing nationalist army leader who is most readily referred to as Pibun. Where Pridi stood for a strong blending of socialism with his nationalism, Pibun presented the image of militarism linked with nationalism. The king, Rama VII, abdicated in 1935 rather than agree to renewed attempts to restrict royal authority, and he was succeeded by a ten-year-old boy and a Regency Council. Pibun became head of the government and Pridi Minister of Finance; the nationalisms of both combined in a drive against the somewhat entrenched positions of the Chinese. Discriminatory legislation against Chinese traders was accompanied by the deliberate government policy of encouraging the Thais to engage in trade and commerce themselves. The government set an example by establishing paper, textile, and rice mills as well as sugar, silk and tobacco factories and other enterprises including tin-mining and smelting and co-operative stores. The Chinese were not easily dislodged from the commanding position which they had built up in the Thai economy but, as the pressure increased, larger numbers of them began to seek the protection of Thai citizenship; at this stage the government increased the barriers to naturalisation.

Subsidies were given to Thai firms, technical training was assisted both at home and overseas, and a strictly controlled system of State education was established. Buddhism was given a patriotic interpretation and the name Siam was replaced by Thailand, or 'the land of the free'. A theoretical framework for the new nationalism was put forward by Prime Minister Pibun in 1939 in the principles of *Ratha Niyom* calling for national rejuvenation. Large numbers of Chinese schools were closed, Chinese newspapers were suppressed, Chinese secret societies investigated and some Chinese community leaders imprisoned.

In politics and trade, Thailand in the late 1930s was looking increasingly towards Japan as a counterweight to the Western powers and a possible insurance policy; thus the way was prepared for a measure of co-operation with the Japanese when they occupied Indo-China and prepared their invasion of the Malay peninsula. The reward for such co-operation was the token restoration to the Thais of territories in Cambodia, Laos and northern Malaya which had once been parts or dependencies of the Thai kingdom. Generally, however, the status of Thailand was little better under the Japanese than that of a conquered country.

Pibun remained in office until 1944, by which time the Thai mood had veered against co-operation with the Japanese and towards an eventual *rapprochement* with the Western allies. Pridi, who had been a wartime organiser of the Free Thai resistance movement, came again to the centre of the political stage at the end of the war and, thanks partly to American mediation, Thailand was able to adjust herself to the changing pattern of international relations and to become (1947) an accepted member of the United Nations. Rapid changes of government followed and there were two civil wars and three *coups* between 1945 and 1951. Pridi's regime was at least semi-liberal but it was overthrown by a military *coup* organised by Pibun in November 1947. By rumour, Pridi and his associates were insidiously connected with the mysterious death of the young king, Ananda, who was found shot in the head (June 1946); the financial corruption of some members of Pridi's government and the occurrence of widespread disturbances and riots combined to weaken the premier's position.

The Pibun administration lasted ten years, though not without internal power struggles among its supporters. Strong rather than liberal government characterised its early years and where the Pridi era had been marked by left-wing tendencies, Pibun was deliberately anti-communist at a time when the communist rebellion began in Malaya and Mao Tse-tung's forces were on the way to victory in China. There were problems enough of internal security and national unity, with large Chinese and Malay minorities in the southern provinces and pro-Viet

Minh Vietnamese in the sensitive north-east areas; moreover supporters of Pridi attempted counter-revolutions in 1949 and again in 1951.

By 1955, Pibun felt able to allow greater expressions of democracy, including the establishment of political parties and the preparation for elections in 1957. A diversity of political parties fought the elections amid great tension and the announced results of a clear government victory were challenged by charges of ballot-rigging. The tide of public opinion went against Pibun in 1957 as it had gone against Pridi ten years earlier and yet another *coup* ended in Field-Marshal Sarit becoming Prime Minister in October 1958. The monarchy itself survived all these upheavals but the government was still an autocracy with a strong military basis.

Unease about minorities and frontier situations brought the Thais into the South-East Asia Treaty Organisation and steered Thai foreign policy into alignment with the West; American influence was particularly strong. Internally, the economically powerful Chinese minority constituted one major challenge to a common nationality within the Thai borders. Beyond the frontiers, the lesson of history pointed to the Thai tradition of self-preservation in a changing world.

Nationalism in Malaya remained relatively undramatic until the Second World War. A number of individual Malayans were affected by nationalist ideas which were current in other Asian countries and Western-type education contributed in Malaya, as elsewhere, to the aspirations for political and social change. Yet neither a strong political party nor an organised popular movement for a self-governing or independent Malaya had emerged before the Japanese invasion.

Several factors help to explain the tardiness of nationalism in Malaya. British rule in the peninsula was both direct and indirect. The Straits Settlements of Penang, Malacca and Singapore constituted a crown colony, but the nine Malay States were technically protectorates which retained their traditional forms of monarchy. It is true that British influence was very strong in the four Federated Malay States and that the practicalities of federal government tended to outdate the role of the monarchies, yet there remained much consultation on both sides. In the other, so-called Unfederated States, the Malay governments were able to preserve a much more independent role. The indigenous political structure of Malaya, though greatly modified in the British period, was still, in the 1930s, sufficiently separatist in character to provide in itself an obstacle to unity. Moreover, even in a protecting role Britain had only entered into the affairs of the Malay States from 1874 onwards and at dates well into the twentieth century in some cases.

The comparative prosperity of Malaya, apart from trade depressions after the 1914–18 war and again in the early 1930s, also served as a brake on nationalist tendencies. Plantation agriculture, especially for rubber-production, and extensive tin-mining were the main sources of Malaya's wealth and though this was not evenly shared, living standards in Malaya were high as compared with neighbouring countries. Business enterprise demonstrated mainly by Chinese and Europeans, but effective only with Malay co-operation, had made the Malay States a land of promise for hundreds of thousands of immigrants from India, the East Indies, and, especially, south China. Until 1931, emigration and immigration proceeded freely and many immigrant families tended to look upon Malaya as a temporary home. Evidence for a plural society exists at a number of stages in Malaya's history but never on such a scale as in the present century. Three main racial groups predominated, Malays, Chinese and Indians, but within each category there were linguistic and other cultural differences and widely varying periods of family domicile in the country.

There were, in fact, many loyalties and patriotisms in pre-1941 Malaya but these were not, in the main, linked with any vision of a new unified and independent nation. Traditionally, the loyalty of the Malay was felt and given towards his own Sultan and State. Small numbers of educated Malays were attracted by ideas of pan-Islamism and this kindled an Islamic revival in the inter-war years and also turned the attention of some Malays to the possibility of a form of union with Sumatra. In political terms, however, the Malays, claiming to be the truly indigenous people, retained several privileges. They had, in many cases, good opportunities for appointment to government service, the government paid for their schools and, in theory at least, helped them to retain their lands. British administrators in high office seldom failed to be aware of their responsibility for safeguarding the special status of the Malays.

An underlying factor in Malay nationalism was a feeling of resentment against the economic encroachments of the Chinese. It would be wrong to over-emphasise this for the inter-war years since there was no major racial clash between the races, but the Chinese exhibited a tendency to remain a self-contained community, or series of communities, preserving their own languages, culture and system of education. Many Chinese openly or privately supported the efforts of Chiang Kai-shek and the Kuomintang Party to reunify China. A smaller number took their inspiration from Chinese communism, and the Malayan Communist Party (M.C.P.) was founded as a separate organisation about 1927 with a largely Chinese membership. Since it did not register publicly its constitution and aims, it remained an illegal organisation until the Japanese invasion; it was, for its size, very active in fomenting unrest and discontent in labour circles. Indians in Malaya were often diverted politically by the independence struggle in their home- or mother-country, and the campaigns of the Congress Party in particular tended to serve as a channel for the political sympathies and aspirations of the Malayan Indian. Inter-marriage between members of different racial groups was a relatively rare occurrence in Malaya and thus nationalism developed along communal rather than pan-Malayan lines.

The Japanese invasion and occupation of Malaya (1941–5) greatly accelerated nationalist developments. It is highly significant to note, first of all, that no party or group existed in Malaya which the Japanese could recognise and sponsor as an 'independent' government. Japanese policy was more accommodating towards the Malays, and the Malay forms of government were kept in being but subjected to Japanese supervision through political agents and the requirements of the Japanese military authorities. The Chinese were generally oppressed, and in many individual cases, persecuted. Communists were especially sought out as active opponents of the regime, and the M.C.P. took to the jungle where it succeeded in leading an armed resistance movement with some contact and assistance from a British 'Special Force'. Indians were recruited for the Indian National Army or for forced labour, and Eurasians were made to suffer for the Western elements in their heredity.

One effect of the Japanese period was a sharpening of racial feeling between Malays and Chinese. This varied from place to place but some of it was deliberately initiated by the Japanese and at the end of the war there were a number of ugly and serious racial clashes. One Japanese administrative experiment was to combine the administration of Malaya and Sumatra through a headquarters in Singapore, and though this had little real success it may have helped to keep alive the pan-Malay concept of fraternal bonds across the Malacca Straits. So far as European influence was concerned, Japanese policy aimed at abolishing the use of the English language and lowering British prestige which had received in any case quite a deadly blow through a rapid military defeat which included the fall of Singapore. The more constructive side of this policy was the arousing of an Asian consciousness which, whatever the attitudes to Japanese rule, could hardly fail to have some long-term significance for the post-war period. Moreover, a country which suffered the hardships of a harsh foreign occupation could hardly emerge with its political outlook unchanged; the Japanese military administration imposed a form of unity on the whole area.

The communist-led guerilla fighters, who had adopted the title of Malayan People's Anti-Japanese Army (M.P.A.J.A.), came out of the jungle as heroes at the end of the war and attempted to set up areas of control. There was just a possibility that the returning British forces might be challenged but the M.P.A.J.A. agreed to come to terms and accept demobilisation conditions. Chin Peng was one leader who was honoured in the victory celebrations in London; his name cropped up in different circumstances later.

As in Burma, the British intention was to retain control for a temporary period through a military administration while preparing the way for a new constitution. A Malayan Union was planned for all the States and Settlements except Singapore, which was to remain a crown colony for the time being. In the view of many Malays and many pre-war British administrators the Union plan, when its terms became known, imposed, even as a transitional stage, too much British control and its citizenship clauses undermined the special protected status of the Malays. Moreover, the agreement of the individual Sultans to the new scheme seemed to have been obtained in great haste and without opportunities for fuller and further consultations. In short, the Malayan Union plan provoked a widespread and determined Malay reaction and to oppose it the United Malays National Organisation (U.M.N.O.) was created in 1946 under the leadership of Dato Onn bin Jaafar of Johore. There were already some political parties in existence and the Malayan Communist Party had been legalised, but the new Malay organisation had the greatest support. Its first success was to obstruct the new Union and help create a second constitution whereby the same territorial area was given a federal framework with Malay rights and privileges more carefully safeguarded. This new Federation of Malaya was inaugurated in February 1948 and it was intended to pave the way towards democratic self-government. Most Malays were probably satisfied with it for the time being; non-Malays, including the almost equally numerous Chinese, had more reason for discontent. Given time and patience, the rights of citizenship could be fully extended to all non-Malays, but many saw themselves temporarily as second-class citizens.

Within a few months, the new government was faced by a communist-led armed revolution operating from jungle bases. M.C.P. leaders had decided that the situation was promising for such a tactical move and they resorted to military supplies which they had taken care to hide some three years earlier. The M.C.P. leaders now posed as the true nationalists seeking to liberate Malaya from the colonial yoke and using every means of persuasion and intimidation to gain support. For the next twelve years the 'Emergency', as it was called, affected virtually every aspect of life in Malaya. At vast cost the rising was gradually controlled and suppressed; on more than one occasion the war was described as a battle for the minds and hearts of the people. The M.C.P. was outlawed but other political parties came together in 1953 in an 'Alliance' which comprised U.M.N.O., a Malayan Chinese Association (M.C.A.) and a Malayan Indian Congress (M.I.C.). Dato Onn had tried to broaden the racial basis of U.M.N.O., and, failing this, left it to found a new party; the leadership was taken over by Tunku Abdul Rahman, a prince of the royal family of the Kedah state. The Tunku, as he was to become known, played the major role in the establishment of Malayan independence. At one stage during the Emergency, in 1955, he and others negotiated under amnesty terms with the communist Secretary-General, Chin Peng, who refused to end the fighting except on terms very favourable to the communist cause. This made the Alliance all the more anxious to secure independence to counter the communists' claim to represent Malayan nationalism.

Malaya became independent on 31 August 1957 with Tunku Abdul Rahman as Prime Minister. Singapore, in the meanwhile, had avoided a shooting war and was moving somewhat uncertainly towards self-government. Singapore differed from the Federation of Malaya in that some eighty per cent of the population was Chinese and that the economy was largely based on free-trade principles. Singapore politics in the 1950s were extremely lively and strikes and riots, many of which were communist-inspired, were frequent features. Several political parties appeared, the most dynamic being the People's Action Party (P.A.P.) which embraced many shades of left-wing opinion and had its own severe internal struggles. By 1959, the P.A.P. had an overwhelming majority in the newly-elected government, and when the new constitution of the State of Singapore was introduced in June of the same year, Mr Lee Kuan Yew as P.A.P. leader became the first Prime Minister. Mr Lee's policy was deliberately Malayan and he kept the idea of a merger with the Federation much to the fore. A major difficulty in the way of merger was the Malay fear that the racial balance would then be tipped in favour of the Chinese; the Federation, itself newly independent, was also anxious to avoid trade union and student troubles of the kind which had disturbed Singapore in the mid-1950s.

A solution to the merger problem was attempted in 1963 when both Singapore and Malaya became part of the larger Federation of Malaysia which also comprised the former British colonies of North Borneo and Sarawak. Viewed in one way, this new federation was an attempt to reach a racial balance more acceptable from the Malay side. It was also aimed against the possibility of any communist *coup* in Singapore. For the Borneo territories and for Singapore it provided a gateway to full independence within a federal framework which still had to make its own checks and balances workable. The internal tensions and difficulties were considerable and Lee Kuan Yew and Abdul Rahman came later to agree, with reluctance, that Singapore should secede from the federation. Externally, Malaysia was challenged by the government of the Philippines which raised old claims to parts of northern Borneo, based on the rights of earlier Sultans of Sulu. A nearer and bigger threat came from Dr Sukarno's Indonesia which proclaimed a 'confrontation' against the new Malaysian State and proceeded to wage diplomatic, economic and limited military warfare against it. Irredentism, political jealousies and the need for an emotional unifying cause in his own country were all part of the background to the Indonesian president's actions.

So far as Malaya and Singapore were concerned the task of nation-making would still require great skill and patience and the passage of time. For the Borneo territories, which were nowhere near so politically advanced, this was even more true.

WESTERN ASIA

It is proposed to confine attention in this region mainly to the modern nationalisms of the Arab and Turkish peoples, and it can be seen that the early years of the twentieth century witnessed significant changes. The Muslim Ottoman Empire lay across the frontiers of Europe and Asia and embraced many races and cultures; its eventual disintegration was brought about by a mixture of foreign wars and internal separatism. Some of the separatist developments belong to European history and can be seen in the context of European nationalism; the growth of modern

Turkey and of the modern Arab states is perhaps best viewed in the context of western Asia, though there are many overlaps and areas of loose definition. The geographical proximity to Europe of the Arab and Turkish lands brought European influences to bear at an early date (and, of course, vice versa) and so far as modern ethnic nationalism was concerned, some of the earlier, mid-nineteenth-century contacts were with nationalists from central and eastern Europe. A Polish refugee, Count Constantine Borzeki, who embraced Islam and became an official of the Ottoman Empire, published in 1869 a book on the Turkish peoples with a historical section which drew attention to a separate Turkish identity. At the government level, the Ottoman Empire was a pan-Islamic State and the Turks had long tended to submerge their separate racial identity in the common brotherhood of their religion. A Polish nationalist interpretation of their historic past together with the findings of oriental scholarship in Europe helped, by the late decades of the nineteenth century, to foster pan-Turkish ideas, in part as a response to the current vogue of pan-Slavism. As the political fortunes of the Ottoman rulers declined, the concept of a new and wide Turkish hegemony stretching across central Asia became all the more attractive for groups of patriotic intellectuals among the Tatars in Russia and among the Turks in Turkey.

Ottoman Sultan Abdul Hamid II, who reigned from 1876 to 1909, appeared at first to move with a current trend of liberalism and constitutionalism when, at the beginning of his reign, he promulgated a new constitution for Turkey. This included a parliament with a nominated senate and an elected chamber. Abdul Hamid viewed this structure, however, more as a façade than a reality and when his parliament showed undue signs of life he dismissed it at the end of two brief sessions. For the rest of his reign, the Sultan demonstrated that reform (non-political) and modernisation were to come from the throne.

In 1908, Young Turk revolutionary officers in Salonika pressed the Sultan, under threat of an army *coup*, to restore the constitution of 1876. The success of the Japanese in 1905 and of a constitutional revolution in Persia in 1906 encouraged a revival of Young Turkism, which had been evident a generation or so earlier, until it reached the point of rebellion. The Young Turks saw their country endangered by further separatism from within and possible further pressures from outside. Reluctantly, Abdul Hamid gave way and a second period of constitutional government was inaugurated in Turkey. The Sultan himself had been a careful exponent of pan-Islamism and a quick 'counter-revolution' against the

Westernising and secularising tendencies of the Young Turks contained a strong and militant religious element. The movement was suppressed in 1909, Abdul Hamid was deposed and his brother, who had spent many years in confinement, ascended the throne rather unwillingly as Mehmed V.

In the years immediately before the 1914–18 War, German interests in Turkey increased steadily. Railway building and planning was one major sphere of activity under German initiative and the Baghdad railway scheme was a largely German undertaking. The new Turkish army was trained by German officers under the supervision of German General Liman von Sanders. As the European powers completed their network of alliances which led to the entanglement of 1914, Turkey's leanings towards Germany became more clearly defined and, in August 1914, a military alliance with Germany was accepted. The Young Turks had feared partition if the Entente powers won the war and, in the event, the defeat of Turkey by 1918 left the way open for a final dismemberment of the Ottoman Empire. The Treaty of Sèvres (August 1920) imposed on the old Empire a very harsh and punitive settlement. Syria, Palestine and Mesopotamia were lost, together with what had long been the very theoretical overlordship of Egypt. By the terms of Sèvres, Smyrna, Armenia and Kurdistan were also removed from the Empire but some of these terms were to be challenged during the next few years, in particular the right of the Greeks to occupy Smyrna and other areas in western Asia Minor. From the shock of defeat and the humiliation of Sèvres a new, smaller but more dynamic Turkey arose from the ruins of the defunct Ottoman Empire. This successful, but often costly, movement was largely the work of a group of rebels led by an army officer, Mustafa Kemal, later known as Kemal Atatürk.

Mustafa Kemal came to prominence in 1919, when, as Inspector-General of the army of the north, he took over the leadership of a nationalist rising which he had been sent to suppress. He and his followers were prominent in the holding of congresses for the ejection of European occupation forces from Turkish soil and the restoration of Turkish sovereignty. They were also the main supporters of a revolutionary Grand National Assembly established at Ankara in April 1920. Kemal organised and trained a new army to defeat the Greeks stationed on Turkish soil. By allowing the Greeks to strike first deep inland he chose the timing of a dynamic counter-attack which ended in their being driven back across the Aegean. A new international treaty signed at Lausanne in 1923 recognised the *status quo* in Asia Minor and crowned the efforts of Mustafa Kemal and his followers for the maintenance of Turkish prestige and the preservation of a Turkish homeland in Asia Minor with a European outlet at Constantinople (Istanbul).

Initially, the Kemalists had a strong pan-Islamic character, their purpose being to free Islamic lands and Islamic populations; they sought also to liberate the Sultan-Caliph and to expel the infidel invader. In his own capital, the Sultan refused to be 'liberated' and clearly regarded Kemal and his supporters as rebels. The Islamic content, as a consequence, began to disappear from the revolutionary programme and nationalism and secularism took its place. The success of Mustafa Kemal against the Greeks and the international recognition gained by Turkey at Lausanne led, in October 1923, to the establishment of a Republic with Kemal as its first President and Ankara the new capital. The Sultanate was abolished and, with it, the Caliphate through which the Sultan had nominally been the chief political figure of the Muslim world. With Kemal as leader, the new Turkey witnessed drastic and far-reaching changes during the next decade and a half. But Kemal's position in the early years of what was really a dictatorship did not go unchallenged and, in 1925, there was a very serious revolt of the Kurdish peoples. The Kurds, or 'Mountain Turks', lived in the eastern provinces of Turkey and had fellow kinsmen in Syria, Iran, Iraq and the North-West Frontier provinces of India. Their rebellion was based on a resentment of Turkish rule and desire for independence, and on outraged feelings at the abolition of the Caliphate by Kemal's government. A separate 'Kurdistan', carved out of the Ottoman Empire, had been envisaged at Sèvres in 1920, but nothing came of this at Lausanne three years later. The rising lasted about three months and it was suppressed ruthlessly, though for many years afterwards there was sporadic unrest among the Kurds. The Turks of the eastern provinces remained loyal but Kemal decided that the time had come to break or weaken the power of religion over his people.

In August 1925, Kemal started his campaign for dress reform including the sensational abolition of the wearing of the fez. This was accompanied by attacks on old Muslim modes of conduct and attitudes towards women. Womens' rights were advocated and polygamy made illegal. Where the new laws met with resistance or caused disturbances, 'Independence Tribunals' moved in to pass sentences after troops or police had restored order. A new code of civil law based on that of Switzerland was introduced, together with a new penal code adapted from the Italian pattern and a new commercial code borrowed from

Germany and Italy. The speed with which these changes were effected is a measure of the disciplined response of the Turks to a strong leader, but Kemal's life was in danger at times. A conspiracy to assassinate him in Smyrna (Izmir) in June 1926 was discovered in time and Kemal used the occasion to effect the arrest and execution of virtually every prominent man known to be opposed to his policies.

The reforms 'from the top' continued along the lines of a new nationalism and secularism. Islam ceased to be the official religion for Turkey in April 1928. A new Turkish alphabet was introduced to oust the Arabic one, and a mixture of government threats and promises helped to speed the change-over. Language reform continued with the eradication of Persian and Arabic words and the coining of new Turkish words, some of which were borrowed from European languages, especially French. Turkish historians inflated the role of the Turks in the history of civilisation, and Kemal gave official support to some of their wilder theories; Islamic history was dropped from the school curriculum in favour of Turkish history.

Technically, Kemal's government was of a one-party kind, the People's Party. The membership was often somewhat mixed, and discredited elements were purged from time to time. An early Progressive Republican Party, formed in November 1924, was suppressed after the Kurdish revolt. By the late 1920s the latent opposition to the government included Islamic, communist and liberal intellectual elements. In 1930 Kemal allowed a Liberal Republican Party to be founded, under the leadership of Ali Fethi Okyar, a former Prime Minister, the function of this Party being to provide a constitutional 'Opposition'. The experiment was, to say the least, premature and, as the new party aroused public demonstrations of support from religious and other dissidents, it was dissolved. It lasted only two or three months and another 'Popular Republican Party' had an even shorter life; there was no further organised opposition until after the Second World War.

During the 1930s the revolution continued through such media as the insistence upon Turkish names for Turkish towns and cities, the formulation of the principles of the Turkish Revolution and the dissemination of these through 'Peoples' Houses' or meeting halls throughout the country, and the institution of a Westernised weekend. Titles were brought into line with the emphasis on modernism and nationalism and, from January 1935, surnames were made compulsory. Kemal added 'Atatürk' ('Father Turk') to his name to lead the way. It was a measure of Kemal's success that there were no great upheavals at the time of his death (November 1938). His successor as President was Ismet Inönü, another ex-soldier and a former Prime Minister, who had been associated with Kemal for some thirty years. The Republican People's Party still formed the government.

Turkey remained neutral during the Second World War, taking precautionary measures in both military and diplomatic spheres but mainly seeking to safeguard Turkish soil from becoming a battlefield. A property tax levied to help pay for mobilisation fell very unfairly on non-Muslims and some observers have seen in this some evidence for the influence of Nazi ideas; it may equally have marked a revival of very old attitudes. In the late months of the war, Turkey declared war on both Germany and Japan and made easier for herself an entry into international affairs in the post-war years. By 1945 there were many signs of internal tension, including a split in the ranks of the ruling party. Four members, including Adnan Menderes, left the Republican People's Party to found a Democratic Party, and President Inönü accepted that perhaps the time had come for an extension of demo-cratic ways. Local authorities, however, especially in the eastern provinces, found it difficult to make a distinction between legal opposi-tion and rebellion and elections (on an open ballot system and open to many pressures) returned the People's Party in overwhelming strength. Both parties had further divisions and a National Party emerged as an offshoot of the Democrats.

The first free elections were held in 1950 and on this occasion all the elements desirous of change came together to strike at the government. These included the political liberals, the religionists and those who wanted a more open policy in relation to foreign trade and investment in Turkey. The Democrats won 408 seats out of 487, and some twenty-five continuous years of Republican People's Party rule came to an end. Celal Bayar was the new President and Adnan Menderes the new Prime Minister. Theoretically, there was now a two-party government but the Democrats acted much more in a one-party tradition. The desire for change which had showed itself at the polls was motivated strongly by the idea of restoring and reviving the Islamic religion, and the govern-ment made some concessions along these lines, sufficient for the moderates but not for the extremists. The wearing of the fez again occurred spontaneously in the eastern provinces, the call to prayer was now allowed in Arabic instead of Turkish, and religious instruction was added to the curriculum of the village community centres. There were increased attendances at the mosques and this was accompanied by a spate of new mosque building. On the other hand, the government kept a close surveillance on the activities of the Republican Party and the National Party, and did not hesitate to act, on occasion, by fine, imprisonment or confiscation of property.

The Democrats again won the four-yearly election in 1954 although other new parties had come into existence by this time. The country's economy was improving and the more liberal policy in religious matters seemed to be paying off. In foreign affairs post-war Turkey looked towards the West, accepted first British, and then American, aid and was cool and cautious towards Soviet Russia. Alliances were seen as one way to national security and these were made through NATO, the Baghdad Pact and CENTO. The Turkish Deputy Prime Minister spoke of Turkey's need for alliances at the Bandung Conference in 1955; he also indicated Turkey's anti-communist attitude. Among the reasons which have been put forward for the absence of a strong communist movement in Turkey are the relative smallness of the industrial proletariat, the lack of revolutionary traditions among the peasantry and the image of Russia as a traditional enemy. In the early days of the Turkish Revolution, Kemal and his followers did look to the Soviet Union for help and regarded the Soviets as champions of the independence of an Eastern people against Western imperialism, but, later Turkey came to look to the West for help and to see in the Western way of life the best hope for the future.

Stability at home and abroad was what Turkey needed most, but a crisis with Greece over Turkish nationals in Cyprus was one feature of the later 1950s, and a military *coup* in 1960 ended the political career of Adnan Menderes who had helped to revive and exploit religious forces for political purposes. After a period of military government, a new constitution brought the Republicans narrowly to power in October 1961.

Nationalism has had a tendency to set off chain reactions and just as pan-Turkism was, in part, a response to pan-Slavism, so pan-Arabism within the Ottoman Empire was almost an inevitable response to the Young Turks. The Ottoman emperor, Abdul Hamid II, had surrounded himself with Arab advisers and when he fell they were removed from office. At the same time, the Arab official class within the Empire found itself without influential patrons at the Sultan's court. Arab nationalism was not a completely new phenomenon in the twentieth century but its manifestations increased within the Ottoman Empire in the years between the revolution of the Young Turks and the outbreak of the First

Communist delegation to armistice talks, Korea, 1951

Combat troops, South Vietnam

Two Arab rulers, Hussein of Jordan and Saud of Saudi Arabia, in 1956

World War. From Egypt, Mesopotamia and Syria, Arab groups began
to voice demands for the autonomy of Arab States within the Empire,
and in the Turkish homeland itself young Arab officers and students
organised themselves into secret societies of a revolutionary nature. In
Beirut and Damascus there were Arab Committees which openly
fostered an awakening of the Arab spirit and a decentralising policy for
the Empire; secretly they planned for Arab independence. Paris, which
had housed the first 'Congress of Ottoman Liberals' in 1902, was host
also to the 'First Arab National Congress' held in 1913.

Thus, when the Ottoman Empire became involved in the war of
1914–18, the situation was ripe for an enemy power to exploit the Arab
movement of decentralisation through military and financial aid and
promises of long-term support. Those Arab leaders who were prepared
to turn the war situation to their own advantage found a ready ally in
Britain, whose government had been following the course of the Arab
awakening for some time. The British occupation of Egypt from 1882
onwards had, among other things, provided Britain with a strategic base
from which to observe and make contacts with the centres of Arab
nationalism at both urban and village level. The suggestion that British
policy in the years immediately before the First World War was
sufficiently realistic to abandon at last the incurably 'sick' Ottoman
Empire and seek to create a new Arab empire to fill the power vacuum
may contain more than a little hindsight but is not too wide of the
mark. When the Arab ruler of the Mecca region, Sherif Hussein, by
title a descendant of the Prophet, decided to oppose the Sultan's
proclamation of a 'holy war' against Russia, France, England and their
allies, he sent emissaries to the British High Commissioner in Cairo.
There followed a lengthy exchange of correspondence between the
High Commissioner, Sir Henry McMahon, and Hussein and, by 1916,
when Hussein declared his revolt openly, Britain was committed to
help and protect the evolution of separate Arab countries. Exception
was made in the cases of the crown colony of Aden, parts of lower
Mesopotamia adjacent to the Persian Gulf where Britain claimed special
interests, and parts of the Levantine coastal territories where French
influences were recognised.

The Arab Revolt was partly anticipated and partly precipitated by the
Turkish governor in Syria, Jamal Pasha, who carried out a series of
treason trials and executions of Arabs who were incriminated by
discovered documentary evidence. A Turkish force was sent southwards
into the Arabian peninsula and Hussein feared that its mission was to

deal with him. As a military operation, the Revolt had only a limited success though it was subsequently highlighted on the British side through the activities of Colonel T. E. Lawrence, who worked as a liaison officer with the Arabs. Neither Syria nor Mesopotamia, though for different reasons, staged a popular uprising against the Turks, and regular British army officers like General Allenby and General Maude led the major campaigns in Palestine and Mesopotamia. But in the psychology of nationalism the Arab Revolt was important, for Hussein and his sons became associated with the victory and one son, Faisal, was particularly linked with the liberation of Damascus.

During the war a number of variously bilateral and tripartite agreements were worked out between Britain and Hussein, Britain, France and Russia, and Britain and France, for the subsequent partitioning of the Arab world under the protection of foreign powers. After much more diplomatic bargaining, the San Remo agreement of 1920 placed Syria and Lebanon under French mandate and Palestine and Mesopotamia under British mandate. The mandate system as defined by the League of Nations to territories of the former Turkish Empire allowed for the provisional recognition of independent nations subject to the rendering of administrative advice and assistance by a mandatory power until they were able to stand alone. This was, to say the least, less than real independence, and ardent Arab nationalists keenly resented the imposition of mandatory conditions. In January of the previous year, Emir Faisal (son of Hussein) had presented to the Peace Conference a demand that the Arabic-speaking peoples of Asia should be recognised as independent sovereign peoples.

The mandate system, therefore, brought a measure of disillusion especially to those nationalists in Syria and Mesopotamia who had survived earlier repressions and witnessed the downfall of the old Empire. An independent kingdom of Greater Syria to include Lebanon and Palestine, with Faisal as king, had already been proclaimed prior to the San Remo agreement. In the Arabian peninsula it remained to be seen how successful Hussein (who had taken the title 'King of the Arabs' in 1916) would be in consolidating a new kingdom and in extending his family and dynastic interests in other Arab regions. Meanwhile, Arab nationalism faced another challenge through British policy enunciated in 1917 in the Balfour Declaration in favour of the establishment in Palestine of a National Home for the Jewish people. The Arabs observed the anniversary of the Declaration as a day of national mourning and, in course of time, Arab and Jewish nationalisms, despite all the British efforts to create a *modus vivendi*, had a highly inflammatory effect one upon the other.

For his advanced years, Hussein was a very ambitious ruler; he was also a rather subtle diplomat. His negotiations with the British in 1916 had been paralleled by countering negotiations with the Ottoman government for money, supplies and recognition of his title in the Hejaz region of the peninsula. After the Republic was established in Turkey, Hussein assumed the title of Caliph with the implication for all Muslims that the mantle of the former Sultans of Turkey had fallen upon his shoulders. The title itself was, of course, an anachronism which had been revived particularly by Abdul Hamid II and it was no longer a sufficiently significant symbol for pan-Arabism or pan-Islamism. At this stage, it simply added to the growing atmosphere of personal rivalry in the Arab hierarchy and, in October 1924, Ibn Saud, Sultan of Nedj, a central area of the Arabian peninsula, drove Hussein out of Mecca and forced him to renounce his recently acquired title. Ibn Saud proceeded to gain control of Jedda and the whole of the Hejaz (1926). In 1932, he joined his name to a kingdom and took the title of King of Saudi-Arabia, proclaiming about the same time a philosophy of Islamic friendship and Arab brotherhood.

Meanwhile, Hussein's son Faisal spent a rather insecure three years as king in Syria before being expelled as a result of clashes between the new French administration and Syrian nationalists. Faisal was already well-known for his appearances in Paris and London and for his wartime role in the Arab Revolt. In August 1921 he became the British-protected sovereign of the new Mesopotamian kingdom of Iraq with Nuri es-Said as his leading minister. The inauguration of this new government followed a period of rebellion against the earlier British military administration and Faisal himself was inclined to sympathise with nationalist aspirations rather than passively accept British advice. The beginnings of nation-making were complicated in Iraq by the existence of a substantial non-Arab minority of Kurdish people and by a division of Muslims into Sunnis (the majority sect) and Shi'is. In Baghdad, the capital, radical nationalists fostered opposition to the new regime. An Anglo-Iraq treaty, signed in October 1922 but not ratified by the National Assembly of the new constitution until March 1924, established the continuity of British influence through a High Commissioner and other officials, and by control over foreign policy and finances and rights over airfields. The treaty was an unequal one and it barely won the necessary support on the Iraqi side; it did, however, point to improved relationships in the future. By June 1930 Iraq had achieved complete independence and Nuri es-Said was exploiting this by promoting the idea of an Arab alliance to include Nedj, the Hejaz and Transjordan (referred to below) with the eventual prospect of all the remaining Arab countries joining. As an interim measure he was prepared to go ahead with a series of bilateral agreements.

Iraq, sponsored by Britain, was the first of the mandated territories to secure independence and might therefore have become a natural focus for pan-Arabism. Its influence was felt especially in Syria among nationalists who were still loyal to Faisal and who regarded a union with Iraq as the best means of ending the French mandate. Dynastic and personal rivalries kept Saudi-Arabia aloof since Ibn Saud, who had replaced Hussein, had no motive for furthering the Hashemite line of Hussein and his sons. Saudi Arabia, in fact, was a rival centre in the trend towards pan-Arabism, and Egypt (whose nationalism is not mentioned here other than incidentally) provided a third and distinctive challenge. Throughout the inter-war years the Iraq government was oligarchical in character, leavened, until his death in 1933, by the benevolent despotism of King Faisal. More extreme forms of nationalism appeared from time to time, the worst feature being a large scale massacre of Assyrians who were non-Arabs and non-Muslims. During the reign of Ghazi, Faisal's son and successor, a short period of military dictatorship was imposed by Bakr Sidki acting on behalf of army elements and dissident politicians. The British hope of a friendly and constitutional Arab state in Iraq was hardly borne out at this stage; the forms of constitutionalism were there but not the substance, and the orientation of the new nationalism remained in the balance.

The lands east of the Jordan were administered in the early post-1914–18 years by Faisal's Arab government from Damascus but then transferred to the British mandate as part of Palestine. Britain set up a self-governing area of Transjordan in 1921 with Abdullah, son of Hussein, as its ruler. Materially, the region was poor and Abdullah followed a policy of accepting British financial and technical help with British army officers seconded to train his Arab Legion. Like other members of his family, Abdullah was not without ambition and he revived the Hashemite dream of a Greater Syria, though not to much practical effect. Until the Second World War Britain retained the prerogatives of a mandatory power in Jordan but was much more occupied with the problems of Arab–Jew relationships in Palestine proper.

The issues raised by modern Zionism and especially that of a Jewish homeland have been extensively written about and can only be given slight mention here. Zionism needs to be studied in its international and its European setting; so far as the course of Asian nationalism is concerned the main interest centres on the creation, from 1948, of a new state of Israel and on the dramatic impact of Jewish nationalism on that of the Arabs. The intention to create a Jewish homeland did not presuppose the creation of a Jewish state but it obviously implied the idea of a largely autonomous region. The principle underlying immigration policy for Jews into Palestine was defined in 1922 as that of avoiding being a burden on the people as a whole. Arab nationalists did not take kindly from the first to the arrival in the Palestine Mandate of Jewish settlers whose numbers added to the small Jewish community already resident there, yet, initially, there was no widespread alarm. A policy of restricted immigration together with the labelling of Transjordan as a specifically Arab area seemed to set limits to the extent and influence of the new Jewish homeland. Early incidents and protestations on the part of the Arabs were probably due as much to religious feelings as to nationalist fervour, but two developments led in time to the bitter clash which was demonstrated by riots in 1929 and widespread disorders from 1936. One of these was the zeal, energy and devotion with which colonising Jews transformed their promised land and the symbol of this progress provided by the modern city of Tel Aviv. The other was the increasing rate of Jewish immigration in the 1930s spurred on by the persecution of Jews in eastern and central Europe and, finally, in Nazi Germany. It was estimated that the Jewish population in Palestine more than doubled itself between 1929 and 1935 and that, by the latter date, it represented a quarter of the whole population.

Thus in the years immediately before the Second World War extremists on both the Arab and Jewish sides turned to violence and sabotage both against the government and against members of the opposite community. Only strong British troop and police reinforcements made any general semblance of order possible, and attempt after attempt to find a compromise political solution, including blue-print plans for partition, ended in failure. A British proposal in May 1939 envisaged a Palestinian State in ten years' time jointly administered by Arabs and Jews and with a preparatory programme which included strict numerical control of Jewish immigration in the meantime. For the Zionists this was, briefly, not enough; for the Arabs it was too much.

The Second World War found the Jews more alert to the international issues especially on the European scene, the Arabs more intensely focussed on the Arab world. Arab nationalist leaders felt disillusioned and embittered towards Britain over the Palestine situation and towards France over Syria and Lebanon where the French had retained more prerogatives than the British in Iraq. In Syria, Arab unrest had been shown in a nationalist armed revolt in 1925 and urban riots in 1936. As a result of all this, Arab nationalists were not primarily disposed to be hostile to the Axis powers and were hardly moved by the plight of European Jews. The government of Iraq under a regent, Raschid Ali, opposed the unconditional transit of Allied troops from India to the Middle East and North Africa via Iraqi territory and declared against Britain, in May 1941, with general Nazi approval and financial support. Raschid Ali's movement was defeated by the resistance which it met at the British air base of Habbaniya, where Kurdish and Armenian guards stood loyally by the R.A.F., by the apathy of the Iraqi people as a whole and by the despatch from Transjordan of a relief column.

As the war progressed and an Allied victory over the Axis powers became more imminent, two main streams of pan-Arabism developed. One originated from Baghdad under the leadership of Nuri es-Said (who was reinstated after the flight of Raschid Ali) and looked for the unification of Palestine and Syria with Iraq. Baghdad was seen as the prospective capital of this pan-Arab state which would allow autonomous regions for minorities in Lebanon and Palestine. Another, and opposing, development came from Egypt where, in October 1944, representatives of Syria, Lebanon, Transjordan, Saudi Arabia and Yemen joined Egypt in an agreement for the independence and territorial integrity of Lebanon and for support for the Palestinian Arabs. Iraq joined with these states, in March 1945, in the pact of the Arab League which aimed at strengthening the relations between its members and co-ordinating their policies; the secretariat of the League was established in Cairo, but otherwise its organisation was loose and it could only act on unanimous decisions. The League, from the beginning, preached a message of Arab unity but this proved easier to talk about than to achieve.

After Raschid's opposition had been overcome in Iraq, British forces continued into Syria and Lebanon and, in August of the same year, 1941, a joint Anglo-Russian invasion of Persia (Iran) took place to counteract pro-Axis forces at work there and open up land communications between Russians and British who were now allies. The Shah was forced to abdicate in favour of a young son but, by a wartime agreement, Britain and Russia undertook to remove their forces from Persia within six months of the end of hostilities. Meanwhile in Palestine, Jewish terrorist activities continued during the war years despite the general co-operation of the Jews in the British war effort. The Jews had rejected the British White Paper proposals of 1939 and they demanded for Palestine a Jewish state, a Jewish army and unlimited immigration under the control of a Jewish agency. In the war years, therefore, and mainly by secret means, Jewish organisations prepared themselves in every way for the fight which they expected later. The years immediately after the war brought no peace to Palestine but rather an escalation of violence. In February 1947 Britain, weary of fighting both Arabs and Jews, put the Palestine problem to the United Nations. A partition plan for two states, Arab and Jewish, was offered in November 1947 with a safeguard of international trusteeship; the Jews were ready to see possibilities in the plan, the Arab states rejected it. When Britain after giving warning, laid down the mandate in May 1948, a Jewish state of Israel was proclaimed at Tel Aviv and a Jewish army emerged to protect it.

It was left to Transjordan to initiate the first Arab attack but Abdullah was clearly not going to be content to fight only in the interests of pan-Arabism. The Arab States failed, in the event, to co-operate effectively and were forced to resign themselves to the existence of Israel though they did not recognise it and adopted tactics of economic blockade against the new Jewish State. Jews were expelled from Arab States for alleged disloyalty and, more significantly still, upwards of half-a-million Arab refugees left Palestine for neighbouring Arab countries. The Arab States claimed that these refugees had the right to return and were prepared to make use of them as a political weapon. There was much nationalistic soul-searching among the Arab States after 1948. A small Palestinian Arab enclave continued to exist near Gaza and Abdullah of Jordan annexed the old city of Jerusalem and adjacent territories to the north and south of it, westwards of his own frontiers; Transjordan then became the Kingdom of Jordan. The failure of the Arab States to prevent the emergence of Israel was marked by internal revolutions mainly led by dissident army officers but influenced by the fluctuations of pan-Arabism. Thus there were *coups* in Syria (1949), Egypt (1952) and Iraq (1958). King Abdullah was assassinated in Jerusalem (1951) and Nuri es-Said was murdered in the Iraqi rising.

By the 1950s the old order of leaders was giving way to a new one but the future of pan-Arabism was still uncertain. In February 1958 Syria and Egypt were fused into the United Arab Republic, and Iraq and

Jordan countered with a short-lived Arab Union. The Iraqi revolt was partly brought about by the influence of the United Arab Republic, and President Nasser of Egypt was aspiring to lead a comprehensive pan-Arab union. Nasser's influence on pan-Arabism was especially strong after the Suez crisis of 1956 but it did not go unchallenged from Baghdad, even after the fall of Nuri es-Said's regime. Lebanon and Jordan invited American and British troops respectively in 1958 to provide security against possible attacks and thus provided another proof of the divisions existing in the Arab world. Russian influence with the Arab States (and especially with Egypt) offered, from 1955 onwards, a striking and significant counterpoise to that of the West which, in the Arab view, was tainted by imperialism and Zionism. Neither the problems of Arab unity nor those of Arab–Israeli relationships seemed to become significantly easier with the passage of time, and outside interference tended only to put them out of focus. Certainly so far as inter-Arab relationships were concerned, a worthwhile and lasting solution was only likely to be found by the Arabs themselves.

Israel continued to live under the shadow of intermittent threats and action from the Arab States. Egypt and Syria were most prominent in a war of propaganda, border incidents and economic blockade. The Israeli response was one of military preparedness and retaliation. Israel's military victories against Egypt in 1956 were followed by peace-keeping measures on the part of the United Nations in the Gaza area and the free passage of Israeli shipping through the Gulf of Aqaba. A decade later, in 1967, Egypt demanded the removal of the peace-keeping force from Gaza and secured the closure of the Gulf; under Nasser's leadership the Arab States mounted a menacing military build-up against Israel. Dramatically, the Israelis fought their third successful war in less than twenty years in the interests of national security. The problem of Arab–Jewish relations still remained as difficult as ever and Israel desperately needed to secure a greater measure of identity with the region in which the country lay.

4 The Springs of Asian Nationalism

MODERN nationalism in Asia is like a stream which has flowed from many springs. The pace and direction of flow have varied in different countries and at different times; cross-currents have occurred frequently and there has been much overlapping. There is no one single way to the sources but there are some features which are sufficiently general and widespread as to allow their identity to be broadly stated and exemplified. At one stage or another a sense of history has entered into the nationalist programme. Ideological concepts imported into Asia and, to some extent, developed within Asia have been highly significant. The 'anti' element in nationalism has also been very strong, often directed against Europeans but perhaps almost equally often against other Asians. Social change, arising from complex factors, brought new leaders and new organisations to the stage of politics and therefore to that of nationalism; social programmes were often part of the new nationalist ideal. The educational factor in all its various manifestations is of the greatest importance in any study of Asian nationalism; so is religion which, to take extreme cases, has blended harmoniously with nationalism or has torn it apart. The pressure of events in other parts of the world and a tendency for political chain reactions to take place within Asian regions themselves are other matters which need to come into the general reckoning. It is virtually impossible to suggest general priorities among all these courses and causes and certainly impossible to give them more than broad treatment and illustration within this present work. It again needs to be emphasised at the outset that Asian nationalism was not merely a revolt against the West; it has had its own cultural roots which lie deep.

Some awareness of a historic past has been one of the driving forces behind most nationalist movements and nowhere more so than in Asia. Japanese nationalism drew strength from the continuity of Japanese political history which was aided by the insular position of Japan and the long tradition of emperors whose origin was traced back by legend to the Goddess of the Sun. Nationalism helped vitally to create a new and modern Japan yet it is very significant that the forward movement of modernisation was often accompanied by a strong appeal to the traditions of the past. A good example of this may be found in the famous Rescript on Education promulgated in 1890. This document, read aloud to schoolchildren and students on a number of occasions each year until 1945, strongly emphasised the legacies and values of Japan's past in the interest of supporting the existing authorities in whatever they might decree. The Japanese people were asked to face both ways at the same time.

Chinese nationalist leaders quite naturally stressed the intrinsic greatness of China and especially in relation to the damage which they detected in the impact of the West. The traditional Chinese Empire had regarded itself as the centre of the world. At times when the old China had a strong government neighbouring Asian States had hastened to pay their respects to the Celestial Court, and diplomatic approaches by the West had been treated with a mixture of hauteur, condescension and plain opposition. The Chinese political heritage was important to nationalist inspiration (though the nationalists were eager to break away from it) but at least equally significant was China's great cultural and civilising tradition. China had not only witnessed great eras of civilisation within its own frontiers; over the centuries the Chinese had civilised and sinicised invaders from the north, and exported elements of Chinese culture to Japan, Central and South-East Asia. It was, therefore, not surprising that the typical Chinese nationalist, proud of the traditions of his people but resentful of the ways in which the Empire had been weakened, should regard Europeans of all kinds as 'barbarians', 'red devils', or merely 'foreign devils'.

India's past contained many cultural strands but the great majority of Indians followed Hindu traditions. Hinduism was not in itself a basis for modern nationalism. The Hindu caste system was a divisive element in Indian society and the Hindu ideal of detachment from worldly matters seemed at cross-purposes with national aspirations. One of the strongest Hindu political legacies centred on the Maratha kingdoms of western India and their long struggle for independence from a Muslim Empire. It was no coincidence that several of the great Hindu nationalists stemmed from western India and that popular Hindu support could be won in the same area by reviving the glories of the Marathas.

In a similar historical perspective, Muslim Indians, and especially those in the north, looked back to the achievements of the great Muslim Empires whose architectural monuments outlived their period of political supremacy. British political power reached India gradually in the eighteenth century at a time when the Moghul Empire was in serious decline and the Marathas were divided among themselves. By the turn of the twentieth century, educated Muslims in northern India emphasised strongly the case that it was Muslim political power and privilege which had been replaced by that of the British Raj. Both Hindu and Muslim nationalists could, on occasion, conjure up different visions of golden ages which had preceded British rule and, in so doing, they helped to inspire a Renaissance element in Indian nationalism.

In South-East Asia, modern nationalism also sought historical support. It has been argued that here, as elsewhere in Asia, the opposition to nineteenth-century Western expansion contained a strong nationalist element. The monuments of past greatness, comparable to anything of their kind in the world, were to be found in the great medieval temple-city of Angkor in Cambodia and the magnificent early temple tomb of Borobodur in central Java. It is not without irony (as Professor D. G. E. Hall has pointed out) that these vastly impressive remains were rediscovered and identified by European archaeologists and historians who also, in some cases, rescued them from oblivion. There is more than a touch of myth about most 'golden ages', and emotion rather than objective scholarship quite naturally guided much of the nationalist view of history. To say this is not to diminish the importance of the historical factor; real or mythical, or a mixture of both, the historical factor has been a major driving force for nationalism in South-East Asia where, by the end of the nineteenth century, all countries except Siam (Thailand) were subject to some form of Western political control.

By the first decade of the twentieth century, the Thai kingdom was about 700 years old and Thai nationalism had recently been sharpened by wars with Burma in the nineteenth century and by skilful political diplomacy to keep the British and French at some distance. Programmes of controlled Westernisation and modernisation were seen in Siam as the politic answer to the difficult and complex dilemma created by the meeting of a dynamic and expansionist West with a much more traditional and conservative East. Burmese nationalists have been particularly conscious of a sense of history. One modern writer, Htin Aung, has cited evidence for Burmese nationalism from the eleventh century and has claimed that, throughout their long history, the Burmese have always been conscious of their nationality, bordered as they have been by great neighbours in China and India. The Burmese monarchy, less flexible than that of Siam, steered a collision course with Britain in the nineteenth century and it took the Burmese some little time to recover from the shock of British annexations and the disappearance of their own monarchy. By the 1920s the historical perspective was restored and a new generation of leaders was ready to make use of it in the nationalist cause.

Among the peoples of French Indo-China the Vietnamese (or Annamites) had one of the strongest senses of history and national identity. They had taken much of their culture from China, but were not Chinese. In the nineteenth century their emperors could, at times, be as disdainful of the West as the Chinese Court itself. The Vietnamese were the most numerous of the Asian peoples in Indo-China and the most politically minded. Their own national traditions included the winning of an independence from China in the tenth century and their own later expansion into Cham and Khmer territories in central and southern Annam and Cochin-China. They mounted very considerable opposition to French advances and, even when subjected to French control, retained a nationalist spirit which manifested itself both in guerilla activities and in a deceptively passive awaiting for the time when the foreigner would withdraw.

In the case of Indonesia (former Netherlands East Indies) with its widely dispersed island territories, the message of history pointed more to regional traditions and loyalties than to any pan-Indonesian legacy. Java had always been an island of great political and cultural importance but there were other islands and peoples with very significant histories. The Achinese of northern Sumatra were proud of their early association with Islam, their military empire in the sixteenth and seventeenth centuries and their thirty years' war with the Dutch at the end of the nineteenth century. The people of the southern Celebes also had their own strong traditions as fighters and traders, while the island of Bali preserved a distinctive culture which owed much to a pre-Islamic past. The political unification of the East Indies by the Dutch, tenuous as it was, provided the precedent for a mainly Java-based modern Indonesian nationalism. Indonesian nationalists wanted the boundaries of the new nation-state to be no less extensive than those of the Dutch Empire in the Archipelago. References were made to a medieval empire of Majapahit which, from a Javanese capital, had claimed control over a large part of the Indies and of the Malay peninsula. That many of these claims lacked solid historical evidence to support them does not detract from the importance of Majapahit to modern Indonesian nationalism, and not least in the years after independence.

In both the Malay peninsula and the Philippines, fragmentation rather than political unity had been the main feature of the pre-colonial era and the nationalist appeal to history was rather less evident in these two areas. That it was not ignored completely was emphasised by a new Malayan Prime Minister's decision in 1957 to proclaim his country's independence at Malacca, the first seaport in Malaya to fall under Western rule and formerly the capital of a Malay empire. The government of the Philippines claimed a certain continuity with the one-time Sultanate of Sulu and its island empire in expressing ancient rights in northern Borneo at a time when the Malaysia federation was rooted.

Among the nationalisms of western Asia, no race had a greater sense of history than the Jews. Religion and history were the two main ingredients of modern Zionism which has been only partly an Asian movement and partly a European and a world one. The tremendous interest in archaeology in modern Israel can be seen both as a stimulus for and a manifestation of national pride. Arab nationalism rested also on a strong sense of cultural identity and, on occasion, on a timely appeal to the historic mission of Islam. The distinctive Arab ideology of the modern nation-state was, however, slow in evolving and seems to trace most clearly from about the end of the First World War. In the inter-war period, Arab writers began to stress the essential historical unity of the Arab region of Arabia and the Fertile Crescent and to claim Palestine as an Arab land from prehistoric times. Turkey reached modern statehood by policies and actions which cut across pan-Islamic traditions and divorced religion and politics at government level. Mustafa Kemal was himself deeply interested in history and saw the decline of the Ottoman Empire in something of its historical setting. He encouraged and patronised an upsurge of activity in matters historical in his new Turkey even to the extent of tracing tenuous links between ancient Hittite and modern Turk. Yet his policies were intensely revolutionary in secular and Westernising ways. He deliberately sought to break with a past from which he had openly drawn some of his nationalist inspiration.

Anti-foreignism as a feature of Asian nationalism has been both common and complex. In China at the time of the Boxer Rising, it can be seen as a rallying cry for many anti-Western elements and for the restoration of proper Chinese pride and prestige. In making a desperate effort to rid China of the foreigner, the Boxers were doomed to failure but in so far as their movements revealed the depth of the Chinese identity they helped to prevent the political partition of their country. In 1919, to take another example, the anti-foreignism of Chinese student demonstrators was directed more particularly against Japan which had made wounding and humiliating intrusions into Chinese sovereignty. In its turn, Communist China was to find no shortage of occasions for promoting anti-foreignism in the interests of Chinese nationalism and of China's bid for leadership in the communist world.

Anti-foreignism aimed at the West could easily arise from resentment at the interference by colonial governments with traditional ways of life. The rights and privileges of class or caste and the time-honoured customs of traditional societies were areas in which colonial governments were well-advised to tread most warily and act only after the ground had been carefully prepared. During a controversy over what became the Age of Consent Act in India (1891), B. G. Tilak, a militant Hindu nationalist, opposed, not on principle but on the grounds of unwarranted interference, the government's proposal to raise the legal age of marriage for Indian girls from ten to twelve years. Six years later, Tilak was in trouble with the authorities for having, among other things, been highly critical of the government's measures against plague in Bombay, again on the grounds of interference with the customs and tenets of Hindu society. Tilak wanted to see reform arising from the people through education and example, rather than being imposed by laws and regulations alien to their traditions. In a more directly political issue, Hindu nationalists of Bengal opposed what they saw as the weakening of that great province when Lord Curzon proposed, in 1905, to divide it into two. The largely Hindu Congress Party came out strongly against partition while the Muslim League owed its origins in part to the fears and suspicions of Muslims (who predominated in areas of eastern Bengal) in the face of outbursts by Hindu extremists. Another instance of resentment in the Curzon era related to the proposed government reform of Indian universities. The resentment here was of a middle-class and not a popular nature; the institutions in question were only traditional in a very limited sense and were, in fact, of British origin. None the less, the small educated Indian middle class which agitated about the government's interference with the universities formed at that time the area of recruitment into the early nationalist political organisations.

The plea of economic exploitation in the interests of Western imperialism was one of the most frequently recurring themes in the literature and speeches of nationalist groupings in Asia. This line of attack was followed particularly by the more ardent revolutionaries and especially by those seeking eventually to achieve radical social and economic change. But even the more moderate and constitutionally-minded nationalists could speak with fervour on the theme of exploitation, and this is instanced in G. K. Gokhale's presidential address to the Indian National Congress in 1905 with references to 'absentee capitalism', 'a great and ruinous drain of wealth' and 'the continuous impoverishment of the mass of people'. The same theme is apparent in the Indian Independence Pledge of 1930 and it is common to all independence movements. It was always easy to point to broad evidence to support it and it had the advantages of both popular appeal and a high emotional content.

The story of individual relationships between Asians and Europeans provides at times fascinating and revealing glimpses of the personal background of Asian nationalist leaders. Tunku Abdul Rahman, the later Prime Minister of Malaya and Malaysia, did not take to politics early in life but he carried memories of his student days in Cambridge and London when, on occasion, he became deeply conscious of his race and country. Indeed, a great number of Asian nationalist leaders shaped some part of their political future, often unconsciously at the time, in the capitals and cities of learning of the West. Incidents of sympathy and friendship on the one hand, as between Ho Chi Minh and the French Socialists, or rebuffs on the other, even of a relatively minor kind, could and did influence the pattern of future events. Highly significant also were the personal relationships between European governing and commercial classes in Asia and the Asians with whom they came into contact. Sir John Kotelawala of Ceylon deplored the attitudes of servitude which some Sinhalese officials adopted towards their European masters; earlier, the Chinese Boxers had been provoked by the pervading and not always tactful influence of the Christian missionaries in the interior of China. After the Amritsar massacre of 1919 in India, resentment rose high because of what was thought to be a cheap view of Indian lives by the British governing side and also on account of the humiliating 'crawling order' imposed on Indians at a spot where a European had been murdered. These are scattered and widely different examples of the personal and racial aspects of anti-Westernism which formed one component of Asian nationalism, and they could be added to extensively. Arrogance and exclusiveness on the part of a European ruling class could provoke deep feelings of resentment and hostility. To keep the balance, it must be said that many liberal Europeans gave sympathy and encouragement to nationalist aspirations, while Marxists and Communists from the Western countries deliberately fostered the more radical and revolutionary kinds of nationalist activity.

But anti-foreignism was only partially an anti-Western phenomenon and modern nationalism in Asia was aroused, as in Europe, by the suspicions, jealousies and hostilities of the peoples within the region itself. In some cases, these antipathies had their origins well before the era of European influence in Asia. Thus, for example the Thais and the Burmese had been traditional rivals, and overseas Chinese communities had incurred the hostility of Indonesians in the seventeenth century. Chinese and Japanese nationalisms reacted one against the other. Chinese resentment against Japanese incursions into Empire territory and against Japan's opportunist demands during the First World War, provided a real basis on which national reunification movements could build in the 1920s. Conversely, the reality of a new and lively nationalism in China, leading to military friction in areas bordering on Japanese-held territory, provided the occasion for the ascendancy of the militarists and ultra-nationalists in Japan. The suffering of China during the long war with Japan (1937–45) also helped to forge the soul of the new China though it did not prevent the internal power struggle which was due to follow.

Both Chinese and Japanese nationalisms provoked opposing nationalist forces in other countries. The links between overseas Chinese in South-East Asia and the Kuomintang or the Chinese Communist Party added a political factor to the mixed atmosphere of mistrust, suspicion and envy which at times characterised the relationships between Thais, Burmese, Indonesians or Malays, and the Chinese communities settled alongside them. Japan started the twentieth century as a shining example for nationalist aspirations elsewhere in Asia, but deep and bitter resentment of Japanese control over South-East Asian peoples in the Second World War speeded up the tempo of nationalism in the countries concerned, quite apart from the effects of a Japanese policy of fostering nationalism from separate motives. Many other examples of inter-Asian friction with effects upon nationalism could be quoted. The Kurds in rebelling against Mustafa Kemal's Turkey in 1925 could be envisaged as supporting a nationalist Kurdistan which had been lost to them between Sèvres and Lausanne; the Karens of Burma were other hill-peoples whose sense of national identity brought them at times into revolt with the major grouping within a common frontier. The stimulus of the new Jewish homeland in Palestine to Arab nationalism and pan-Arabism can be amply illustrated, and the growth of Arab nationalism itself in opposition to Turkism, despite the common bond of Islam, gives another indication of the ways in which anti-foreignism can be interpreted.

In very many ways education was linked with the growth of national-ism in Asia. In those countries which came to be administered by Western powers, government and missionary schools and colleges provided a wholly or partly Western-type education with emphasis upon a European language and European concepts in the realms, for instance, of literature, history and law. In the colonial age in South-East Asia, Western-type education reflected a variety of outlooks, each contributing in its own way to ideals such as patriotism, liberty or democracy. American traditions in the educational field could hardly fail to pass on to young Filipinos the message of the American War of Independence and the great issues of nation-making which followed. The French ideals of liberty, equality and fraternity were understood by Vietnamese, some of whom saw no reason why they should not be just as valid for the people of Vietnam as for the people of France. The starting point of modern Dutch history was the long and eventually successful revolt against the rule of Habsburg Spain, and the Dutch also exhibited a legitimate pride in the world-wide achievements of their small nation. In educational institutions which bore the British stamp the freedom of the individual, the equality of different peoples before the law, and the love of one's own country, were all themes which protruded from the curriculum at different stages and in different ways and it would have been strange indeed had these provoked no response from Indians, Burmese, or Malayans.

It is possible, of course, to imagine that young Asians often regarded the Western-centred areas of their studies as something of an academic exercise only, useful mainly as a means to an end, and there is some truth in this. Yet the challenge was often presented to the Asian mind in the contrast between ideals and practice on the part of a Western ruling-class and in particular where any form of racial discrimination by Europeans or Americans could be detected. As larger numbers of

Asians living under colonial regimes came to attend institutions of higher education, nationalist politics could, as at Hanoi and Rangoon, became extremely lively in student circles, and university graduates in general could become very frustrated and politically-minded where they saw themselves faced with limited career prospects.

The part played in the nationalist movements by South-East Asians who had received their higher education in Europe is impressive. Mohammed Hatta and Sœtan Sjahrir of Indonesia were conspicuous examples of student backgrounds in Holland; Tunku Abdul Rahman of Malaya and Lee Kuan Yew of Singapore had experienced the academic environments of London and Cambridge. Ho Chi Minh was in large measure self-educated in Paris and Moscow. Even more striking in this connection was the Indian nationalist movement with British-trained lawyers of the calibre of Gandhi, Nehru and Jinnah. The impact of the West at first-hand and the close associations formed between Asian students in Western centres of learning, had a dynamic effect on future nationalist leaders.

The interaction between education and nationalism was not confined to Western-type education or to those Asian countries which were subject to Western control. One of the dangers, nationally-speaking, of a Western-educated elite was that it might turn out to have more in common with other Western-educated people than with fellow-Asians as a whole. B. G. Tilak, in calling for a more popular approach on the part of Indian nationalists in the first decade of the twentieth century, pointed to the barriers which existed between Congress leaders and the mass of the people. Those whose nationalism stemmed in part from religious or cultural revivalism sometimes attacked the secularising effects of Western education or condemned it for its eroding influence on traditional concepts. In one form nationalism created a demand for more vernacular or 'national' schools and colleges to preserve and pass on the vital elements of national culture in a national tongue. The young Nehru, for example, speaking in Brussels in 1927, accused the British of having uprooted India's ancient educational system and replaced it by something 'which is ridiculously meagre'. In Burma in the early 1920s, the issue of national and vernacular education was raised vigorously as part of a nationalist programme to defy the apparent extension of government control over the educational system.

Many nationalist movements were concerned about educational opportunities from their very beginning. *Budi Utomo* (1908) in Java aimed at organising schools on a national basis, and leading Indian

Muslims until the turn of the century were concerned more with educational matters than with politics in a broader setting. The demand for free and compulsory primary education figured frequently among the resolutions of the Indian National Congress in the inter-war period. Colonial regimes were not over-anxious to provide vernacular education at secondary and higher levels and 'wild' schools started by nationalists in Indonesia represented an attempt to extend educational provisions.

The clash between Western-type education with its missionary schools and colleges in China and a reawakened and aggressive national consciousness has been noted earlier. Student nationalism was another aspect of the Chinese scene, focussed early in our period on the University of Tokyo and, by 1919, taking the form of anti-Japanese demonstrations in China. By tradition, Chinese education was rigid in structure and method and it could easily adapt itself to the spreading of patriotic and political ideas both by the Kuomintang and the communists. Patriotism and anti-Japanese feelings were sponsored in Chinese schools in the 1920s and 1930s and the same attitudes were deliberately evoked through the China-centred schools among the overseas Chinese in South-East Asia. The new official language, *Kuo Yu*, was one feature of this movement which included the despatch from China of teachers who were party members and the use of text-books printed in China in which the Kuomintang and the principles of Sun Yat-sen figured prominently. Communist influences also penetrated into the schools of the overseas Chinese, mainly, it has been argued in the case of Malaya, through the work of Hainanese teachers in night-schools. Political agitation among Chinese students in Singapore schools in the 1950s could be seen against a set of conditions which, with variations, had existed for a generation or so. The orientation of Chinese education among the Chinese in South-East Asia helped, through separatism, secrecy and suspicion, to stiffen the nationalisms of the other peoples – Burmese, Thai, Malay, Indonesian – in the countries where the Chinese formed minorities.

Inherent in the modern Japanese educational pattern was a strong sense of patriotism and duty. The famous Imperial Rescript has been mentioned earlier. The Japanese were an era ahead of the rest of Asia in providing universal and compulsory primary education, but for Japanese leaders education meant less the development of young minds for a fuller life than the training of efficient and obedient citizens for a strong State. In time, the young were indoctrinated by ultra-nationalist and militarist ideas and one of the major tasks which the American occupation authorities set themselves after the defeat of Japan in 1945 was the liberalising of the educational system. Text-books were revised to eliminate 'propaganda' elements and courses in 'ethics' were replaced by new ones in the social sciences.

Nationalism in student circles and through the medium of state education was discernible also in Western Asia. There was interaction also between education and religion and nationalism; Cairo, a great Moslem university centre, was also a nursery of new politics and new nationalisms. Two instances, each to be taken only in its own context, may suffice to show some links between education and pan-Arabism. Arab nationalists in the government of Iraq in the 1930s worked to disseminate feelings of Arabism in the schools and in the army. Secondary school students were introduced to military studies and reminded that economic independence was not enough; what Iraq needed was military strength. Just as Prussia had dreamed sixty years earlier of uniting the German people, Iraq, already independent, might dream of uniting all the Arab countries. Young men in schools and colleges were exhorted to prepare themselves for military service and sacrifice, the 'profession of death'. In 1938, the 'First Arab Students' Congress' was held in Brussels. Many Arab nationalists made a deliberately strong appeal to the young and this students' congress concerned itself much with definitions and principles for the new Arabism. In the 'Arab Pledge' which was one of its creations, the Arabs were held to constitute one nation and Arab nationalism was required to liberate and unite the Arab homeland. The raising of living standards and improvements in the material and spiritual well-being of the Arab peoples were other objectives and the pledge ended with a personal dedication to help bring all this about and to maintain the national interest above all other considerations.

Patterns of social and economic change were interwoven with the growing fabric of nationalism in Asia. In territories under Western rule a small but relatively influential middle class arose through government service or trading. This class sent some of its sons for higher education and professional training and some of these became the nuclei of early nationalist groupings. The extending range of government activities called for an expanding civil service; the increasing provision of social services, however inadequate this remained, meant more doctors and teachers; greater literacy was both cause and effect for more newspapers and journalists; Western-trained lawyers were in demand for the

Western-style administration of the law and the increasing litigation of a more complex business world. These occupational opportunities were only partly open to Asians but precisely on this account they provided a cause which nationalists could take up with vigour. The early Congress Party in India spent much time and effort on such matters as the nature and timing of the Indian Civil Service examinations, trying to improve the conditions for Indian candidates; equality of status between British and Indian magistrates was another issue of great importance from the Indian point of view. Commissions in the army offered another career area for Indian middle-class families and, not unnaturally, the nationalists saw the process of 'Indianisation' of the officer ranks moving far too slowly.

The relative size of the middle class and the opportunities, political, social and economic, open to it varied from country to country as did the extent of its commitment to nationalism. It needs also to be remembered that well-established, more aristocratic families like the Nehrus in India could provide ardent nationalists. Often the major urban centres provided the setting for 'middle-class nationalism' while the surrounding countryside was virtually untouched by the movement. In the story of Arab nationalism, Damascus, Baghdad, Cairo and Ankara all loom large and this pattern is paralleled elsewhere, from Bombay to Rangoon and from Bangkok to Tokyo. The vastly increasing size of Asian towns from the late nineteenth century onwards reflected both overall population increases and the evolving complexity of the functions of the towns themselves as government, trade, and industrial centres. Large urban communities tended to develop a character of their own and to concentrate some of the tensions which were elsewhere dispersed; much of the anti-Chinese feeling and activity in Thailand, for instance, was centred in and around Bangkok. The towns provided the natural centres for political demonstrations, attacks on the property of alien governments or groups and internal revolutionary plotting and activity; the urban universities nurtured the student leaders.

There has been a very considerable urban element in the growth of Asian nationalism but this is by no means the whole story. In his long planning and struggle for the achievement of a communist republic in China, Mao Tse-tung deliberately abandoned the idea of basing the early stages of his revolution, as in the Russian pattern, on an urban proletariat and turned instead to promoting a massive revolutionary sphere among the peasantry of the Chinese countryside. Communist organisations elsewhere in South and South-East Asia, although starting with urban roots, did not fail to give attention to country areas through a variety of tactics which included persuasion, promises of land reform, intimidation and guerilla warfare. Chiang Kai-shek, to take another case from China, gained part of his support for the reunification of China from the wealthier merchant groups in the eastern cities and towns and another part from the rural landlord class.

Economic developments, such as the growth of mining and plantation agriculture through foreign enterprise and capital, were also connected in several ways with the rise of nationalism. The miners and plantation-workers represented, for the most part, new-style communities in South and South-East Asia, and as such, and like the growing towns, they were open to new influences. Looked at in one way, the workers on tea and rubber plantations were a kind of rural proletariat, uprooted from their traditional origins and subject, economically, to distant forces over which they could have no control; in this context they attracted the attention of communist agents. Viewed in another way, the mining and plantation groups were often made up of immigrants whose separateness and relative well-being might be a cause of resentment among indigenous peoples. Nationalists in dependent countries were quick to point to grievances such as the impoverishment of peasant proprietors at the hands of alien money-lenders, the decline of village industries and handicrafts through the unfair competition of favoured imports and the burden of taxation which, it was held, served mainly to support a top-heavy, expensive and foreign administration. In India a great deal of Gandhi's energy and time was devoted to the 'constructive programme' of promoting the home spinning and weaving of *khaddar* or traditional cloth, by villagers.

The pace of nationalist developments was greatly quickened by the existence or growth of modern communications and mass-media. Gandhi's call for a simpler and more self-sufficient society in India did not square easily with the modern and sophisticated organisational apparatus of the Congress Party itself, with its links between branches and centre, its annual conferences at one town after another, its Press backing and publication of papers and reports. The Press in India and elsewhere reached an ever-expanding readership and was highly influential in the spread of nationalist viewpoints and ideas. In general, the more advanced the pattern of communications in a country the earlier was the growth of nationalism and the quicker its pace. For this reason alone, some parts of the Arab world of western Asia were rather late in entering the nationalist arena; the reunification of China by the Kuomintang was, on the other hand, helped in more than one way by attention to improved communications. In time, the power of the radio at periods of crisis came to supplant that of the Press, and the seizure and control of the national radio apparatus was a key operation in any successful revolutionary *coup*. Oratory and the transmission of personality were of great importance too in an Asian world accustomed by tradition to recognising human and personal qualities. Titles of affection and esteem were accorded both in life and afterwards to the great nationalist leaders. Many of the leaders, Nehru, Jinnah, Ho Chi Minh, Sukarno and Abdul Rahman among them, could impress Westerners as well as Asians with their great personal charm and courtesy and, on occasion, personalities rather than politics might dominate the nationalist scene, just as unexpected or unpremeditated incidents might become turning points in the nationalist cause. Not all the springs of nationalism lend themselves to rational analysis.

Until Asian nationalism was well advanced the ideological concepts which helped to inspire it were mainly borrowed or adapted from the West. It has been argued for instance, that there was no specific ideology of Arab nationalism until after the First World War and that only in the 1930s was the first serious attempt made to define the meaning of Arab nationalism and what constituted the Arab Nation. New nationalist versions of Arab history were produced to show the antiquity of the Arab people. The ideologies taken up by Asian nationalists were by no means always clear-cut and often involved something of a mixture which was then grafted on to a specific Asian background. Two broad types of political philosophy were involved, that of liberal democracy and that of Marxism, the latter both with and without Leninist–Communist interpretations. Both English and Continental European political philosophers and statesmen influenced Asian intellectuals, especially in the earlier stages of the nationalist movements. John Stuart Mill was often quoted, especially in India; Locke and Rousseau were referred to and Mazzini had a particular attraction for those who felt motivated to start 'Young' movements and for the secret types of organisation. In the case of India, there was a long and interesting association between English Liberal politicians and Indian nationalists of the more constitutional kind.

Marxism had a widespread appeal among Asian nationalists who were strongly inclined towards social reform and social justice or who were attracted to the idea of a new, secular and philosophical basis for nation-building. For some, Marxism was attractive either because it offered a kind of secular religion or because it promised tangible economic results. Among those on whom Marxist ideas had a formative effect were India's Nehru, Indonesia's Sukarno and Sjahrir, Burma's Aung San and China's Sun Yat-sen. At the western end of Asia, Marxism, in any version, played a relatively minor role in the main nationalist developments; in Japan it permeated intellectual circles in the inter-war period but different elements took what they wanted from it. It contributed both to military extremism and to communist and socialist groupings in opposition to militarism. After the war, the communist and socialist aspects of Marxism gained strength from having, as it were, been proved right in their anti-militarism while classical Marxism acquired further respectability.

Marxism became more than an academic source of inspiration for Asian nationalists from the time of the establishment of the Soviet Union and the international organisations of communism. The new nation-making in former Tsarist Russia was watched with the greatest interest and sympathy by those Asian leaders who aspired to help build new nations themselves out of the existing colonial regimes. Anti-imperialist statements and policies actively propagated by the Soviet Union were not unwelcome in many parts of Asia and for some Asians there were opportunities of visiting Moscow and seeing the new Russia at first hand. By 1936 Nehru could write that whereas the younger men and women of the Congress used to read Bryce, on democracies, and Morley and Keith and Mazzini, they were now reading, when they could get them, books on socialism and communism and Russia.

The setting up of communist parties in Asia in the 1920s can be seen in one sense as a move to influence and direct nationalism towards communist republicanism. In China, and at the price of civil war, this was eventually successful and the Chinese developed their own inter-pretations of Marxist–Leninist ideology. Elsewhere, only in North Vietnam and North Korea was communism able to capture new States. In their anti-imperialism and their emphasis on a new social and economic order, the Asian communists had much in common with nationalists in general but they often lacked a subtlety of approach and a flexibility which harmonious relationships with non-communist nationalists required. They were positively hampered at times by following a 'Leftist' line as directed by Stalin's Russia and by concentrating too much on class-struggle and too little on anti-imperialism. Communist parties in Asia made immense gains during the time of the

Second World War and in the years immediately following, but these were, in some cases, squandered by violent revolutionary tactics which were over-optimistically based on hopes of wide popular support.

In India in 1945 Nehru denounced the policies and tactics of the Indian Communist Party. Until 1935, he said, the communists had worked against the Congress from underground; from 1936 until the early years of the Second World War, there had been a joint front between Congress and communists, but, during the war, their ways had parted as Congress leaders suffered imprisonment while communists, in the interests of Soviet Russia, actively supported the war effort. Nehru claimed that, for the Congress, national independence was always the prime objective whereas the communists gave primary importance to other issues.

The Malayan communists made a tentative but short-lived bid to take over the country at the end of the Japanese occupation and led a full-scale insurrection in 1948. Their claim to be the true nationalists in Malaya was not substantiated and, in this context, one weakness of the communists was that they were mainly Chinese, a fact which inevitably aroused suspicion among the Malays. In Indonesia, the communists were an important element of the anti-imperialist front and the new State-making, but here again the disproportionate Chinese contribution to communism provoked hostility, and an added danger to any communist–nationalist merger came from the more militant Islamic groups. The failure of a pro-communist *coup* in 1965 was followed by an all-out and massive purge and blood-bath against alleged communists and communist sympathisers which was not untinged both with aspects of racialism and of 'holy war'.

The dialogue between communism and nationalism in Asia continues. Marxism, in various socialist interpretations, has at least had wide partial and nominal acceptance and the concept of planned national economies is virtually universal. The question of specifically Asian ideologies in the new nation-making will bear fuller investigation, but some noteworthy contributions may be seen in the Gandhian philosophy of non-violence and in the various blendings between imported ideas and the appeal to traditional society.

Religion has been both a binding and a dividing force in the evolution of Asian nationalism. Islam, viewed in its wider setting, has been international in character and the ties and sentiments of the Islamic world have ranged far beyond national boundaries. For strict Muslims the brotherhood of the faithful had, traditionally, much more significance than national divisions, and pan-Islamism in the Ottoman Empire ran contrary to the new Turkish and Arab nationalisms. The architect of the new Turkey deliberately secularised his State and reduced the political role of ardent religionists. The Islamic religion was one of the greatest bonds among the Arab peoples. Early Arab nationalist writers began to draw a distinction between Arab Islam and that of the Turks, and to claim a continuity in purity of practice for the Arabs as the true inheritors of the homeland of the faith. In 1919, King Faisal of Syria publicly declared the Arabs to be one people living in a defined region, and went on to say of the Arab people that they were Arabs before being Muslims and that Muhammad was an Arab before being a Prophet.

In India, the case for the separate identity of the Indian Muslims succeeded in the end although Congress, which wanted no such separation, had always claimed to be open to all Indians. Islamic interests could at times divert even politically-minded Muslims from a nationalist goal and a good case in point was the preoccupation of sections of the Indian Muslim community with the Khalifate movement on behalf of the Sultan of Turkey in the period immediately following the First World War. After independence the leaders of Pakistan gave attention to the possibilities of some form of pan-Islamic union which might stretch from North Africa to Indonesia, but nothing came of this. An early Indonesian nationalist party, Sarekat Islam, was inspired in part by Islamic revivalism, and Islam continued to play an important role in Indonesian politics both in the years of nationalist struggle and after independence. Early Malay nationalism also owed much to Muslim inspiration but was somewhat diverted by pan-Islamic aspirations. Later, though an independent Malaya took Islam as the national religion, the Pan-Malay Islamic Party attracted only minority support, much of it from the more traditional village societies of the east coast States.

The student of modern nationalism in Burma and Ceylon must take careful account of the role of Buddhism. One of the effects of the British regime in Burma had been to create a new educational system which directly and indirectly hastened the decay of the Buddhist monastic schools. The links between the Burmese government and Buddhism had earlier been broken by the British annexations and the deposition of the monarchy. Buddhism at this point ceased to be the state religion in Burma, a position which it had held for eight centuries. It was, therefore, not surprising that Buddhist revivalism was strongly woven into the fabric of Burmese nationalism, though Marxism was there too. U Nu, one of the founders of modern Burma, combined a devout Buddhism with a shrewd appreciation of nationalism and skill as a statesman. Most Burmese political leaders in the later 1930s made an appeal to religion, though Aung San and some of the Thakins were cynical about this. During the Japanese occupation Buddhist Burmese provoked a conflict with Christian Karens (a minority people) which embittered relationships into the post-independence era.

In Ceylon there were religious riots between Buddhists and Muslims in 1915 but this was a relatively isolated example of communal strife and the possible impact of religion on politics. The political motivation and use of Buddhism in Ceylon was much more apparent after independence, in the 1950s. Buddhist revivalism was then partly centred on the celebration of the 2500th anniversary of the Buddha's attainment of nirvana but partly linked also with a cultural, social and economic movement of the vernacular-educated Sinhalese against the privileged positions of their Western-educated fellow-countrymen and against that of the Ceylon Tamils. Buddhism came to be used emotionally and violently in a power struggle in which other very complex forces were involved. At least equally tragically, Buddhists in South Vietnam felt impelled less than a decade later to come out in violent and self-immolating protest against the more Westernised and Catholic administration of President Ngo Dinh Diem. The concept of Buddhism as a gentle and tolerant religion received some shocks in an age of transition, revolution and violence.

The whole subject of the interplay between religion and nationalism in Asia is very large and complex. Christianity is often readily seen in an 'anti' sense, in so far as it was regarded as 'Western' or 'colonial', but there is a more positive side to its contribution to nationalism. The first modern nationalists in western Asia included Lebanese Christians; a number of Asian nationalist leaders, including, for example, Dr Sun Yat-sen, had at least part of their upbringing in the Christian tradition, and the influence of Catholicism in the former French territories, and especially in the Philippines, has been too great to be viewed only in a negative role. Strictly orthodox Hinduism, particularly in its more militant forms, tended to impede the achievement of political unity in India and it ran counter to Nehru's conception of a secular State. The new Israel, secular and nationalist as it appears, is not yet fully secular. It has been pointed out that a Jew there may be an agnostic or even an atheist without losing his place in the community, but that the same would not be true should he adopt another religion.

Japan offers several interesting case-studies of the dialogue between religion and modern nationalism, and some aspects of this can be traced back to the nineteenth-century persecutions of both Buddhism and Christianity. One striking case, however, was that of the revival of Shintoism and especially of State Shintoism. Early Shintoism in Japan was a simple form of nature and ancestor-worship. Its relationship, in course of time, to nationalism was related to its antiquity, the reverence accorded to its shrines and the work of Shinto scholars who attempted to penetrate its myths and traditions in order to find a Japanese 'soul' which pre-dated the cultural influence of China. A proliferation of popular Shinto sects in the first half of the nineteenth century was an indication of national consciousness and the state cult of Shintoism was centred on the idea of a semi-divine emperor and imperial line. From the time of the Meiji Restoration (1867) the state cult was built up and carefully separated from popular Shintoism. It has been estimated that, by the 1930s, State Shintoism was supporting over 15,000 priests and more than 100,000 shrines, organised into twelve grades which culminated in that of the Sun Goddess, who could, by tradition, be regarded as progenitress of the Japanese imperial family. Attendance by loyal citizens at the shrines was seen as a Japanese duty whatever religious convictions were held. The emperor's divinity stemmed from his embodiment of Japan's divine ancestors, and the Japanese people and their country were considered to be under the special protection of the gods. All of this increasingly permeated the schools and the army and must be seen in the context of Japanese militarism and ultra-nationalism. Of particular significance to events in the Second World War was the widespread theory of deification for the souls of those who died in the cause of the emperor.

State Shintoism in Japan suffered a shattering blow through Japan's defeat in the Second World War and it became a key target for the American occupation government. While freedom of religion was to be guaranteed to all, no religion was to be state-aided and no person was to be compelled to take part in any 'religious act, celebration, rite or practice'. The Japanese emperor added his contribution to the ending of State Shintoism by publicly repudiating the idea that he was divine and rejecting any divinely-ordained mission whereby the Japanese people were destined to bring the whole world under their own rule.

It must be said, finally, that there were many nationalist leaders in Asia who were not deeply committed on specific ideological or religious issues. Many indeed, working from a mixture of conviction and politics, sought a middle way between extremes. In this connection, Nehru's concept of a secular State for India was a remarkable example of the personal courage and determination of one leader in restraining Hindu religious political forces at a time of the greatest possible tension. Where secularism did triumph, it did not remain unchallenged, and where imported ideologies were rejected or only partially accepted they were sometimes transformed into new political syntheses.

5 Some Problems of Asian Nationalism

ALL nation-states have 'problems' and the new or transformed nation-states of Asia are no exception. Where the achievement of independent political status has been recent, it has to be remembered that independence is no ready guarantee of nationhood. When the Federation of Malaya became independent in 1957, its new Prime Minister, Tunku Abdul Rahman, publicly declared that 'Merdeka', or freedom, was not the end, it was only the beginning. Some of the problems of the new States of Asia have had their counterparts in the new States of Africa, many of which are of even more recent origin, and thus the concept of 'emerging nations' has arisen, with both political and socio-economic connotations. It has often been pointed out that, in a world of increasing internationalism, the nation-state has an anachronistic look about it, but few Asian leaders would be ready to subscribe strongly to this view. They would instead feel themselves more readily in sympathy with a declaration made by Dr Sukarno in 1956, in which he acknowledged that there could be some in the West who held the view that nation-states were out-dated, but that this attitude could never be shared by present-day Asians, for whom nationalism was all-important.

The heredity of the new (or transformed) States had a great bearing on their early growth. Those whose origins were due to bitter physical struggle generated a revolutionary momentum which sustained in their leadership a struggle-consciousness or revolution-consciousness with a mystique of its own. It is not surprising to find that this kind of momentum appeared in Communist China after the long years of internal tension, foreign war and civil war, followed by the practical and vigorous working out and application of ideological concepts. But the spirit of struggle and revolution continued to exist in several other countries, often quite independently from any one distinctive ideology. In Burma and Indonesia, both countries in which the army had played a significant part in the independence movements, the new nation-making was marked by frequent appeals to the spirit of liberation or revolution.

In Ceylon, independence had been achieved along undramatic and constitutional lines, but the internal power struggle came later. Some major crisis involving the whole country seemed to be a necessary early stage in the evolution of the new State and there was a great prestige symbolism about the whole 'struggle' concept. During the 'confrontation' with Malaysia which began in 1963, Dr Sukarno's Indonesia could be made very conscious of the virtues of its revolutionary struggle as compared with the 'neo-colonial' status which it ascribed to the new Malaysia Federation and to the Federation of Malaya. Malaya, it is true, did not fight the British for independence but had its own civil war against communist rebellion. Since this involved massive British and Commonwealth participation, it did not, perhaps, have quite the full value of a nation-making struggle, and the external danger from Indonesian threats may itself have provided a further worthwhile national bond, though this is debatable.

The constructive work needed to establish the new patterns of government offered stiff challenges to Asian leaders, especially in those countries which were relatively ill-prepared for their new status. So far as constitution-making went – and most countries were concerned with this – there was a variety of Western models to choose from but no guarantee that any of them, or any mixture of them, would fit the case in any particular country. The idea, for example, of a mainly two-party system of government and opposition was by no means suited to many Asian countries. Kemal Atatürk experimented unsuccessfully with the idea of a constitutional 'Opposition' in Turkey as early as 1930 and, twenty years later, after Turkey's first free elections, there was still one-party rule in a theoretically two-party State. In Pakistan, to take another case, new forms of government after independence had to be built up almost from nothing; there was virtually no basis for a parliamentary system. The Muslim League was firmly led by Jinnah and his short period of Governor-Generalship continued a marked trend to authoritarian rule. Jinnah was, of course, a Western-trained lawyer and his own vision of the future Pakistan may well have been that of a secularist, nationalist, and in some form, democratic State, but there were few leading Pakistanis who were ready to agree fully to such a political blueprint and there was no impelling movement towards it from the broad masses of the people. The early constitution-making in Pakistan offers less guidance to the student of new-state politics than do the movements of power groups and personalities in that country and the role of the army.

The ingenious title of 'guided democracy' was used in Indonesia to describe a system whereby Dr Sukarno, balancing the main parties against each other, could speak directly to the nation and make use of mob violence when it suited his purpose. This remained an inherently dangerous and unstable political concept despite the very great skill of its chief protagonist. Yet in the attempts to identify the leader with the most ordinary levels of society and vice versa, and in the implied idea of reaching consensus-type agreements from a variety of viewpoints, could be discerned features which had for several years quite a wide appeal, and not only in Indonesia.

Where forms of democratic government proved ineffective or corrupt or both, there arose at times the possibility of a military *coup* in the interests of order, authority and integrity, a practice which was to have its counterparts in the new African States. The experiments of the Turkish Republic with party systems and free elections have been referred to earlier. In 1960, the army gained political control, giving way, within two years, to a new constitutional form of government. The new government, uncertain from the start, was challenged by army officers in 1962 and again in 1963. The view has been expressed by Professor Tinker, a contemporary scholar in Asian political affairs, that revolutionary military regimes have served at best only to deal with immediate and temporary issues and that they have provided no solution to the long-term question of national development.

Japan might seem at first glance a country which, in certain circumstances, could be ripe for forms of military revivalism. Japanese militarism received an overwhelming blow in 1945 and anti-militarism was further developed by American occupation policy and finally written into the new constitution. Japan renounced war as a sovereign right together with the threat to use force as a means of settling international disputes. The Japanese were never to maintain land, sea or air forces or other war potential. By 1960, however, the position had been modified and reinterpreted in such a way that the Japanese army totalled 180,000 men and Japan also had a navy of 125,000 tons' displacement and an air force of 13,000 planes. It has been argued that these figures were not in themselves highly significant but that they represented a possible base for further expansion. The question of any real or potential liaison between the armed forces and politics seems, to some observers, to have been raised anew.

There were many factors in Japan working in the opposite direction. The constitutional limitations serve as some kind of brake on the influence of militarism on politics, though it must be added that, in themselves, they hardly provide any guarantees. There would seem to be little prospect of Japan's playing an independent military role overseas. Ex-servicemen's leagues have, however, been concerned with helping to restore the prestige of the armed forces and, in some cases, sponsoring the election of ex-military men to the government. They have also been anxious to uncover and denounce forms of corruption and political subversion and to meet the challenge of communism. Outside of military associations there are civilian forms of right-wing nationalism in Japan, but there has been a fragmentation about the whole movement which has tended to reduce its significance. Should a sufficiently dynamic and uniting cause present itself in Japan, democratic processes may come under very heavy pressure and the prospect of widespread revival of Japanese ultra-nationalism cannot, it would seem, be entirely ruled out.

Many post-independence Asian countries have been beset by problems inherent in plural societies and by the particular problems which relate to the government of minorities. The pattern of independence itself has often been accompanied by bids for political self-determination on the part of minority peoples who were sufficiently integrated and organised to take action. Irredentism is a phenomenon which can be observed at times in the large nation-state but it may also be identified in the outlook of smaller minority peoples with distinctive characteristics, and especially, perhaps, in that of hill and frontier peoples. Thus the authority of the new Burma was challenged both by the Shans and the Karens just as, a generation earlier, the new Turkey had been challenged by the Kurds. Similar claims for self-determination were heard in India from the Nagas and the Kashmiris. Generally speaking, the new States were prepared to take a strong and repressive line with 'rebel' movements, though, in the case of Burma under U Nu, this attitude was tempered by feelings of compassion.

Communism was not slow to ally itself with minority grievances and active pro-communists were recruited, for instance, from among Shans, Karens and Kurds. The support won at different times for communism among the Chinese minorities in South-East Asia cannot be ascribed to one single cause, but minority feelings and complaints of 'second-class citizenship' have often been part of the background. The problem for these Chinese minorities was not one of irredentism – unless seen in any wider irredentism of China itself – but of establishing a new political identity in a rapidly changing situation. The communist-led guerilla

H

war which broke out in Malaya in 1948 pre-dated national independence but continued for some years after this event. Since the Malayan communists were predominantly Chinese, any constructive programme to end the war had to examine the question of Chinese sympathies and loyalties. The existence of a legal Chinese political party did much to ease the communal tensions, but communalism in Malayan politics continued long after the 'Emergency' period had ended. One observer of the Malayan scene has seen the need to break down political pluralism while acknowledging that social pluralism was likely to continue for some considerable time.

The occasional persecution of minority groups is one of the less pleasing forms of the new nationalisms in Asia though, so far as the Chinese in Thailand or Indonesia are concerned, there have been many precedents from earlier times. The whole tenor of nationalism encourages a heightening of the qualities and aspirations of a majority grouping and puts minorities on the defensive. The successful absorption and integration into the new nations of peoples with immigrant backgrounds is a matter requiring both delicacy of judgment and level-headed statesmanship. A measure of patience and a recognition that some changes, if they are to occur smoothly, will need time are other necessary attributes for those concerned with nation-making in multi-racial societies. The danger often lies in the fact that nationalism can appear to be as impatient in a post-independence era as it was in the earlier years of struggle. Another minority case can be illustrated from the post-independence era in Ceylon. Here the main minority issues have centred on peoples of Indian descent. The Ceylon Tamils have been long established in the country and their claims to political citizenship in the new State were recognised, though they were to have grievances on cultural and linguistic grounds. The Ceylon Indians, on the other hand, were immigrant peoples who had arrived in Ceylon mainly for plantation work at various dates in the nineteenth and twentieth centuries. Generally, they were much less integrated into the wider society of their adopted land (if this term can be used to include several generations) than were the Ceylon Tamils, and they often retained connections with south India. The new political order in south Asia posed for the Ceylon Tamils the crucial and difficult problem as to whether, under one set of conditions, they should apply for citizenship rights in Ceylon, or whether, under a different set of conditions, they should attempt to become citizens of India. Equally, there was a danger that many of them might remain virtually stateless persons for a considerable period. This question of citizenship in Ceylon for peoples of south Indian background, and the even more vexed and emotional issues raised over national language, brought the grievances of Ceylon Tamils and Ceylon Indians into Indian politics and served to sharpen relationships between the new India and the new Ceylon.

Only in one Asian region has a large minority succeeded in creating its own nation-state, and this was split into the widely separated components of West and East Pakistan. Pakistan has faced so many problems of nation-building that it is a little artificial to isolate its own main minority problem, that of the large Hindu community in the area of East Bengal, but this is relevant to any study of the problems raised by minorities in the new states of Asia. As political divisions developed in the Muslim community itself, a substantial Hindu electoral element gained an importance beyond mere numbers. Moreover, the Hindus were a source of tension between Pakistan and largely-Hindu India; their presence in an Islamic country raised a very difficult problem of assimilation and tended to keep alive memories of the communal troubles at the time of Partition. The main minority question in Pakistan has to be seen against a complex of other factors. The strictly orthodox Muslims tended to see non-Muslims as second-class citizens and were opposed to those who would support the idea of a secular State. Others again would hope to encourage modernising and secularising influences within a broad Islamic framework. The fact that the main Hindu community in Pakistan is resident in East Bengal at once introduces a regional element into the situation, and regionalism is another divisive element with which some of the new States have been obliged to contend.

Pakistan itself is perhaps the most obvious example of acute regional division. Eleven hundred miles of Indian territory divide the two parts of the State and normal movement between the two is by air or the long sea route via southern India. Rather more than half the population lives in East Pakistan, while West Pakistan has remained the main centre of the government and the army. Viewed from East Pakistan, the western province has seemed at times to wield an influence out of proportion to its contribution to the overall economy and well-being of the two-part State. Cultural differences between even the Muslim peoples of the two affect such matters as language, dress and customs and there are differences of temperament between the West Pakistani and the Bengali. Given these divisions, the basis of modern nationalism in Pakistan must be seen as insecure. A widespread acceptance, to one degree or another, of Islam, fear of Hindu domination from India, and memories of communal clashes from the past, have contributed to the structure of the State, and acceptance of forms of authoritarian rule has helped to keep the country going. Alignment with the West in defence arrangements which affect both the Middle East and South-East Asia has served to raise Pakistani morale, and new industrial projects have also had a prestige value. When all has been taken into account, Pakistan has been less unstable than might perhaps have been expected. One shrewd observer of the Pakistani political scene has seen the best hope for the future in the production and dissemination, first through the educational system, of a principle revived from the days of the Moghul Empire, whereby honour was to be achieved through services to the State.

Political India has not escaped the tensions of regionalism. The extent to which the constitution was, and has remained, federal has been much discussed, together with the tendency for political power to shift from the centre to the States or vice versa. Jawaharlal Nehru saw provincialism in India as one of the elements disruptive to national unity, linking it in this context with caste and communalism; in 1961, he authorised the setting up of a National Integration Council. Since Nehru's time, Indian provincialism has shown itself to be quite lively. The central government has intervened at times in the States for what were seen as security reasons, as in Kerala and in the Punjab. The Sikh demand for a Punjabi-speaking separate State has had to be listened to and met, and parts of southern India have also pressed strong claims for further regional identity.

The conception, inauguration and only partial success of the Federation of Malaysia provides a case-study in regionalism and minority problems combined. The starting point of this federation was in the attempt to find a generally acceptable form of merger between the independent Federation of Malaya and the self-governing colony of Singapore. A straightforward union between the two very closely related areas would have given a slight overall majority in the population to the Chinese; this was a situation which politically-minded Malays in the Federation were not yet willing to accept. In terms of potential voting power and citizenship rights the communal influence was still strong and it was going to take time and patience before a fully 'Malayan' consciousness was developed. At the same time, the Prime Minister of Malaya was deeply concerned about the possibility of a government in Singapore which might, at a future time, prove hostile or subversive to his own. After considerable investigation and negotiation the new political entity of Malaysia emerged in 1963, with Malaya and Singapore constituted into a wider federal framework which included the former British colonies of North Borneo and Sarawak, but not, as had been hoped, the British protectorate of Brunei. Britain and the Borneo territories were involved in all the discussions and planning and Dr Sukarno's Indonesia took the attitude that this was all a sinister piece of 'neo-colonialism'.

Curiously, in terms of races, the new federal agreement added more Chinese than Malays to the population of Malaysia, but this was seen to be offset by the larger elements of Borneo peoples who were mostly of Malay type but who saw themselves as separate communities with traditions of their own and in many ways distinct from those of the Malays of the peninsula. To add to the spread of communal problems, there were very considerable differences in the stages of political and economic advance reached by North Borneo (re-named Sabah) and Sarawak on the one hand, and between either of these territories and Singapore or the Federation of Malaya. It could be argued, however, that so far as the Borneo territories were concerned the new Malaysia gave them an opportunity for political independence at a much earlier date than they might otherwise have expected it. Safeguards had to be written into a complex constitution in many places.

In certain ways, the establishment of the Malaysia federation tended only to exacerbate the very communalism and separatism which it was designed to reduce. The leading political party (People's Action Party) in Singapore was more radical in character than the Alliance government in Malaya and there were troubles when, in 1964, the two parties began to put up electoral candidates in the elections held within each country. Economic policy for the new federation was a real problem since Malaya derived large revenues from imports and exports, whereas Singapore had mainly held to a free trade outlook. In foreign policy, Tunku Abdul Rahman of Malaya, with a recent history of communist-led civil war to influence him, was more virulently anti-communist than the Singapore Premier, Mr Lee Kuan Yew. The tensions, in short, became such that in August 1965 Singapore seceded from Malaysia, a step agreed by Tunku Abdul Rahman and Lee Kuan Yew as, regretfully, the best solution to immediate troubles. By this measure, though not intentionally from the outset, Singapore became fully independent and the federation was weakened in the eyes of Sabah and Sarawak. The Borneo territories presented a real challenge in terms of political integration and social and economic development.

Complexities of new nation-making to take into account the combined political future of a colony and protectorate states have also been evident in southern Arabia. Britain took the main initiative in mooting the idea of a federation between the protectorates known collectively as the Western Protectorate and the colony of Aden. By 1958 this concept was sufficiently advanced to alarm the ruler of neighbouring Yemen and provide a major reason for his alliance with the Egyptian-led United Arab Republic. In turn, the protectorate rulers became more whole-hearted about the plan for federation. Politically and economically, the Aden colony was relatively advanced while the protectorates were relatively backward. About a quarter of Aden's population was non-Arab and a substantial proportion of Yemeni people was resident in the colony. The hostility of the Yemen to its southern and eastern neigh-bours was increased by the establishment of a new revolutionary and republican government there in 1962 and the invasion of the Yemen by Egyptian troops ostensibly to support the new regime. The Federation of South-Arabia, born in 1963, was thus confronted by external enemies from the start, while having problems enough within its own boundaries. Pro-Yemeni republicans and pro-Egyptian agents formed part of the confusing background of militant nationalist organisations which did not hesitate to use terrorism as a political weapon. The prospect of in-dependence for the Federation aroused wide speculation about its future.

Religious and other cultural issues, and especially that of language, have raised almost continual problems in some new States. Religion normally has a reference in the constitutions of States and it can be a focal point for certain political parties. Buddhism is the state religion for Cambodia and Laos and has a special position as the religion of the majority in Burma. The Thai king is required to be a Buddhist and uphold the religion. In Ceylon, Buddhism has been a strong element in Sinhalese nationalism and in the relationships between Sinhalese on the one hand and Ceylon Tamils and Ceylon Indians on the other. In South Vietnam Buddhism has been invoked in protest against a regime which was held to be unrepresentative of the national outlook. A new and militant Buddhist grouping in Japan, one of several 'new religions', was becoming a political force in the country by the early 1960s. In Pakistan and in Malaya, Islam was adopted as the state religion. Pakistan, in view of the history of Partition, would have found it difficult, initially at least, to take any other decision; the Malayan situation was more con-troversial in view of the balance of communities and cultures there.

The Indonesian constitution expressed belief in God but was not specifically Islamic in character. In India and the Philippines and in Japan religious freedom was expressed in more secular terms. In Communist China ideological revisions and 'cultural revolutions' have had something of the fervour of a religious struggle.

Right-wing Hinduism, militant at times, showed itself periodically in the unfolding of the Indian nationalist movement. The Hindu Mahasabha party dated back to the years of struggle for independence but the Jan Sangh, formed in 1951, became the most powerful of the Hindu communalist parties. Its programme called for a universal ban on cow slaughter, the reunion of India and Pakistan, the dropping of English as an official language and greater control by the Indian government of foreign capital investments. Minorities, in the Jan Sangh view, would receive no special privileges. Congress stood firmly opposed to Hindu orthodoxy in politics and Nehru frequently condemned communalism of this kind. After Nehru's death, the Jan Sangh and other communal parties became still more prominent in political activities which included demonstrations, sometimes ending in violence. The activities of the Jan Sangh could alarm Sikhs and Muslims in the 1950s and 1960s in ways reminiscent of the reactions of minorities to militant Hinduism in India a generation earlier.

Where Islam was the dominant religion of a country, sectarianism within its own ranks could create new tensions and rifts. The orthodox Sunnis have, on occasion, shown their hostility to other sects such as the Shi'is and the Ahmadiyas. This type of sectarianism existed in the Yemen where peoples with Sunni traditions lived along the coastal plains and Shi'is occupied the uplands. This situation offered an extra inducement to the Egyptian invasion, the Egyptians posing as allies of the Sunni tribespeople against their hereditary overlords from the uplands.

The impact of Buddhism in Ceylon and South Vietnam has been mentioned earlier. In the new nation-states religion could be an explosive force but of at least equal portent was the question of language. Western-educated nationalists, had, in the dependent territories, extensively used the language of the imperial country, English (or American), French and Dutch. The case for a continuation of the use of English after independence was overwhelming, though it could never be, in an Asian country, a national language. The case for the French language was less strong and for the Dutch language very slight. English had become the universal language *par excellence* and thus had very considerable prestige as well as a practical value. In a multi-racial 'ex-colonial' country like Malaya, English had the added advantage of being the free tongue of all Western-educated people, whether they were Malays, Chinese, Indians or others. In political India a wide variety of regional language was in normal use and English had been the main medium of communication in the growth of the Indian National Congress movement. It is clear that in countries like India and Malaya, and also in Burma, which provided a Secretary-General (U Thant) for the United Nations, there was a considerable future for the use of English, but this only begged the question of the establishment of national languages. Only in a few countries such as Japan, Thailand and Vietnam, did the whole population virtually speak one tongue.

In Burma and Ceylon the language of the majority became the national language, with consequences, especially in Ceylon, which included an attack on the favoured positions held by some members of English-speaking minorities. When Malaya became independent in 1957, Malay was declared to be the official language, but English was equally placed for a ten-year transitional period. In Singapore, Lee Kuan Yew worked hard for the adoption of the Malay language, setting an example himself in its use. When the wider Federation of Malaysia was inaugurated, Malay was named as the official language but additional reservations for the continuing use of English were particularly specified for the Borneo territories. All multi-linguistic countries show that it is one thing to name an official language and another to implement this quickly. A Malayan child who is not of Malay race will speak, as likely as not, a mother-tongue at home, will learn Malay at school as the national language, and English as a first foreign language which may have a vital career importance.

Indonesia created a new Malay language by synthesis to avoid the choice between many regional languages, and in the Philippines the language of the central island of Luzon was selected as the official language, though, in fact, English still held the main place in the upper forms of schools and in higher education as well as in politics and government. The geographical and racial divisions of Pakistan were partnered by linguistic differences. Bengali was the principal language of East Pakistan but Urdu, originally a mixture of Hindi and Persian, had a strong following in influential circles in West Pakistan. Both Urdu and Bengali became national languages but English continued to fill a major role in many spheres.

In the field of language controversies India is a special case because of its size, its federal-type constitution and the very large number of different languages (over sixty) spoken in its states. English had been the most significant language of the independence movement and it continued to be indispensable, but the need for a national language with Indian roots was a strong one. A northern Indian language, Hindi, was put forward as a claimant to the national title and it was adopted by Congress as the official language. Hindi, however, has not been welcomed in southern India which has its own range of Dravidian languages. Any hard driving to establish Hindi all over India has only provoked signs of separatism especially in the largely Tamil south. Moreover, militant right-wing Hinduism has taken up the cause of Hindi and sought to purify the language, a move which has helped to strengthen particularism and regionalism rather than promote national acceptance. Bengali and Punjabi-speaking regions have been among those which have shown sturdy resistance to the spread of Hindi. The result of all this debate, some of it literally riotous, has been the reorganisation of states on a linguistic basis and the use of regional vernacular languages by state governments. Thus, while Hindi still remains perhaps the likeliest aspirant to the national language title, and has some sanction from Congress, it stops short at many state boundaries, not all of them in the south. English is an upper-class language which can still effectively cut across barriers of state and caste and seems likely to do so for some time. The principle of linguistic states can be seen as part of a process of decentralisation which seems to have speeded up since the death of Nehru but which may still be comfortably contained within the federal framework.

When, in the European setting, the political connotations of names like Alsace-Lorraine, the Versailles settlement and the Saar are remembered, it need be no matter for surprise that irredentism, a feature of modern European nationalism, could also arise from the military and diplomatic legacies of the past in Asia. Some of this irredentism was directed against the continuation of western rule in those parts of Asia where a transfer of power had not taken place. Thus the new India, after mounting considerable diplomatic and psychological pressures, forcibly occupied (1961) the former Portuguese territories of Goa, Damao and Diu, having accepted the transfer of the former French territories of Pondicherry, Karikal, Mahé and Yanaon. The Indonesian revolution, so it was argued, could not be complete while Dutch rule still held in western New Guinea, known to the Indonesians as West Irian. This territory, which the Dutch claimed to be ethnically and economically different from the rest of the former Netherlands East Indies, was excluded from the agreements over transfers of sovereignty to Indonesia in 1949, and remained a controversial issue until 1962 when the Indonesian view, aided by the United Nations, prevailed.

The attitude of Indonesia to the future of former British territories in North Borneo could also be seen to contain an irredentist element. The argument here was based on the indivisibility of the island of Borneo (Kalimantan) and on the historic claims of a traditional pre-colonial Indonesian empire which had allegedly held sway over the Malay archipelago. The inclusion of some of these Borneo territories in the Malayan-inspired and British-sponsored Malaysia could thus be interpreted, in one sense, as an affront to the irredentist mood of Dr Sukarno's Indonesia. Indonesia was the main Asian protagonist in active opposition to Malaysia but not, initially, the only one. The government of the Philippines protested over the inclusion of the former British North Borneo (Sabah) in the Malaysia federation on the grounds that this territory had once formed part of the domains of the Sultan of Sulu whose rights had passed down to the nation-state of the Philippines. A great deal of diplomatic activity accompanied all these arguments and, at one period Japan, offering facilities in Tokyo for summit conferences, took on the role of honest broker. This kind of irredentism – admittedly mixed with other motivating factors – could be serious enough, accompanied as it was, in the case of Dr Sukarno's Indonesia, by acts of sabotage, armed infiltrations and threats of invasion of the Malayan homeland.

The nature and extent of Japanese irredentism in the post-Second World War world offers a case for delicate assessment. It seemed unlikely that Japan would again aspire to a new vision of empire-building or that the Japanese would raise serious claims to former territories either on the Asian mainland or as far distant as Formosa (Taiwan). There were, however, island areas like the southern Kuriles to the north-east of Japan's main islands, and the Ryukyus (Okinawa group), to the south-west, which could be more justifiably claimed as Japanese territory. So far as the Japanese government has been concerned the temperature of irredentism in relation to both these areas, would appear to have been well controlled in conjunction with Japan's great efforts for recognition and friendship since 1945. The Ryukyus were first built up into an important base by the United States; the northern sector of the chain was then subsequently transferred to

Japan, while the southern islands remained an area in which the Americans and Japanese co-operated in economic developments, pending a suitable timing in the world situation, for their hand-over to Japanese rule. The Kurile islands were a matter for negotiation between Japan and the Soviet Union. Here there were differences of opinion on what constituted the Kuriles and, though the Soviet Union was prepared to make small island concessions, on certain terms, these hardly went far enough to meet the Japanese case.

Not all modern Asian irredentism has stemmed directly from anti-colonialism or from the case for reviewing imposed peace settlements. Some of the most serious issues, though linked with Western influence in the past, have appeared in the form of boundary disputes between the new or revived States themselves. Two cases may suffice for illustration; first that of the China–India frontier dispute and, secondly, the case of Kashmir in the dispute between India and Pakistan. The Chinese challenge to India's frontier is not to be explained entirely in terms of irredentism but it was justified and accompanied by versions of old maps which showed some 50,000 square miles of contemporary Indian territory as lying on the Chinese side of the border. The China–India frontier issue was preceded (1950) by the Chinese invasion of Tibet, itself an irredentist move, and an unsuccessful Tibetan rebellion (1959) which brought Tibetan refugees to India. The whole basis of the frontier dispute which brought Chinese troops into India (1962) was very complex, but the Chinese case rested mainly on the view that the existing Himalayan frontiers had been established at a time when the British Empire was strong and the Chinese Empire weak. To Nehru's argument that the McMahon Line, marking part of the boundary been India and Tibet, was established and right by usage, treaty and geography, the Chinese answer was that the Line was a legacy of Western imperialism and that China was only seeking to establish its own historic territorial rights. On the same general basis, China negotiated frontier adjustments also with Burma and Pakistan.

In a politically-divided Indian subcontinent from 1947 onwards, the position of the princely state of Jammu and Kashmir became delicate in the extreme. It is worth noting at the outset that parts of Kashmir were both hill and frontier country and might be expected to show a sturdy individuality. Moreover some of the Chinese territorial claims related to what was seen from the Indian side as Kashmiri territory. The essential difficulty over Kashmir at the time of Partition, however, arose from its tradition of Hindu princely rule over a population which was predominantly Muslim. An accession to political India seemed more in accordance with the nature of the government, but represented a clear negation of the Pakistani principle of the 'two nations' in India. Faced by a Pathan invasion which crossed Pakistani territory in 1947, the Hindu Maharaja of Kashmir acceded to India and invited Indian troops to repel the tribesmen. From this time onwards Kashmir remained a bitter bone of contention between India and Pakistan with charges and counter-charges on both sides, United Nations missions and, on occasion, direct diplomacy between representatives of Delhi and Karachi.

As the years passed it became clear that any solution to the problem of Kashmir would be likely to involve some form of compromise and partition. Pakistan pressed for the use of a plebiscite in Kashmir, confident of a Muslim majority vote for union with a Muslim state. India repeatedly protested about the presence of Pakistani troops on Kashmiri territory. India's Prime Minister, Nehru, had a strong personal feeling for Kashmir which was the traditional homeland of his own Brahmin family; he was ready, moreover, to support the constitutional right of a ruler to accede to India as the Maharaja did in 1947. For Nehru, and for Congress, India was a secular state open to all Indian peoples and creeds. A plebiscite in Kashmir, as Nehru saw it, would not only raise communal tensions there but would bring dangerous repercussions to other parts of India. Kashmir carried less prospect of internal communalist strife in Pakistan, for the Hindu population was mainly in East Bengal where it felt no strong attachment to Kashmir. For West Pakistan in particular, Kashmir became a rallying cry, almost a crusade call, which remained constant whatever the governmental changes.

The tragedy of the Kashmir dispute in terms of Indo–Pakistan relations lay in the increasing military expenditure in both States, the reduction of trade between them and the build-up of a propaganda campaign which eventually, in 1966, broke out into an open, if short-lived, war, to the great amazement and concern of the friends of both countries. Though a reconciliation was effected through the good services of the Soviet Union, the wounds were deep and the scars were likely to remain for a long time.

Most of the new nation-states in Asia have had problems enough to occupy them for many years in the internal sphere alone. Among the more obvious but heavy tasks were those concerned with political integration and with programmes of social and economic development.

At the same time they have had to establish relationships with neigh-bours often as new as themselves and to define their standing in international affairs. How far, they could ask themselves, were regional political or economic agreements necessary or desirable? What specific measures, if any, should they take for their own security in an unstable world? What attitudes, many might ask, should be taken towards that old giant, China, now clothed in modern and dynamic ideological dress? The answers to questions of this kind have varied with the passage of time. In western Asia the pact of the League of Arab States has been noted earlier. In south and South-East Asia in particular, two organisa-tions have assisted in programmes of economic development, namely E.C.A.F.E. (The United Nations Economic Commission for Asia and the Far East) and the Colombo Plan. Neither of these bodies is ex-clusively regional or even exclusively Asian, and the same is true of the security alliance, S.E.A.T.O. (South-East Asia Treaty Organisation). The three Asian members of S.E.A.T.O. were Pakistan, Thailand and the Philippines, but the nature of the agreements reached left the effectiveness of the alliance greatly dependent on Western Powers.

Relationships between new Asian States and Communist China since 1949 provide a wide selection of case studies. At one period (about 1950) the new Israel and the new China seemed to befriend each other in an un-friendly world, but China later paid more attention to the Arab States, much to Israel's discomfiture. India's friendly attitude towards China and support for China's entry into the United Nations received some hard shocks in the border dispute, as did the whole concept of Indian neutralism. Cambodia, influenced in part by memories of Chinese claims from the past and by considerations of the potential of Thai and Vietnamese irredentism in the present or the future, has behaved very diplomatically towards Peking. Some countries managed to combine friendliness towards the new China with an element of hostility toward the overseas Chinese in their midst. Indonesia's orientation towards China was periodically upset by internal attitudes to the Chinese minority, especially in Java. A dramatic change was effected through the process, in 1965, of a pro-communist *coup* and a military and pro-Muslim counter-*coup*, which brought diplomatic contacts with Communist China almost to breaking point. This sequence of events had a par-ticularly ironic twist in view of the great publicity given ten years earlier to the holding, at Bandung in Java, of an impressive Afro–Asian conference to express something of the common spirit of the new (or re-born) states of Asia and Africa. Wide differences of outlook were, not surprisingly, evident enough even at Bandung in 1955 and the patterns continued to change in the years which followed.

The problems which new Asian States have faced in dealing with disruptive forces within their boundaries and in adapting themselves to a new and changing world outside have sometimes been described by the phrase, 'second stage of nationalism.' In their search both for security and economic aid, new countries have looked to the United States of America and the Soviet Union. American resources and strategy have been especially active in the pursuit of a 'containment' policy towards communism and Chinese expansionism. This build-up has occurred not only in direct confrontation areas such as Formosa (Taiwan), South Korea and South Vietnam but also, for instance, in Thailand and the Philippines. The extent of the impact of massive and dynamic American influence on both the regimes and the national entities of the countries most concerned will be a matter for later assessment. So long as there has been fear of external dangers to parts of the region the American presence in South-East Asia, for example, has shown no signs of diminishing.

In this second stage of nationalism several of the old leaders are still at the helm though many very notable ones have gone. A new generation of politicians has been emerging for whom the first stage of independence movements, revolution, civil war and foreign war, belongs to the lore of the past. The new nationalism often seems less dogmatic, less sure of its aims and direction. It frequently faces at the same time the most acute kinds of external and internal change. There have been some indications of a more flexible outlook on the possibilities of inter-Asian regionalism, though more, as yet, in the economic than the political sphere; where security is a major issue this tendency may increase. Present-day nationalism in Asia can still profit from some of the idealism of earlier years and from the lessons of the very recent past. If it is to fulfil the hopes of some of its first and greatest protagonists it will, however, continue to demand constructive statesmanship of a very high order.

Part Two

Source Readings

Source Readings

I

THE INDIAN SUBCONTINENT

SOUTH-EAST ASIA

WESTERN ASIA

Note. The page references given in all cases are 'outside' ones, the extracted text starting within and finishing within the pages given.

Every care has been taken not to lift anything out of context. The readings are chosen to illustrate aspects of Asian nationalism but they are not the subject of specific commentaries, being left, in the main, to speak for themselves.

Asia in General

1. ASIAN NATIONALISM:
AN ASIAN VIEWPOINT, 1953

[K. M. Pannikar, Indian historian and diplomat, published a wide-ranging study of the impact of the West on Asia (and to a lesser degree of Asia on the West) taking as his starting point the famous voyage of Vasco da Gama to India in 1497–8]

... The growth of national feeling was the direct result of the reaction against Western aggression. It should be remembered – this is a point to which we shall revert – that the sense of exclusive nationalism is not very old either in Europe or in Asia. In Europe the conceptions of the Middle Ages did not include the ideas of individual nationality. Its growth synchronised with the period of European expansion, and it became the accepted creed of Europe only after the Napoleonic era. In Asia, while Japan because of its insular position developed a certain sense of nationality – limited it should be emphasised by a strong sense of feudalism – what existed in China was a feeling of imperial greatness, comparable to that of the Roman Empire, and what kept India alive was a tradition of continuity through Hinduism. The transformation of these feelings into a sense of nationhood was an essential aspect of Asian renaissance.

Within the framework of these general characteristics the problem differed greatly in complexity. The reorganisation of Indian life was much more difficult, for in India a sense of political unity which existed both in China and even to a greater extent in Japan had to be created anew. Also Hindu religion with its wide ramifications touching every aspect of life, and with its caste system and its inherited customs and laws, presented a problem of immense complexity for the reformer. Also, the necessity for reform was greater in Hinduism than in the other social structures of Asia. Political conditions under which the reforms had to be undertaken also differed radically. Japan and Siam under their national monarchies were able to direct the process and to work out the adjustments with minimum social disturbances. In India, the existence of a single government over the whole area, maintaining law and order and providing a uniform education, made it possible for the forces generated by the impact with Europe to work themselves out without interference. In China, on the other hand, the breakdown of the Central Government, the limitations imposed on the sovereignty of the Empire by the unequal treaties, and especially by extraterritoriality, the uncontrolled activities of missionaries of various Christian sects and creeds, and finally the rivalry and intrigues of the Great Powers, all anxious to establish spheres of influence and exercising power without any sense of responsibility, led to a breakdown of both the political and social structure which led to the Revolution of 1911–12. The immense significance of this difference which left China without a strong and established social order and with its renaissance uncompleted when the new ideas of the Russian Revolution began to spread, will be dealt with later. For our present purpose, it is sufficient to note that while the movement towards reorganisation was universal in Asia, and was motivated by similar factors, its results were uneven, depending largely on the political circumstances in which each country was placed and the strength of the pressure exercised on it. . . .

K. M. Pannikar, *Asia and Western Dominance*, pp 317–18

2. ASIAN NATIONALISM: A WESTERN VIEWPOINT, *c.* 1950

[Christopher Dawson, a British writer and historian with a strong attachment to cultural themes, wrote a mid-century essay on 'The Problem of Oriental Nationalism' which was published with another essay under the title given below]

. . . Oriental nationalism does not mean, as one might suppose, a reaction in defence of traditional oriental culture; on the contrary it means the adoption or appropriation by the Eastern peoples of Western culture. It stands for a new way of life which is as a rule secularist and anti-traditional. The communist states are the most extreme examples of this, since they deliberately aim at rebuilding the whole social edifice on the basis of an ideology which originated in London in the Victorian age, and was developed down to the smallest detail in twentieth-century

Russia. But the same occidentalising tendency is to be seen in purely nationalist states which are not in any way contaminated by communist ideology. Thus, the introduction of the new order in Turkey was marked by the systematic secularisation of the Turkish state and culture – the abolition of Islam as the state religion, the introduction of a new legal code based on European models and the substitution of the Latin alphabet for the Arabic script.

When one considers the strength of the forces that these movements had to contend with – the organised political and economic power of the European world on the one hand and the age-long influence of religion and custom and law on the other – their success seems almost miraculous. There were, however, two great factors in their favour. In the first place, the ordinary man had become convinced of the efficacy of Western techniques. He had learnt the lesson in the hard school of war. Even the most conservative, who remained entirely convinced of the superiority of oriental religion and culture, could not shut their eyes to the military and economic power of the West, and at a very early date they recognised that it was necessary to learn the secrets of Western technical efficiency if they were to survive.

To do this they had to accept some degree of Western education. But it proved impossible to limit education to purely technical subjects. Western techniques were inseparable from Western ideas, and the students who were trained in Europe and America or under Western teachers became converts to the Western way of life and apostles of Western social and political ideas. Thus there grew up all over the East, and at a later period in Africa also, a new educated class which was entirely alienated from the old learned classes – the Confucian scholars in China, the Brahmins in India and the Ulema in Islam – and which shared the culture of the student class of the West and especially of the liberal and revolutionary intelligentsia.

It was this new class that created the modern nationalist movement in the East. Their indoctrination with Western ideas only made them more determined to assert their equality with the European and to claim the right of national self-determination. . . .

C. Dawson, The Revolt of Asia, pp 15–16

Japan

3. JAPANESE IMPERIAL RESCRIPT ON EDUCATION, 1890

[In 1889, Japan established an oligarchic type of constitution which could be regarded as a concession to the demand for some kind of democratic participation in the government. A year later, the following document was issued under the seal of the Emperor. It asserts the importance of traditional Japanese morality, derived from Confucianism and Shintoism, and it was to serve as a check against dangerous political or moral ideas from the West. The rescript was publicly read to school pupils and college students in Japan on five or six commemorative occasions each year during the years between 1890 and 1945; it had a powerful impact]

Know ye, Our Subjects!

Our Imperial Ancestors have founded our Empire on a basis broad and everlasting and have deeply and firmly implanted virtue; Our subjects, ever united in loyalty and filial piety, have from generation to generation illustrated the beauty thereof. This is the glory of the fundamental character of Our Empire, and herein also lies the source of our education. Ye, Our subjects, be filial to your parents, affectionate to your brothers and sisters; as husbands and wives be harmonious, as friends true, bear yourselves in modesty and moderation; extend your benevolence to all; pursue learning and cultivate arts, and thereby develop your intellectual faculties and perfect your moral powers; furthermore, advance the public good and promote common interests; always respect the Constitution and observe the laws; should any emergency arise, offer yourselves courageously to the State; and thus guard and maintain the prosperity of Our Imperial Throne, coeval with heaven and earth. So shall ye not only be Our good and faithful subjects, but render illustrious the best traditions of your forefathers.

The way here set forth is indeed the teaching bequeathed by Our Imperial Ancestors, to be observed alike by their Descendants and subjects, infallible for all ages and true in all places. It is Our wish to lay it to heart in all reverence, in common with you, Our subjects, that we may all thus attain to the same virtue.

The 30th day of the 10th month of the 23rd year Meiji.

A. Tiedemann, Modern Japan, pp 113–14

4. JAPANESE VICTORY AT TSHUSHIMA, 1905

The day promised to be fine and clear, which was exactly what the Japanese needed. The curtain was about to rise on Act Five.

Deployed as a wide fan of flotillas and single ships, the Imperial Fleet swept the sea in the general direction of Matsushima. At five twenty Togo received a signal from Kataoka that the Fifth Division, steaming sixty miles south of the Admiral, had sighted several columns of black smoke on the horizon, bearing east. A few minutes later came more details; *Four enemy battleships and two cruisers in sight, course northwest*. The surviving Russians were making another attempt to reach Vladivostok. Once again, Togo steamed to cross their course.

This time he had everything in his favour, both strength and speed. The First and Second Divisions received orders to intercept the enemy: the Fourth, Fifth, and Sixth to harry him from the south. A little after ten o'clock, the enemy came in sight. The old *Nicholas I*, flying an admiral's flag, was leading the line followed by the *Orel* and by two armoured coastguard ships, *Apraxine* and *Seniavine*. The cruiser *Izumrud* was steaming abeam of the line and a little ahead of the flagship.

At ten thirty-four the *Kassuga*, followed at once by all the other Japanese battleships, opened fire. The *Izumrud*, immediately increasing to full steam ahead, left the line of Russian ships, steering due east. She was making her escape. Togo saw that she was doing so, and that the *Chitoze*, in prompt pursuit of her, was being out-distanced. It did not matter. One or two smaller fry were bound to get away, what mattered was the main body of the enemy, the remnant of his battle line. What remained of that could not escape, it was there, in front of him, encircled and again suffering a devastating bombardment.

This had lasted exactly nine minutes when one of the officers of Togo's staff said something about the *Nicholas I*. He had noticed something happening aboard the Russian flagship. He had seen the battle flag at her mainmast top jerking up and down in a peculiar manner. Next, it was seen to be running down to half-mast. At the same time, an international code signal was run up: *X G H*. The signals officer of the watch immediately translated: *We ask to negotiate*.

Togo made no move. He seemed to turn to stone. The officers surrounding him were equally motionless, equally silent. They looked at the admiral and they looked at the Russian ships, still under heavy Japanese fire. But more than one mouth was opened in amazement or to utter an exclamation at what came next.

The other Russian ships, acting almost together, were striking their colours. And when the Russian flags had disappeared below their bridges, another flag was run up on every ship: the Rising Sun, national emblem of Japan. The Russians had struck their colours and run up their enemy's flag to make it quite clear that they were surrendering. It was a heartbreaking spectacle. Even on Togo's bridge there were officers whose hearts were thumping uncomfortably, officers with lumps in their throats and tears in their eyes.

Togo's eyes were dry. He still said nothing. He stared at the Japanese flags fluttering from the Russian mastheads. Russian guns were no longer firing but Japanese shells were still exploding on the Russian ships.

'Admiral, they are surrendering', said one of the officers. 'Should we cease fire?'

Togo made no move, said no word. Was he going to sink an enemy disarmed? Or could he not believe his own eyes? Every second that passed seemed unbearable to his expectant staff officers.

'Admiral, they are surrendering,' said his chief of staff in a voice that was unsteady, almost shrill. 'Does not the spirit of Bushido require us to cease fire?'

Togo took one more look at the signal flying from the mast of the *Nicholas I* and at the Japanese flags on the other ships. 'Cease fire', he said.

And he ordered all the ships to form a circle round the enemy. This scene was played out on May 28, 1905, at a quarter to eleven in the morning in waters situated approximately eighteen miles southwest of the Liancourt rocks.

G. Blond, *Admiral Togo*, pp 231–3

5. JAPAN'S WAR AND PEACE POLICIES, 1905

[The author (born 1863) was at one time director of the Imperial
Art School in Tokyo and a member of the Imperial Archaeological
Commission to preserve ancient Japanese art, architecture and
archives. He was a keen supporter of Japanese cultural traditions]

It was then (1895) that the triple coalition interfered with the just
fruits of our victory. In the name of peace, Russia, upheld by Germany
and France, forcibly demanded that we give up our newly acquired
possessions in Manchuria. This unexpected blow was a severe one,
considering the great sacrifices we had made in the war. We were,
however, in no position to refuse the combined demands of the three
powers, and had only to submit; moreover, as their intervention came
in the sacred name of peace, the nation had to be content. The fact that
the Muscovite Empire soon after coolly took possession of Port Arthur,
which she had asked us to evacuate, seemed a queer proceeding, but we
offered no opposition to her action, for, as novices in European diplomacy, we still believed in international morality and relied on the fair
words of the Russians when they declared that their intention was to
hold that place merely in the interests of universal commerce. Nine
years elapsed, during which their real designs became revealed. The
greatest shock came to us, however, when we found that they were
determined not only to possess Manchuria, but also to annex Korea.
Protest after protest was made on our part. Promise after promise was
given by Russia, never to be fulfilled. Meanwhile, she was pouring huge
armies into Manchuria, and her advance-guard entered Korea itself.
The throat of the dragon was touched, and we arose. Among the crags
of Liao-tung and the billows of the Yellow Sea we closed in deadly
conflict. We fought not only for our motherland, but for the ideals of
the recent reformation, for the noble heritage of classic culture, and for
those dreams of peace and harmony in which we saw a glorious rebirth
for all Asia.

Who speaks of the Yellow Peril? The idea that China might, with the
aid of Japan, hurl her hosts against Europe would be too absurd even
to notice were it not for those things from which attention is drawn by
the utterance. It may not, perhaps, be generally known that the expression 'Yellow Peril' was first coined in Germany when she was preparing
to annex the coast of Shantung. Naturally, therefore, we become
suspicious when Russia takes up the cry at the very moment when she

is tightening the grasp of her mailed hand on Manchuria and Korea.

The Great Wall of China, the only edifice on earth of sufficient length to be seen from the moon, stands as a monumental protest against the possibility of such a peril. . . . This cry of a Yellow Peril must, indeed, sound ironical to the Chinese, who, through their traditional policy of non-resistance, are even now suffering in the throes of the White Disaster.

Again, the whole history of Japan's long and voluntary isolation from the rest of the world makes such a cry ridiculous. However changed modern conditions may be, there is no reason for supposing that either Japan or China might suddenly develop a nomadic instinct and set forth on a career of overwhelming devastation.

Okakura-Kakuzo, *The Awakening of Japan*, pp 216–21

6. THE 'NATIONAL CONGRESS' MANIFESTO IN SEOUL, KOREA, 1919

How miserable are our 20,000,000 compatriots. Do you know the reason for the sudden demise of His Majesty the Emperor? He has always been healthy and there was no news of his illness. But he has suddenly expired at night in his sleeping chamber. Would this be ordinary? As we advocated the national independence in the Paris Peace Conference, the cunning Japanese produced a certificate stating that 'The Korean people are happy with Japanese rule and do not wish to separate from the Japanese' in order to cover the eyes and ears of the world. Y Wan-yong signed it as the representative of the nobility: Kim Yun-sik signed it as the representative of the scholars; Yun T'aek-yong signed it as the representative of the royal relatives; Shin Hŭng-u signed it as the representative of educational and religious fields. It was then submitted to His Majesty for his royal seal – the worst crime possible. His Majesty was most enraged and reprimanded them. They did not know what to do, and fearing other incidents in the future, they finally decided to assassinate His Majesty. Yun Tŏk-yong and Han Sang-hak, two traitors, were made to serve His Majesty's dinner, and poison was secretly added to his food at night through the two waiting women.

The Royal Body was immediately torn by agony and soon the Emperor took his last breath. There is no way to describe the pain and agony in our hearts. The two women were also put to death by poison, immediately, so that the intrigue might not be leaked out. The hands of the brigands are becoming more obvious, and cruelty is running to extremes. We have not yet revenged the humiliation of the past (the murder of the queen). And yet another calamity is brought upon us. Ask the blue sky who is incurring these misfortunes. If our people still exist, how could we neglect to cleanse these humiliations? Since the American President proclaimed the Fourteen Points, the voice of national self-determination has swept the world, and twelve nations, including Poland, Ireland, and Czechoslovakia, have obtained independence. How could we, the people of the great Korean nation, miss this opportunity? Our compatriots abroad are utilising this opportunity to appeal for the recovery of national sovereignty, but the compatriots within our country are still unmoved. Support is not very strong, and opinions are not decided. Think, our compatriots! Now is the great opportunity to reform the world and recover us the ruined nation. If the entire nation rises in unity we may recover our lost national rights and save the already ruined nation.

Also, in order to revenge the mortal foe of His Majesty and Her Highness, our 20,000,000 compatriots, arise!

January, thirteenth year of Yung-Li (1919).

Kungmin Taehoe (Seal).

Chong Sik Lee, *The Politics of Korean Nationalism*, pp 111–12

7. JAPANESE SECRET SOCIETIES, *c.* 1921

The most vicious method of intimidation and control over the Japanese was exercised by secret societies, or Kais. For centuries the kai formed part of the Samurai stranglehold on the people of the soil. More recently, the Black Dragon (Roku-Ryu-Kai) Society – associated with the name of Toyama Mitsuri – and the Black Ocean Society (Gen-yo-sha) founded by him in 1879, were the most active.

The Gen-yo-sha was the model for the Gestapo, of the Nazi, and the Ogpu, of the Soviet police system. In early Meiji days, the Gen-yo-sha was the directing force behind the kempei. Then the population was harassed by political bullies, Soshi, and their hirelings the Goro-Tsuki hooligans. After Meiji, the kais shared out the work in hand with the various criminals, kidnappers, assassins, blackmailers and thugs who were directly – and indirectly – employed by Gumbatsu and Zaibatsu to ensure the smooth running of the Tokyo administration.

Since the Sino-Japanese War the kais have been responsible for the assassination of four or five Prime Ministers and a round dozen Cabinet Ministers who would not come to the heel of their masters. To detail each incident would add nothing to what was made public at the time but it may still be worth while to try and explain the inability of the extensive ramifications of the Japanese press, and literature of Japan, from 1900 to 1941, to create a public opinion capable of expressing itself with realism against the Gumbatsu and their kais.

In the first place. The Kempei-Tai, by a special law, were responsible directly to Imperial Headquarters as Special Police to guard the security of the State. They had the right to hold their prisoners for one-hundred-and-twenty-one days without a warrant or a formal charge being preferred. Acting in close co-operation with the Home Office and the civil police they applied most terrible methods of torture to obtain confessions of guilt out of innocent Japanese, Chinese, Koreans or foreigners arrested on information supplied by any member of a kai. In the second place, Japanese journalists, educationalists and authors combined their talents to spread State Shintoism as a necessary co-efficient of expansion of Empire.

Such editors, professors or authors who held to a contrary opinion were deemed, by the kais, to be guilty of the crime of *lèse-majesté* and this in their opinion warranted severe punishment which was inflicted without recourse to the law courts.

In the judgement of the kais they were journalistic-eta – the outcasts whose touch would defile Shintoism – socialists, communists, labour leaders, all of them harbouring dangerous thoughts.

When Toyama founded the Gen-yo-sha his personal objectives were in Korea, Formosa and North China. Members of the Roku-Ryu-Kai were planted in these centres to operate much as Communist cells do outside the U.S.S.R. today. By 1894, kais were already fully recognized as a secret agency of the government, and it was the tripartite intervention, 1895, which brought many embittered Japanese supporters into Toyama's movement. They were the ready tools for creating incidents in Korea and Manchuria, incidents which were made the most of by the Gumbatsu.

I shall give one personal illustration of their methods. It concerns the first quasi-democratic Prime Minister of Japan, Mr Hara, and the labour movement in 1921.

Hara's term of office – 1918–1921 – coincided with the rise of labour unions in Japan. I was interested as an onlooker. Through Count Soyejima I passed on the suggestion to Mr Hara that he should abolish Clause 2, para. 17, of the Police Regulations and thereby permit labour to organize into unions with the right to use the strike weapon when negotiating with employers. As the matter stood, 'those who, with the object of causing a strike, seduce or incite others, shall be sentenced to major imprisonment of one to six months with additional penalty of three yen to thirty yen', and this Police Regulation was to break up ordinary labour meetings.

Mr Hara replied, through Count Soyejima, that he was well aware of the repressive nature of the Regulations but he did not intend to commit political hara-kiri by acting on the suggestion just then.

As Prime Minister there were many other things of benefit to the country he could accomplish before he died, or lost office.

That was in July, 1921 when we had labour trouble in Kobe shipyards, and labour disputes in many cotton and spinning mills in Osaka and Tokyo. I went to Borneo and South China for a few months and returned with Lord Northcliffe on 2nd November, 1921. Hara was already a marked man: he had not helped the unions but he had violated the rule that Naval and Military portfolios must be held by serving naval or military officers. He had taken over, as a civilian, the Naval Office when the Navy Minister – Admiral Kato – went on to the Washington Conference.

Lord Northcliffe, at my suggestion, had arranged to meet Mr Hara outside of Tokyo if possible, to discuss the abolition of the police regulation I have mentioned and also the non-renewal of the Anglo-Japanese Alliance which was no good to either country in their relations with China. No good that is to the spread of democratic ideas as opposed to imperialism.

But there was to be no meeting between Hara and Northcliffe. On the evening of 4th November, just before Hara's train was due to leave Shimbashi Station, Tokyo, for Kyoto, a patriotic member of the kai stabbed him to death. Police Regulations banning the trade unions continued to function long after Hara was buried.

The assassin was canonized as a patriot who killed in order to preserve the sanctity of the Constitution. That was the fiction to cover the fact that Hara's removal was necessary in the interest of the suppression of the labour movement. The Army and Navy could have forced his resignation with ease but then he would have lived on to be a nuisance.

D. H. James, *The Rise and Fall of the Japanese Empire*, pp 161–4

8. THE BASIS OF EDUCATION IN JAPAN, 1928

[The writer was a former College and School Principal and Member of Parliament in Japan]

Forty years ago our Empire at a single stroke abandoned the ancient culture of the East and took its place upon the swift current of modern civilisation. Education became essential and soon flourished in every part of the land. It became the most important means of guiding and directing our lives. Without it we were not able to enter good society. Wealth and birth alone without education were found to be insufficient. Without distinction of rank or wealth, therefore, all the citizens of the Empire devoted themselves with the utmost diligence to the cultivation of learning and the acquisition of an education. By this means they demonstrated their single-hearted devotion to the Imperial Line. Such devotion is the glory of our ancestral tradition and the true adornment of the present age.

The purpose of education is to provide nurture for men of character. This cultivation has a two-fold object. One kind of education is designed to produce the great leader, the man of all time. The other kind is for the purpose of producing the man adapted to the requirements of the age. When education realises this dual objective it is successful. In order to produce his superman the educator must not consider the achievements of any one nation, he must not be swayed by international rivalries. He must consider neither merit nor renown, neither the handful of rice nor the gourd of wine. He must concentrate on producing the man who will be great for all time. His task is to produce material which will ensure the permanent peace and prosperity of the nation. The second great object of education is to produce men who are suited to the changing times and who are able to adapt themselves with ease to the immediate emergency. By producing people who are thus adaptable, educators will enable the citizens to fulfil their duties to the nation.

Our Empire is not limited to any ephemeral existence. It will achieve an immortal and everlasting destiny. It must possess in its history the elements of both permanent and temporary existence. Educators must not fail to adapt their methods to this end. To ensure both present and future prosperity they must carefully nourish and produce such men as will secure the true progress of the Empire and who will be trained at the same time to take advantage of the changing conditions in the world. I have designated one type of education immediate or practical education and the other potential or ideal education. I consider these two types of education to be essential to the maintenance of a flourishing and peaceful Empire. The direction of education with a view to producing either the superman or the practical man, the choice of practical or ideal methods must be left to the wise leadership of our educators. They must be careful in their choice. At the same time those who receive their instruction must consider their own capacities in order to choose aright between the two alternative types of education available. If care is taken in making suitable choice then although the paths of ascent are different all may unite in admiration of the view from the summit, and the merit of their several efforts shall be of equal value. All will rank as equals for they must all be regarded as equally fulfilling their full duties as subjects. . . . Through following in the footsteps of occidental nations and vigorously entering the sphere of western culture, our Empire has enjoyed great prestige and renown. Emerging from her period of immaturity her present intellectual and material achievements are inferior in no way to those of foreign nations. To maintain their present rank among foreign peoples and to sustain for ever undiminished their glorious heritage is the true task of the citizens of the Empire. The fulfilment of this mission calls for the provision of an education which is both ideal and practical, both temporary and enduring in character. To perceive these points with clarity is to see penetratingly into the future. To fulfil this mission is the true task of the citizens of the Empire. To perform these tasks is to offer true service to the Emperor above and to fulfil our obligations to our ancestors.

Y. Hibino, *Nippon Shindo Ron, or The National Ideals of the Japanese People*, pp 76–9

9. SECRET ORGANISATIONS IN THE JAPANESE ARMY BETWEEN THE WORLD WARS

False Pride of the Japanese

As a result of the First World War, Japan came suddenly to rank as one of the five, if not of the three, major world powers, and she attained the responsible position of leader of the Western Pacific. Japan's standing in regard to world peace was important and her responsibility towards the civilization of mankind was an onerous one. But the future development of the Japanese State, the advance of the Japanese themselves, could have been furthered only if they had fully realized their responsibility. So far from doing so, the Japanese let themselves drift with the tide of new-found prosperity, they thought only of their own *amour-propre*, though what was within, their own merits, did not keep pace. The standing of Japan had improved but they forgot the simple truth that Japan, whether the individuals or the state, could attain greatness only in a spirit of humility and by unremitting effort. They lacked the voice of conscience to teach them what constituted lasting peace and what should be the ideals of the individual and of the state. This was the cause of the *Showa* upheaval.

Contempt Shown for the Military

The military caste had grown out of the former strength of the clans which from time immemorial had held the reins of power in the administrative organization. But in proportion as the spirit of a free democracy gathers force, the political parties strove to overthrow the military caste just as the military on their side strove to stave off their own decline. After the war the political parties, which had long suffered under the arrogance of the military, seized the opportunity to cut down military expenditure. Thus they proposed to destroy the power of the military, and leaders of the political parties openly denounced the Army in the Diet. The nation in general jumped to the conclusion that to show their contempt for the military by stripping them of their privileges, something they had never dared to do before, was itself to breathe the air of untrammelled freedom. A narrow-minded desire to pay off old scores also played its part. It was the manifestation of a people that had emerged from feudalism via clan government to a capitalist era of which

K

it had no experience; it was indicative of the gap between the Government and political power on the one side and the nation and public opinion on the other. As for the military, they considered themselves a privileged class and they purposed to retain the power they had enjoyed under clan government. The political parties, again, ignored the fact that their mandate came from the people; they were engrossed in the task of extending their own influence and advantage. Both parties were inured to old habits acquired under clan government. They failed to appreciate the concept that in common with others they themselves were a section of the state and the nation. They failed to see that it was their duty to fulfil the charge laid upon them.

So the military became a target for insults wherever they went. They were made to feel small when they got on the trains in uniform. They had to listen to such remarks as 'What use are spurs in a tram-car?' or 'Big swords are a nuisance to fellow passengers'. The Army were indignant. Whatever their rank, they mostly came from farming villages which formed their background. And it was these villages that were impoverished and withering away because of the prosperity and corruption of the towns. The claim gathered strength that they could not stand by and watch the foundations of military caste being destroyed.

Young Officers form the 'Society of the Sword of Heaven'

The fighting services felt that it was they that defended the state. This contempt for those who were in simple loyalty building the foundations of the empire arose out of the high-handedness of the political parties and the self-assertion of the moneyed interests. Their claims of liberalism and capitalism were in fact the direct cause of the corruption of society. That being so, it was necessary to cure the disease from which the state was suffering by removing the elements that were poisoning the system. Could there be any hesitation in killing such traitors?

Such were the thoughts that little by little began to fill the minds of Army and Navy officers. In the upper and middle ranks of the General Staff Offices, of the War Ministry, even in the Staff College, there were not wanting those who preached such ideas. The blood of the cadets in the Military Academy and of young officers boiled.

Many years ago the Reform of *Taikwa* had been effected when Prince *Naka no Oye* had drawn the 'sword of heaven' and cut down *Soga-no-Iruka* in the Palace of the Emperor. In order to effect the Reform of *Showa*, should there be any hesitation to resort to emergency measures?

Such action was rather the supreme act of a loyal patriot. The time had come to lay down one's life in order to save the country.

So ran the thoughts of the high-spirited young officers. The summons went forth from Tokyo to every headquarters and formation in the country: gather together fellow-thinkers united in the aim of killing traitors and reforming the Government. Many young officers of every Division and of the naval depots signed in blood as they joined the pact and swore to sacrifice their lives as volunteers in reforming the state. This secret society of young officers, that planned direct action, took to itself the title 'Society of the Sword of Heaven'.

It is lamentable to think that the idea of reform in the *Showa* era should have gone back to reactionary principles and adopted as its means the lesson of *assassination* learnt from historic times 1300 years previously.

Young Officers become the Tool of the Senior Staff Officers

These 'young officers' were all subalterns, probationary officers and cadets. One and all held the simple desire to serve their country. And that being so, most of them put aside the traditional Japanese idea of marrying and settling down. Without radical reform, Japan, they thought, could not be saved. They themselves, therefore, would pay the sacrifice and settle the matter. The brains of the Army viewed the trend with some disquiet but none the less they used it for their own ends, so that it became a driving force that fostered the high-handedness of the military.

The object of the young officers was to cure the national malady by direct action, to be pushed to the bitter end – a simple destructive operation that was to be the spear-head of reform. As to a plan to build up after the destruction, they had none. Nor had they the power. They would have to rely on outside sources for constructive plans. They intended to hand over the work of building up again to seniors whom they could trust to do it. This fact was utilized by the senior staff officers to formulate and carry out the Army's own particular plans.

The man that provided the most powerful ideological background to the conduct of the 'Society of the Sword of Heaven' was Ikki Kita. He was a born revolutionary, a planner and executor of dark sordid plots. In youth he had drifted to China where he threw in his lot with the revolutionary movement.

The basis on which stood his plan for revolution, 'Principles govern-ing a measure for the Reorganisation of Japan', is itself clear enough. The ultimate aim is obscure but the plan itself can be readily recognised as a mixture of right and left thinking.

That what he wrote on the reorganisation of Japan constituted a text-book for the young officers of the Society and of revolutionaries in the Army cannot be gainsaid. For them his parlour was a forcing house of revolutionary thought. The hold he maintained over the minds of the young officers became manifest later at the time of the February 26th revolt (1936).

M. Shigemitsu, *Japan and Her Destiny*, pp 28–31

10. THE JAPANESE POLITICAL SCENE, 1932

[Joseph C. Grew was United States Ambassador to Japan from 1932 to 1942. The following account was based on his diaries and papers about the time of his appointment to Japan]

The Mission Begins

May 14–18, 1932   *On the Overland Limited, Chicago to San Francisco.* We're off. A new adventure in this kaleidoscopic life of ours – our fourteenth post and our fourth mission, and it promises to be the most adventurous of all. For five years we've watched the Turkish Republic digging out from the ruins of a defunct Ottoman Empire and hewing its way, painfully, to a new salvation. Now we enter a much bigger arena, on which the attention of the world is going to be centred for many years, and perhaps for many decades, to come. Almost anything may happen except one thing: the abandonment by Japan of her investments, her property, her nationals, and her vital interests in Manchuria. She is there to stay, unless conquered in war, and the interesting question is the policy and methods she will pursue to meet international susceptibilities and what camouflage she will employ to cover uncomfortable facts.

Indeed, many interesting questions present themselves. Will Japan be content with safeguarding her present rights in Manchuria or, as some would have it, does her programme include ideas of far-flung empire throughout Asia, with Korea the first step and Manchuria the second? Can she avoid a clash with Soviet Russia, with America? The big issue is whether this irresistible Japanese impulse is eventually going to come up against an immovable object in world opposition and, if so, what form the resultant conflagration will take, whether internal revolution or external war. It will depend largely on how Japan plays her cards, and this is the problem which we are going to be privileged to watch from the inside, I hope for a long time to come.

I shall do my utmost to keep a detached and balanced point of view. An ambassador who starts prejudiced against the country to which he is accredited might just as well pack up and go home, because his bias is bound to make itself felt sooner or later and render impossible the creation of a basis of mutual confidence upon which alone he can accomplish constructive work. On the other hand, there is always the danger of becoming too much imbued with the local atmosphere. However, I know the minds of the President, the Secretary, and the Department pretty well, and that should help to keep a straight course. To begin with, I have a great deal of sympathy with Japan's legitimate aspirations in Manchuria, but no sympathy at all with the illegitimate way in which Japan has been carrying them out.

One can have little sympathy with the Twenty-One Demands, formulated when the world was busy with the Great War, or with the typically Prussian methods pursued in Manchuria and Shanghai since September 18, 1931 in the face of the Kellogg Pact, the Nine-Power Treaty, and the Covenant of the League of Nations. The purely Sino-Japanese problem has so many complicated features – the interpretation of treaties, what treaties were valid, and who broke the valid treaties first – that one can regard that phase of the situation only as a technically insoluble puzzle. But fortunately our position is clear as crystal: we hold no brief for either side in the Sino-Japanese dispute; we hold a brief for the inviolability of the international peace treaties and the Open Door, and on that issue we have carefully registered our opinion and position before the world and will continue to do so when necessary. So much by way of preface to what may come.

At the very start the pot begins to boil. A correspondent of the *Herald Examiner* met us at the station in Chicago with the Sunday evening paper of May 15 bearing flaring headlines: *Japanese Premier Slain, Serious Revolt; Palace in Peril.* This is the fourth important assassination. The military are simply taking the bit in their teeth and running away with it, evidently with a Fascist regime in view. But in spite of the press reports, I can't believe that the Emperor is threatened, considering the supposedly universal veneration for the throne. There must be something wrong there. If this latest demonstration of terrorism – the murder of Premier Inukai and the exploding of bombs in various public buildings – is the work of a group of fanatics, I wonder whether such extremes may not possibly have a steadying effect on the military themselves. We shall see in due course. . . .

J. C. Grew, Ten Years in Japan, pp 13–14

11. THE JAPANESE ARMY, *c.* 1940

The Japanese Army, in the judgment of most foreign military observers, is stronger in morale than in material equipment. A Japanese who had been a fellow student at college in America told me that he was amazed at the amount of political training which went on during his period of military service. In the Young Men's League to which he belongs before he is called to the colours, in the army itself, and later in the Reservists' Association, the Japanese conscript receives a very thorough indoctrination in nationalist ideas. The army is perhaps the best propaganda agency in Japan, and the young peasant who is the preferred type of soldier probably absorbs more ideas during his period of service than at any other time in his life.

Discipline is of a curiously paternalistic type, which is only understandable if one remembers how deeply the family system dominates Japanese psychology. The new recruit is gravely told that the company commander is his father and the sergeant is his mother. This kind of appeal would not go very far with the American Marines; but it works well in Japan, so far as the maintenance of discipline is concerned. Courts martial are almost unheard of; cases of drunkenness and disorderly conduct, among the troops in Japan, are almost unknown. The severest punishment for the soldier is to have his officer write to his family and complain about his behaviour. The officers take a keen interest in their men's affairs: the mail of the company commander is filled with letters from the families of the men under his command, asking advice on all kinds of problems, from how to meet debt charges to the choice of a bride for their son. The radicalism of some of the younger officers is partly the result of their intimate knowledge of the hardships in some of the country districts.

Morale is also sustained by an extremely high-flown standard of military ethics. It is an indelible disgrace for a Japanese soldier to be captured; an officer who falls into the hands of the enemy is obliged to commit suicide at the first opportunity. A Japanese officer once told a foreign colleague who inquired why there was never any practice in retreating operations that these were unnecessary because a Japanese army would never retreat.

Two features of Japanese military action which have won the praise of foreign military observers have been the extreme mobility of their infantry (thanks to their ability to subsist and fight on minimum simple rations) and their skill in utilizing flatbottomed boats on small waterways to facilitate their advance. This also speaks for the effectiveness of their previous espionage in China and for the care with which plans for future invasion had been worked out.

The war has indicated that Japan is not so weak in the air as had previously been believed. The very conditions of air combat make for utter unreliability in reports of enemy aircraft destroyed; and it would certainly be unwise to accept at face value the Japanese claims of ten Chinese aeroplanes destroyed for every one of their own that has been lost. But Japan certainly has retained the mastery of the air, despite Chinese purchases of British and American aircraft and the five hundred aeroplanes which the Soviet Union, according to a reliable foreign observer, sent to China during the first eighteen months of the war. In the air, as in other fields, Japanese fighting dash and initiative, the traditional willingness of the Japanese aviator, if he can reach his objective in no other way, to crash into it at the sacrifice of his own life, have given them a certain advantage over the more passive Chinese.

W. H. Chamberlin, *Japan in China*, pp 77–9

12. THE 'ULTIMATE MADNESS': JAPANESE ULTRA-NATIONALISM AND MILITARISM, 1940

The Foreign Minister, Matsuoka Yosuke, was an admirer of Hitlerian tactics; shrewd, ambitious, voluble, he had been educated in the United States, was a career diplomat, had accompanied Prince Saionji to the Versailles Peace Conference, had acquired fame in leading the Japanese delegation out of the League of Nations, and obtained a taste of dictatorship, which obviously pleased him, during his tenure of office as president of the South Manchuria Railway. It was no doubt the pressure brought to bear upon Prince Konoye through Matsuoka, the War Minister General Tojo Hideki, and Navy Minister Oikawa, who represented the extremist factions, and also the machinations of Herr Stahmer, later to be German ambassador at Tokyo, who had been sent on a special mission by Hitler, that Konoye was finally compelled to give way, and in September Japan became a signatory to the Tripartite Military Alliance with Germany and Italy.

Matsuoka, who was in the habit of proclaiming that everything he did was in the interests of peace, in one of his first acts on becoming the head of the Foreign Office recalled some forty diplomats from abroad, giving as his reason the necessity for ridding it of those who were considered to have leanings towards Great Britain and the United States. One writer has asserted that Matsuoka was not popular in the Foreign Office. He was certainly not popular with some diplomats, but with the officials in general he was the hero they hoped would clear out all who were considered deadwood and encourage those of totalitarian inclinations.

The new policy was based on the will of the Imperial Ancestors, or Hakko Ichiu, which in the Chinese characters means Eight Points Under One Roof, a theory which had been sold lock, stock and barrel, through the nationalist societies and the works of such intellectual fanatics as Okawa Shumei, long a dabbler in ultra-nationalism and supporter of assassins, whose *History of Japan from 660 B.C.* treated all the legends and myths as gospel. The reference to Hakko Ichiu occurs in the Nihongi and had been dug out to impress the nation but, as Aston comments, 'The whole speech is thoroughly Chinese and it is preposterous to put it into the mouth of an Emperor who is supposed to have lived more than a thousand years before the introduction of Chinese learning into Japan'.

The nation, especially the young, appeared to be thoroughly indoctrinated with the sense of the superiority of Japan over all, including even the Nordic paragons presided over by the maniac Hitler, its mission ordained by the gods, and in October the Imperial Rule Assistance Association was established to stifle criticisms of those who expressed fears that the Imperial prerogative was being ignored. This one party – Taisei Yokusan Kai – now exercised control over all national activities, and all that was allowed to constitutional politics was a Diet Bureau. And on November 10th the greatest tribute to mythology was made in a grand ceremony to celebrate the 2,600th anniversary of the foundation of the Empire by Emperor Jimmu at which, before the Emperor and Empress, Prince Konoye made a speech in which he eulogized the Imperial Virtues, and counselled the nation to observe the lofty ideals of Hakko Ichiu; but it was observed that he spoke like a man giving hypocritical advice to his son, and his bearing was as casual as if it might have been just another unimportant social occasion.

All Shinto priests were now classified as government officials, hitherto this had only applied with those of the most important State Shinto shrines. Buddhism was helpless, or rather made no attempt to restrain the extremism which was engulfing the nation and justified every single act against all that Gautama Buddha had preached. Christianity was almost as hidebound and helpless and, of course at the mercy of the 'dangerous thoughts' ordinances; there was not even a Japanese Pastor Niemoller, none came forward to demonstrate that the much vaunted Bushido, which apparently declined at the end of the Meiji era, did not have the monopoly of courage.

L. Bush, *The Land of the Dragonfly*, pp 193–4

China

13. THE BOXER UPRISING, 1900

[A divine rhyme, said to have been composed in Peking on 17th July, 1900, by the demi-god, Chi Kung, the hero of three novels published in the Ch'ing dynasty. The 'Boxers' sang or recited this type of rhyme with its anti-foreign, anti-Christian, but at the same time, nationalistic and patriotic message]

There are many Christian converts
Who have lost their senses,
They deceive our Emperor,
Destroy the gods we worship,
Pull down their temples and altars,
Permit neither joss-sticks nor candles,
Cast away tracts on ethics,
And ignore reason.
Don't you realise that
Their aim is to engulf the country?

No talented people are in sight;
There is nothing but filth and garbage,
Rascals who undermine the Empire,
Leaving its doors wide open.
But we have divine power at our disposal
To arouse our people and arm them,
To save the realm and to protect it from decay.
Our pleasure is to see the Son of Heaven unharmed.
Let the officials perish.
But the people remain invincible.
Bring your own provisions;
Fall in to remove the scourge of the country.

V. Purcell, *The Boxer Uprising*, p 224

14. CHRISTIAN MISSIONS AND 'ANTI-FOREIGN' ACTIVITIES IN CHINA, 1900

There seems to be a disposition to make the labours of Christian Missionaries responsible for the violent hostility expressed by the Chinese against foreigners. They have been seriously cautioned and counselled by H.M. Secretary of State for Foreign Affairs. The newspaper and periodical press have pointed out in varying terms their power for mischief and the perils which constantly threaten all foreigners in consequence of their action.

In regard to the complaint that missionaries by their enterprise and indiscretion involve themselves in difficulty and then appeal to their own Government for protection and vindication, it may with truth be said that the cases in which this has happened, at least in Protestant Missions, have been so rare and exceptional that no general complaint against Missions can fairly be based upon them. . . . It must, however, be remembered that while missionaries are pursuing their lawful calling they have an equal right with all others to claim the protection of their Government.

It is further complained that missionaries have excited against themselves the hostility of the official classes in China by their habit of interfering in the law-suits of their converts, the just administration of the law being constantly prevented by the powerful pressure of the foreigner's influence. A distinction ought to be drawn in regard to this complaint between the Roman Catholic and the Protestant Missions. The former appear to act on the principle that it is the duty of the Church to act as the protector of its members, and its priests have become conspicuous by their general action as advocates of the causes of their converts. The Protestant missionaries, on the other hand, have thought that to adopt this course would not only arouse the hostility of the magistrates, but would also be a strong temptation to unworthy persons to profess themselves converts to Christianity for the purpose of obtaining the help of the missionary in law-suits. As a rule, therefore, they have steadfastly, and often to their own disadvantage, declined to interfere. Yet the Chinese administration of justice is so venal and corrupt that it is often exceedingly difficult for the missionaries to stand passively by and see their converts suffering from the grossest injustice without making an effort to help them. . . .

There is no evidence that the persecution of the Christians, and attacks on missionaries have any religious basis such as was so prominent a feature in the Indian Mutiny. . . . The complaint against Christianity has been mainly that it was a foreign superstition. The Christians have been persecuted because they had adopted a faith which came from foreigners. The missionaries have been objects of attack because they were foreigners.

China is a huge anachronism. . . . They have grown strong and haughty in their isolation and have looked with supercilious contempt on the foreign barbarians. The gates of their exclusiveness were shattered and forced open by cannon to compel them to receive a commerce they did not want, and to share in an intercourse they despised. . . . Under such circumstances it seems scarcely necessary to saddle on the Chinese missionary the responsibility of anti-foreign feeling among the Chinese. . . . China cannot shut out the tide of the world's life, however much she may desire to do so. . . . The best thing Europe and America can do for China at the present crisis is to give it the gospel of Jesus Christ more freely.

A Statement of Protestant Missionary Societies, 'The Times',
24th August, 1900

.

15. THE PUNISHMENT OF
BOXER LEADERS, 1900–1

China's officials may be said to be a class of individualists, incapable, as a rule, of collective heroism or any sustained effort of organised patriotism; but it is one of the remarkable features and results of her system of philosophy that the mandarins, even those who have been known publicly to display physical cowardice at critical moments, will usually accept sentence of death at the hands of their Sovereign with perfect equanimity, and meet it with calm philosophic resignation. The manner in which the Boxer leaders died, who were proscribed in the course of the negotiations for the peace Protocol at Peking, affords an interesting illustration of this fact; incidentally it throws light also on a trait in the Chinese character, which to some extent explains the solidity and permanence of its system of government, based as it is on the principle of absolute obedience and loyalty to the head of the State as one of the cardinal Confucian virtues.

Despite the repeated and unswerving demands of the foreign Powers that the death penalty should be inflicted upon the chief leaders and supporters of the Boxers, the Empress Dowager was naturally loth to yield, inasmuch as she herself had been in full sympathy with the movement. It was only after many and prolonged meetings with her chief advisers, and when she realised that in this course lay her only hope of obtaining satisfactory terms of peace, that she finally and most reluctantly consented, in February 1901 to the issue of a Decree (drafted by Jung Lu) in which she abandoned to their fate those who, with her full knowledge and approval, had led the rising which was to drive all foreigners into the sea. With the knowledge in our possession as to Her Majesty's complicity, and in some cases her initiative, in the anti-foreign movement, it is impossible to read this Decree without realising something of the ruthlessness of the woman and her cynical disregard of everything except her own safety and authority. Even so, however, Tzu Hsi could not bring herself at first to comply with all the demands of the Powers, evidently hoping by compromise and further negotiations to save the lives of her favourites, Prince Tuan, Duke Lan and Chao Shu-ch'iao. The Decree, issued in the Emperor's name, was as follows:

In the summer of last year, the Boxer Rebellion arose, which brought in its train hostilities with friendly Powers. Prince Ch'ing and Li Hung-chang have now definitely settled the preliminary conditions of the Peace Protocol. Reflecting on the causes of this disaster, we cannot escape the conclusion that it was due to the ignorance and arrogance of certain of our Princes and Ministers of State who, foolishly believing in the alleged supernatural powers of the Boxers, were led to disobey the Throne and to disregard our express commands that these rebels should be exterminated. Not only did they not do this, but they encouraged and assisted them to such an extent that the movement gained hosts of followers. The latter committed acts of unprovoked hostility, so that matters reached a pass where a general cataclysm became inevitable. It was by reason of the folly of these men that General Tung, that obstinate braggart, dared to bombard the Legations, thus bringing our Dynasty to the brink of the greatest peril, throwing the State into a general convulsion of disorder, and plunging our people into uttermost misery. The dangers which have been incurred by Her Majesty the Empress Dowager, and myself are simply indescribable, and our hearts are sore, aching with unappeased wrath at the remembrance of our sufferings. Let those who brought about these calamities ask themselves what punishment can suffice to atone for them?

Our former Decrees on this subject have been far too lenient, and we must therefore now award further punishments to the guilty. Prince Chuang, already cashiered, led the Boxers in their attack upon the French Cathedral and the Legations, besides which, it was he who issued a Proclamation in violation of all our Treaties. [This refers to the rewards offered for the heads of foreigners.] He too it was who, acting as the leader of the savage Boxers, put to death many innocent persons. As a mark of clemency unmerited by these crimes, we grant him permission to commit suicide, and hereby order that Ko Pao-hua shall supervise the execution of these our commands.

Prince Tuan, already cashiered, was the leader and spokesman of the Imperial Clan, to whom was due the declaration of war against foreigners; he trusted implicitly in Boxer magic, and thus inexcusably brought about hostilities. Duke Lan, who assisted Prince Chuang in drawing up the proclamation which set a price on the head of every foreigner, deserves also that he be stripped of all his dignities and titles. But remembering that both these Princes are our near kinsmen, we mitigate their sentence to exile to Turkestan, where they will be kept in perpetual confinement. The Governor of Shensi, Yu Hsien, already cashiered, believed in the Boxers at the time when he held the Governorship of Shantung; when he subsequently came to Peking, he sang their praises at our Court, with the result that many Princes and Ministers were led astray by his words. As Governor of Shensi he had put to death many missionaries and native converts, proving himself to be an utterly misguided and bloodthirsty man. He was undoubtedly one of the prime causes of all our troubles. We have already decreed his banishment to Turkestan, and by this time he should already have reached Kansu. Orders are now to be transmitted for his immediate decapitation, which will be superintended by the Provincial Treasurer.

As to the late Grand Secretary, Kang Yi, he also believed in the Boxers, and went so far as to set a price on the lives of foreigners so that, had he lived, he too would have been sentenced to death, but as matters stand, we order that he be posthumously deprived of his rank and summarily cashiered.

We have already cashiered Tung Fu-hsiang. While permitted to retain his rank as a military official, he cannot escape a certain share of responsibility for the siege of the Legations although his orders emanated from Princes and Ministers of State; and because of his ignorance of foreign affairs, slack discipline, and general stupidity, he certainly deserves severe punishment. But we cannot overlook the services he has rendered in the Kansu rebellion and the good name which he bears amongst our Chinese and Mahomedan subjects in that province, so that, as a mark of our favour and leniency, we merely remove him from his post.

Ying Nien, Vice-President of the Censorate, was opposed to the issue of the proclamation which offered rewards for foreigners' heads, and for this he deserves lenient treatment, but he failed to insist strongly on his objections, and we are therefore compelled to punish him. He is hereby sentenced to be cashiered and imprisoned pending decapitation.

As regards the Grand Councillor Chao Shu-ch'iao, he had never, to our knowledge, shown any hostility to foreigners, and when we despatched him on a special mission to confer with the Boxers, the report which he submitted on his return showed no signs of sympathy with their proceedings. Nevertheless, he was undoubtedly careless, and we therefore, acting in leniency, decree that he be cashiered and imprisoned pending decapitation.

The Grand Secretary Hsu T'ung and Li Ping-heng, our Assistant Commander-in-chief, have both committed suicide, but as their behaviour has been very severely criticised, we order that they be deprived of their ranks; and all posthumous honours granted to them are hereby cancelled.

The Ministers of the friendly Powers can no longer fail to recognise that the Boxer Rebellion was indeed the work of these guilty officials, and that it was in no way due to any action or wishes on the part of the Throne. In the punishment of these offenders we have displayed no leniency, from which all our subjects may learn how grave has been the recent crisis.

As the terms of this Decree still failed to satisfy the foreign Ministers, especially as regards the sentences passed on Prince Tuan and Duke Lan, another Decree a week later, ordered that both these Manchu leaders should be imprisoned pending decapitation, a sentence which was eventually reduced to one of perpetual banishment to Turkestan. Posthumous decapitation, a grievous disgrace in the eyes of Chinese officials, was decreed as a further punishment upon Kang Yi, while Chao Shu-ch'iao and Ying Nien were ordered to commit suicide. Finally, the Grand Councillor Ch'i Hsiu, and a son of the Grand Secretary Hsu T'ung (who had closely followed in his father's footsteps as the most violent opponent of everything foreign), were sentenced to decapitation, and were duly executed at Peking.

J. O. P. Bland and E. Backhouse, *China under the Empress Dowager*, pp 363–7

16. CHINESE INTELLECTUALS AND WESTERN CULTURE, *c.* 1910

During the last years of the nineteenth century a new outlook had rapidly made way among the young Chinese intellectuals. Convinced of the futility of the 'ultra' party and their hope of expelling the foreigner, convinced, too, that the cautious modernizers were going too slowly, and could not in reality protect Chinese civilization by using Western technology, they now believed that a much more drastic change was essential. China must give up much that she had always cherished, including her belief in her traditional form of government. An attempt was made to use the Throne in the manner of the Meiji Restoration in Japan to sanction and direct a programme of sweeping reforms (1898). This was frustrated by the reactionary party, and thenceforward the advanced reformers, abandoning any hope of support from the dynasty, campaigned for a revolution and a republic.

The rapidity and the thoroughness of the change in outlook which then took place in the Chinese educated class is a phenomenon which deserves more attention than it often receives. Shortly after the Boxer Movement had been crushed, and already some years earlier than that, the great majority of the younger generation of Chinese scholar gentry had become revolutionary in outlook, some willing to go farther than others, but all eager to 'drink foreign ink' – to learn Western knowledge, to study abroad, acquire the secret of Western power. Only a generation earlier the fathers of these men had mostly opposed any admission of foreign learning, had derided the knowledge of the West, had harried the missionary, held off the trader, and, even when personally more friendly to individual foreigners, remained in profound ignorance of Europe, its civilization and its thought.

The father of an eminent Chinese of our own time was astonished, when conversing with a missionary doctor with whom he was friendly, to learn by chance that England produced poetry as well as guns, and had a wide literature and a deep scholarship. He was himself a high official of the empire and an accomplished scholar. In 1870 only a tiny handful of Chinese knew any European language (except the 'pidgin' of the merchants). By 1910 at the latest English was the second language of the schools, and very many more Chinese could read and speak it than there were Europeans who could speak (let alone read) Chinese. The Old China Hand of the early twentieth century was content to pass thirty years in China without learning a word of the language.

But this urge for foreign learning was curiously limited. The young Chinese intellectual who went abroad to study, or made do with instruction at home (often beginning in a missionary college), concentrated on science, or still more on political economy and political theory. The writings of John Stuart Mill, the exponents of Western democratic ideas, the economists, the scientists were eagerly studied. Very few, by comparison, were interested in European history, poetry or literature. Nor did the great and continuing missionary endeavour bring in many converts to Christianity. Young Chinese attended missionary schools to learn English, the key to further foreign learning. They went abroad to Western universities, but did not read theology. At a time when the thought of the West was at last open to China and in part willingly accepted, the religion of the West, which an earlier generation of Westerners had regarded as the one real contribution that Europe could make, was no more acceptable than it had been to the old conservative scholars. The enthusiastic teachers of Chinese youth, who found them such admirable and intelligent pupils, may have deplored this lapse, but perhaps did not fully understand the reasons behind it.

The Chinese educated class had been converted, suddenly enough, to a realization that European learning was valuable and essential: essential to 'save China'. Not valuable in itself, not necessary for a full and wider understanding of the whole achievement of the human race, but necessary to give back to Chinese the power to compete on equal terms with the West. In a new, more comprehensive way, the urge to acquire Western learning was a form of the older approach, the use of Western learning to preserve Chinese values. It was now understood that mere products of industry without knowledge of the science and technology which lay behind them were useless. It was also seen that the Europeans had more than science and technology; they had political ideas, methods of social control, techniques of government which also contributed mightily to their power. These, too, China must learn, so that China could beat them at their own game.

C. P. Fitzgerald, *The Chinese View of Their Place in the World*,
pp 38–40

17. DR SUN YAT-SEN AND THE WEST,
1918–24

[Dr Sun Yat-Sen was in political 'retirement' from about 1914 until the end of the First World War; part of this time was spent in Japan. Greatly disappointed by the failure of his hopes after the revolution of 1911, Sun Yan-Sen awaited an opportunity to pursue again his revolutionary and republican ideals. By 1921, he was organising in Canton the basis of a new administration through his revived Kuomintang party. In the following passage, a Western observer surveys this period half a generation later]

He [Dr Sun Yat-Sen] set himself, when nearly fifty years of age, to a detached study of the economic conditions of his country and to a more realistic comparison of China and the West. Nothing could cure him of being a visionary, but he became at last a visionary striving to found his dreams on social and political facts. In one sense he succeeded, for he came to know his own people very much better, both in their weakness and their strength. His earlier admiration of the West, however, was seriously affected. The years of his retirement coincided with the years of the Great War and when he emerged from that retirement with his changed outlook, he came back into a world which was also radically different.

The effect which the war (1914–18) years had on Dr Sun's view of the West is particularly significant because many of his countrymen were suffering from a like disillusionment. The shock which the War gave to Chinese minds was a staggering one. Coming at the time it did, when enthusiasm for Western civilisation was like a flowing tide, it took time for the full seriousness of what was happening to get home, but in the end, thanks to sedulous propaganda, at first by the Germans and then by the British, all China came to know the horrors that were being enacted in these civilised Christian lands. The large-scale slaughter, not of professional soldiers but of ordinary men drafted off by the thousands, attacked the Chinese moral sense in a particularly sensitive spot. To them, with their ancestor worshipping, filial-piety soul, the family was at stake, for youth was the repository of the sacred life handed down from the past. The moral prestige of Europe suffered very badly. Other events, notably the sacrifice of China's interests at the Treaty of Versailles, also conspired to make the Chinese cynical about the peoples whom they had been admiring.

The vein of cynicism was very noticeable in Dr Sun after 1918. He did not expect the 'friendly Powers' to act except for their own interest, and it was on this ground alone that he appealed for help for China. Also he came to see that democracy after the Western pattern was open to criticism in a number of ways. He never lost his faith in the democratic principle, but he felt that for his own country it would have to be abandoned for the time being in face of the need for national unification.

Most striking of all was the change which he advocated in the policy of the Kuomintang (Nationalist Party) in 1921, when Adolf Joffe came offering the help and co-operation of Soviet Russia. Whereas in 1905 the oath of the Revolutionary Party contained the words 'The spirit and binding principle of our various aims are Liberty, Equality, and Universal Love', in 1924 Dr Sun urged that 'there is one thing of the greatest importance in a political party, that is, all members of the party must possess spiritual unity. In order that all members may be united spiritually, the first thing is to sacrifice freedom, the second is to offer his abilities. If the individual can sacrifice his freedom, then the whole party will have freedom. If the individual can offer his abilities, then the whole party will possess ability.' There was thus a swing back to the ingrained tradition of the Chinese family and state, that unity and harmony are the ultimate requisites for which, if necessary, the liberty of the individual must be sacrificed.

Dr Sun told Joffe candidly that he did not consider Communism suited, as a form of social order, to the mentality of the Chinese people, but since their common objective was to save the proletariat from their oppressors there was no reason why China and Russia should not work together. That his relegation of individual freedom to the second place should also be characteristic of Soviet politics was a bond of sympathy and mutual understanding. This was no capitulation to the Soviet idea: on the contrary it was the legacy of generations, and the Secret Societies of the last hundred years had enlisted it in the sacred cause of revolution. . . .

E. R. Hughes, *The Invasion of China by the Western World*, pp. 142–4

18. DR SUN YAT-SEN'S LINKS WITH SOVIET RUSSIA AND THE CHINESE COMMUNIST PARTY, 1923

Joint Manifesto of Sun Yat-sen and A. A. Joffe (January 26, 1923)

1. Dr Sun is of the opinion that, because of the non-existence of conditions favourable to their successful application in China, it is not possible to carry out either Communism or even the Soviet system in China. M. Joffe agrees entirely with this view; he is further of the

opinion that China's most important and most pressing problems are the completion of national unification and the attainment of full national independence. With regard to these great tasks, M. Joffe has assured Dr Sun of the Russian people's warmest sympathy for China, and of (their) willingness to lend support.

2. In order to eradicate misunderstandings, Dr Sun has requested M. Joffe to reaffirm the principles enunciated by Russia in its Note to the Chinese government of September 27, 1920. M. Joffe accordingly reaffirmed these principles, and categorically declared to Dr Sun that Russia is willing and ready to enter into negotiations with China on the basis of Russia's abandonment of all treaties, and of the rights and privileges (conceded by China) under duress, secured by the Tsarist government from China. Among the above-mentioned treaties are included the treaties and agreements concerning the Chinese Eastern Railway. (The administration of this railway has been specifically dealt with in article VII of the said Note.)

3. Dr Sun holds that the Chinese Eastern Railway question in its entirety can be satisfactorily settled only by a competent Sino-Russian Conference. But the key to the current situation lies in the fact that a *modus vivendi* ought to be devised for the administration of the said railway at present. Dr Sun and M. Joffe are of the same opinion that the administration of this railway should be temporarily reorganized after an agreement has been reached between the Chinese and Russian governments, but (on condition) that the real rights and special interests of either party are not injured. Dr Sun also holds that the matter should be discussed with Chang Tso-lin.

4. M. Joffe categorically declares to Dr Sun (and Dr Sun is entirely satisfied with regard to this point): that it is not, and never has been, the intention or the objective of the present Russian government to carry out imperialistic policies in Outer Mongolia, or to work for Outer Mongolia's independence from China. Dr Sun therefore does not deem the immediate evacuation of Russian troops from Outer Mongolia to be urgently necessary or to the real advantage of China. This is due to the fact that, the present Peking government being weak and impotent, after the withdrawal of the Russian troops it would most likely be unable to prevent the activities of the Russian Whites from causing fresh difficulties for the Russian government, thereby creating a situation even graver than that which exists at present.

Manifesto of the Third National Congress of the CCP (June 1923)

The Chinese people are doubly oppressed both by foreign powers and by warlords, and the nation's existence, as well as the freedom of its people, are in an extremely precarious state. Not only the workers, peasants, and students, but also the peaceful and moderate merchants feel (oppressed).

The farcical confusion of the present Peking regime; the increasing oppression and destruction of trade unions and students' federations by the Northern warlords' regime; the unruliness of soldiers and bandits in Shantung and Honan; the threats by foreign powers to retract, on various pretexts, benefits granted by the Washington Conference; the atrocities committed by the Japanese sailors at Shasi and Changsha; the powers' forced cotton exports from China; the Kwangtung fighting engineered by Wu P'ei-fu and Ch'i Hsieh-yuan; disorders in Szechwan fostered by Wu P'ei-fu and Hsiao Yao-nan; civil war looming between the Chihli and Mukden factions, and imbroglios among the various cliques within the Chihli faction: all these show how internal and external troubles have again beset the people. There is no salvation unless the people muster up their own strength in a national movement for self determination. (All) this also demonstrates that the national revolutionary movement led by our Party with the slogans 'down with warlords' and 'down with international imperialism' is on the right path.

The KMT should be the central force of the national revolution and should assume its leadership. Unfortunately, however, the KMT often suffers from two erroneous notions. Firstly, it relies on foreign powers for help in the Chinese national revolution. Such requests for help from the enemy not only cost the (KMT) to lose the leadership of the national revolution but also make the people depend on foreign power, thus destroying their confidence and spirit of national independence; secondly (the KMT) concentrates all its efforts on military action, neglecting propaganda work among the people. Consequently, the KMT loses its political leadership, because a national revolutionary party can never succeed by relying solely on military action without winning nation-wide popular sympathy.

We still hope that all the revolutionary elements in our society will rally to the KMT, speeding the completion of the national revolutionary movement. At the same time, (we also) hope that the KMT will resolutely discard its two old notions of reliance on foreign powers and concentration on military action, and that it will pay attention to political propaganda among the people – never missing an opportunity for (such) propaganda in order to create a true central force for the national welfare and true leadership for the national revolution.

Considering economic and political conditions at home and abroad, and the sufferings and needs of (those) classes of Chinese society (workers, peasants, industrialists, and merchants) which urgently need a national revolution, the CCP never forgets for one moment to support the interests of the workers and peasants. It is our special task to do propagandistic and organizational work among the workers and peasants. Still more central is our task to lead the workers and peasants into joining the national revolution. Our mission is to liberate the oppressed Chinese nation by national revolution, and to advance to the world revolution, liberating the oppressed peoples and oppressed classes of the whole world.

Long live the national revolution of China!

Long live the liberation of the oppressed peoples of the world!

Long live the liberation of the oppressed classes of the world!

C. Brandt, B. Schwartz and J. K. Fairbank, *A Documentary history of Chinese Communism*, pp 70–2

19. MAO TSE-TUNG ON THE LONG MARCH, 1935

We say that the Long March is the first of its kind ever recorded in history, that is a manifesto, an agitation corps, and a seeding machine. . . . For twelve months we were under daily reconnaissance and bombing from the air by scores of planes; we were encircled, pursued, obstructed and intercepted on the ground by a big force of several hundred thousand men, we encountered untold difficulties and great obstacles on the way, but by keeping our two feet going we swept across a distance of more than 20,000 *li* through the length and breadth of eleven provinces. Well, has there ever been in history a long march like ours? No, never. The Long March is also a manifesto. It proclaims to the world that the Red Army is an army of heroes and that the imperialists and their jackals, Chiang Kai-shek and his like, are perfect nonentities. It announces the bankruptcy of the encirclement, pursuit, obstruction and interception attempted by the imperialists and Chiang

Kai-shek. The Long March is also an agitation corps. It declares to the approximately two hundred million people in eleven provinces that only the road of the Red Army leads to their liberation. Without the Long March, how could the broad masses have known so quickly that there are such great ideas in the world as are upheld by the Red Army? The Long March is also a seeding machine. It has sown many seeds in eleven provinces, which will sprout, grow leaves, blossom into flowers, bear fruit and yield a crop in future. To sum up, the Long March ended with our victory and the enemy's defeat.

. . . the Red Army has failed in one respect (in preserving its original bases), but has achieved victory in another respect (in fulfilling the plan of the Long March). The enemy, on the other hand, has won victory in one respect (in occupying our original bases), but has failed in another respect (in realising his plan of 'encirclement and annihilation' and of 'pursuit and annihilation'). Only this statement is correct that we have in fact completed the Long March.

J. Chen, *Mao and the Chinese Revolution*, pp 199–200

20. MAO TSE-TUNG ON HIS CHILDHOOD, 1936

I began studying in a local primary school when I was eight and remained there until I was thirteen years old. In the early morning and at night I worked on the farm. During the day I read the Confucian Analects and the Four Classics. My Chinese teacher belonged to the stern-treatment school. He was harsh and severe, frequently beating his students. Because of this I ran away from the school when I was ten. I was afraid to return home, for fear of receiving a beating there, and set out in the general direction of the city, which I believed to be in a valley somewhere. I wandered for three days before I was finally found by my family. Then I learned that I had circled around and around in my travels, and in all my walking had got only about eight *li* from my home.

After my return to the family, however, to my surprise, conditions somewhat improved. My father was slightly more considerate and the teacher was more inclined to moderation. The result of my act of protest impressed me very much. It was a successful 'strike'.

My father wanted me to begin keeping the family books as soon as I had learned a few characters. He wanted me to learn to use the abacus. As my father insisted upon this I began to work at those accounts at night. He was a severe taskmaster. He hated to see me idle, and if there were no books to be kept he put me to work at farm tasks. He was a hot-tempered man and frequently beat both me and my brothers. He gave us no money whatever, and the most meagre food. On the 15th of every month he made a concession to his labourers and gave them eggs with their rice, but never meat. To me he gave neither eggs nor meat.

My mother was a kind woman, generous and sympathetic, and ever ready to share what she had. She pitied the poor and often gave them rice when they came to ask for it during famines. But she could not do so when my father was present. He disapproved of charity. We had many quarrels in my home over this question.

There were two 'parties' in the family. One was my father, the Ruling Power. The Opposition was made up of myself, my mother, my brother and sometimes even the labourer. In the 'United Front' of the Opposition, however, there was a difference of opinion. My mother advocated a policy of indirect attack. She criticized any overt display of emotion and attempts at open rebellion against the Ruling Power. She said it was not the Chinese way.

But when I was thirteen I discovered a powerful argument of my own for debating with my father on his own ground, by quoting the Classics. My father's favourite accusations against me were of unfilial conduct and laziness. I quoted, in exchange, passages from the Classics saying that the elder must be kind and affectionate. Against his charge that I was lazy, I used the rebuttal that older people should do more work than younger, that my father was over three times as old as myself, and therefore should do more work. And I declared that when I was his age I would be much more energetic.

The old man continued to 'amass wealth', or what was considered to be a great fortune in that little village. He did not buy more land himself, but he bought many mortgages on other people's land. His capital grew to $2,000 or $3,000.

My dissatisfaction increased. The dialectical struggle in our family was constantly developing. One incident I especially remember. When I was about thirteen my father invited many guests to his home, and while they were present a dispute arose between the two of us. My father denounced me before the whole group, calling me lazy and useless. This infuriated me. I cursed him and left the house. My mother ran after me and tried to persuade me to return. My father also pursued me, cursing at the same time that he demanded me to come back. I reached the edge of a pond and threatened to jump in if he came any nearer. In this situation demands and counter-demands were presented for cessation of the civil war. My father insisted that I apologize and k'ou-t'ou as a sign of submission. I agreed to give a one knee k'ou-t'ou if he would promise not to beat me. Thus the war ended, and from it I learned that when I defended my rights by open rebellion my father relented but when I remained meek and submissive he only cursed and beat me the more.

Reflecting on this, I think that in the end the strictness of my father defeated him. I learned to hate him, and we created a real United Front against him. At the same time it probably benefited me. It made me most diligent in my work; it made me keep my books carefully, so that he should have no basis for criticizing me.

My father had had two years of schooling and he could read enough to keep books. My mother was wholly illiterate. Both were from peasant families. I was the family 'scholar'. I knew the Classics, but disliked them. What I enjoyed were the romances of old China, and especially stories of rebellions. I read the *Yo Fei Chuan* (*Chin Chung Chuan*), *Shui Hu Chuan*, *Fan T'ang*, *San Kuo*, and *Hsi Yu Chi*, while still very young, and despite the vigilance of my old teacher, who hated these outlawed books and called them wicked. I used to read them in school, covering them up with a Classic when the teacher walked past. So also did most of my schoolmates. We learned many of the stories almost by heart, and discussed and re-discussed them many times. We knew more of them than the old men of the village, who also loved them and used to exchange stories with us. I believe that perhaps I was much influenced by such books, read at an impressionable age.

I finally left the primary school when I was thirteen and began to work long hours on the farm, helping the hired labourer, doing the full labour of a man during the day and at night keeping books for my father. Nevertheless, I succeeded in continuing my reading, devouring everything I could find except the Classics. This annoyed my father who wanted me to master the Classics, especially after he was defeated in a lawsuit due to an apt Classical quotation used by his adversary in the Chinese court. I used to cover up the window of my room late at night so that my father would not see the light. In this way I read a book called *Words of Warning* (*Shen Shih Wei-yen*) which I liked very much. The authors, a number of old reformist scholars, thought that the weakness of China lay in her lack of Western appliances – railways, telephones, telegraphs, and steamships – and wanted to have them introduced into the country. My father considered such books a waste of time. He wanted me to read something practical like the Classics, which could help him in winning lawsuits.

I continued to read the old romances and tales of Chinese literature. It occurred to me one day that there was one thing peculiar about these stories, and that was the absence of peasants who tilled the land. All the characters were warriors, officials or scholars; there was never a peasant hero. I wondered about this for two years, and then I analysed the content of the stories. I found that they all glorified men of arms, rulers of the people, who did not have to work the land, because they owned and controlled it and evidently made the peasants work it for them.

My father Mao Jen-sheng, was in his early days, and in middle age, a sceptic, but my mother devoutly worshipped Buddha. She gave her children religious instruction, and we were all saddened that our father was an unbeliever. When I was nine years old I seriously discussed the problem of my father's lack of piety with my mother. We made attempts then and later on to convert him, but without success. He only cursed us, and, overwhelmed by his attacks, we withdrew to devise new plans. But he would have nothing to do with the gods.

My reading gradually began to influence me, however; I myself became more and more sceptical. My mother became concerned about me, and scolded me for my indifference to the requirements of the faith but my father made no comment. Then one day he went out on the road to collect some money and on his way he met a tiger. The tiger was surprised at the encounter and fled at once, but my father was even more astonished and afterwards reflected a good deal on his miraculous escape. He began to wonder if he had not offended the gods. From then on he showed more respect to Buddhism and burned incense now and then. Yet, when my own backsliding grew worse, the old man did not interfere. He only prayed to the gods when he was in difficulties.

Words of Warning stimulated in me a desire to resume my studies. I had also become disgusted with my labour on the farm. My father naturally opposed this. We quarrelled about it, and finally I ran away from home. I went to the home of an unemployed law student, and there I studied for half a year. After that I studied more of the Classics under an old Chinese scholar, and also read many contemporary articles and a few books.

E. Snow, *Red Star over China,* pp 127–31

21. MAO TSE-TUNG ON THE REVOLUTIONARY STRUGGLE, 1939

From *The Chinese Revolution and the Communist Party of China*, November 1939

[By this time, the Japanese controlled all the principal ports and cities of China and effectively occupied Chinese territory east of a line Peking–Hankow–Canton. The Chinese Nationalist capital was Chungking in the province of Szechwan and the Chinese Communists had their headquarters at Yenan in the province of Shensi. Communist leader Mao Tse-tung foresaw a long struggle]

... Because our enemies are so powerful, our revolutionary forces can only be strengthened and accumulated over a long period of time so that it may become an invincible force in achieving ultimate victory over our enemies. And while these enemies ferociously suppress the Chinese revolution, our revolutionary force must be persistent and strong in guarding its own camp and defeating the enemy. It is incorrect to imagine that our revolutionary strength will quickly become overwhelming or that the Chinese revolution will succeed easily.

Faced with such enemies, it is clear that the method to be adopted and the predominant pattern of the Chinese revolution cannot be peaceful. Success can be achieved only through armed struggle. Our enemies do not allow the Chinese people to carry out peaceful activities or to possess any political freedom. Stalin has rightly said: 'The special feature of the Chinese revolution is the revolt of the armed masses against the armed reactionaries'. It is incorrect to ignore the principles of armed struggle, revolutionary wars, guerilla warfare and political work in the army.

Faced with such enemies, questions arise concerning the special revolutionary bases. The great imperialist powers, and their reactionary allied armies in China have always indefinitely occupied the important Chinese cities. If the revolutionary force refuses to compromise with foreign imperialism and its servile underlings, but, contrarily, struggles to the very end, and if the revolutionary force is to accumulate and nurture its own strength and avoid fighting decisive battles with powerful enemies when its own strength is not yet ascertained, then it must turn the backward, remote areas into progressive, strong bases, making them great military, political economic and cultural revolutionary strongholds. Then from these strongholds, the revolutionary force can start to drive out those malicious enemies who are based upon the large cities and who encroach upon the villages. Also from these strongholds, the revolutionary force may, through prolonged struggle, gradually achieve total success. Under such conditions, and because of the unbalanced nature of Chinese economic development (the rural economy is not entirely dependent upon the urban economy), and because of the vastness of China's territory (there are immense spaces for the revolutionary forces to fall back on), and because of the disunity and conflict existing within the anti-revolutionary camp, and because the main force of the Chinese revolution, which is the Chinese peasantry, is under the leadership of the Communist party: so there arises the great possibility that the Chinese revolution will succeed first and foremost in the countryside. Thus the revolution is driven to its conclusion within a totally unbalanced atmosphere, which increases our difficulties and causes the prolongation of the revolution. Thus, too, we are enabled to understand why it is that these prolonged revolutionary struggles, starting out from such special strongholds, are composed chiefly of peasant guerilla wars under the leadership of the Communist party. It is incorrect to ignore the principle of making and establishing revolutionary bases in the countryside, and it is equally incorrect to ignore the need for strenuous work among the peasants, and the need for guerilla wars. . . .

> R. Payne, *Portrait of a Revolutionary: Mao Tse-tung*, pp 197–8

22. CHANGES IN RELIGIOUS LIFE IN CHINA (by 1945)

The years after 1895 witnessed marked changes in the religious life of the country. These were in part due to the total impact of the Occident – political, economic, and intellectual – and in part to the labours of Christian missionaries.

To the first cause must be ascribed the weakening of Confucianism. Even before the fall of the Ch'ing dynasty, the abolishment of the traditional system of civil service examinations (1905) shook to its foundations the form of education which had done so much to perpetuate Confucianism. Other innovations in education brought in new subjects to study and ended the concentration on the old learning. The substitution, in 1912, of the Republic for the Empire, dealt Confucianism another blow. The form of government was swept aside with which, since the Han dynasty, Confucianism had been almost inextricably associated. Some of the religious ceremonies maintained by the state disappeared, notably those which had been performed by the Emperor, and many others gradually lapsed. Confucius himself was unacceptable to numbers of the new student class, for he had supported monarchical institutions and his name was identified with the now discredited conservatism and the discarded system of education. With the growth of popularity of Western science and other studies from the Occident, interest in the Classics waned. Experts in the older literary pursuits were respected but few were willing to pay the price of emulating them.

Confucianism did not succumb without a struggle. Attempts were made to show that it was not incompatible with the new order and to have the Republic adopt it as the official cult. Here and there officials and associations of scholars maintained the customary rites in honor of Confucius and his disciples. Study of the Classics was embodied in the new curricula. Moreover, a philosophy which had become part of the very bone and sinew of the nation could not at once disappear. In the China of the 1940s Confucianism was still an important influence. It had, however, suffered greatly.

To the general impact of the Occident, moreover, were to be ascribed a widespread loss of interest in and an antagonism to religion. The twentieth century witnessed in many countries a decline in religion. To thousands the great increase of knowledge of his physical environment which man had achieved through scientific methods had made religion intellectually untenable. To even larger numbers, absorption in the pursuit of physical comforts made possible by this new knowledge rendered religion unimportant and irrelevant or even an enemy. This scepticism and preoccupation with material concerns found in China peculiarly fertile ground, for much of the traditional philosophy tended to make China's scholars agnostic: one of the most prominent of the younger thinkers declared that China's educated class had outgrown religion earlier than any other large group in the history of mankind. The militant anti-religious convictions of Russian Communism were especially influential. In 1922 an organized anti-religious movement came to birth, and the radical elements in the Kuomintang were vigorous in their anti-religious activities, especially during the days of their power in 1926 and 1927. Most of the agitation was focused against Christianity, for the latter was palpably foreign in its origin and in much of its leadership and it was associated with the 'capitalistic' nations for which Communism had so strong an aversion. Some of it, however, was directed against other forms of religion. More than one temple was converted into a school, and even the Taoist 'Pope' was forced to flee from his accustomed residence.

The religious spirit here and there showed signs of a fresh awakening. In some sections a reform movement galvanized the somnolent Buddhism into new activity. For a time, especially before 1922, new and unusually ephemeral syncretic sects such as the Tao Yuan, interested small minorities. For a few years, too, after 1926, it looked as though Sun Yat-sen would become the centre of a new state cult. A weekly ceremony in his honour was required in all schools and his tomb near Nanking became a kind of shrine. Yet by the 1940s enthusiasm for this innovation had decidedly waned.

Most of the earnest and aggressive new life entered through Christianity. After 1895 and until about 1925, Christianity had a phenomenal expansion. The persecutions of the Boxer year proved only a temporary check: in the long run, through the added zest which came to the Church from the heroism of the martyrs, they probably stimulated the spread of the faith.

The reasons for this growth were to be found partly in China and partly in the Occident. Conditions in China were favourable. The old structure of Chinese life was crumbling and with it went much of the resistance which it offered to Christianity. Things Western were popular. In many places the Christian missionary was the only resident Westerner. As a representative of the Occident, therefore, he was given a hearing and was often influential. Repeatedly the altruistic services of the missionary won respect for the Christian message. Moreover, numbers of thoughtful Chinese, eagerly seeking means of extricating the nation from its confusion and weakness, and taught by their Confucian rearing that the salvation of the state and society depended ultimately upon the moral character of the individual, wondered whether the needed dynamic might not be found in the Christian Gospel. Never since the period of disunion between the Hans and the T'ang had conditions in China been so favourable for the acceptance of a foreign faith, and at no time in the more than twelve centuries since it first reached China had Christianity there been confronted with so great an opportunity. As, between the Han and the T'ang, Buddhism won a lasting place in China, so Christianity might now establish itself as an integral part of Chinese life.

K. S. Latourette, *The Chinese, Their history and culture*, pp 465–8

The Indian Subcontinent

23. G. K. GOKHALE AND THE SERVANTS OF INDIA SOCIETY, 1905

For some time past, the conviction has been forcing itself on many earnest and thoughtful minds that a stage has been reached in the work of nation-building in India, when, for further progress, the devoted labours of a specially trained agency, applying itself to the task in a true missionary spirit are required. The work that has been accomplished so far has indeed been of the highest value. The growth during the last fifty years of a feeling of common nationality based upon common traditions and ties, common hopes and aspirations, and even common disabilities, has been most striking. The fact that we are Indians first, and Hindus, Mahomedans, Parsees or Christians afterwards, is being realised in a steadily increasing measure, and the idea of a united and renovated India marching onwards to a place among the nations of the world worthy to her great past, is no longer a mere idle dream of a few imaginative minds, but is the definitely accepted creed of those who form the brain of the community – the educated classes of the country. A creditable beginning has already been made in matters of education and of local self-government; and all classes of the people are slowly but steadily coming under the influence of liberal ideas ... (but) the great work of rearing the superstructure has yet to be taken in hand, and the situation demands on the part of workers devotion and sacrifices proportionate to the magnitude of the task.

The Servants of India Society has been established to meet in some measure these requirements of the situation. Its members frankly accept the British connection as ordained, in the inscrutable dispensation of Providence, for India's good. Self-government within the Empire for their country and a higher life generally for their countrymen is their goal. This goal, they recognise, cannot be attained without years of earnest and patient effort and sacrifices worthy of the cause. Much of the work must be directed toward building up in the country a higher type of character and capacity than is generally available at present and the advance can only be slow. . . . One essential condition of success in this work is that a sufficient number of our countrymen must now come forward to devote themselves to the cause in the spirit in which religious work is undertaken. Public life must be spiritualised. Love of country must so fill the heart that all else shall appear as of little moment by its side. A fervent patriotism which rejoices at every opportunity of sacrifice for the motherland, a dauntless heart which refuses to be turned back from its object by difficulty or danger, a deep faith in the purpose of Providence which nothing can shake – equipped with these, the worker must start on his mission and reverently seek the joy which comes of spending oneself in the service of one's country.

The Servants of India Society will train men prepared to devote their lives to the cause of the country in a religious spirit, and will seek to promote, by all constitutional means, the national interests of the Indian people. Its members will direct their efforts principally towards creating among the people, by example and by precept, a deep and passionate love of the motherland, seeking its highest fulfilment in service and sacrifice; organising the work of political education and agitation, basing it on a careful study of public questions, and strengthening generally the public life of the country; promoting relations of cordial goodwill and co-operation among the different communities; assisting educational movements, especially those for the education of women, the education of backward classes and industrial and scientific education; helping forward the industrial development of the country; and the elevation of the depressed classes.

S. A. Wolpert, *Tilak and Gokhale*, pp 159–60

24. G. K. GOKHALE ON THE AIMS OF THE INDIAN NATIONAL CONGRESS, 1905

[G. K. Gokhale led for many years the 'moderates' or 'liberals' in the Indian National Congress. He stood for gradual political advance through constitutional means]

. . . The goal of the Congress is that India should be governed in the interests of the Indians themselves and that in course of time a form of Government should be attained in this country similar to what exists

M

in the self-governing Colonies of the British Empire. For better, for worse, our destinies are now linked with those of England and the Congress freely recognises that whatever advance we seek must be within the Empire itself. The advance, moreover, can only be gradual, as at each stage of the progress it may be necessary for us to pass through a brief course of apprenticeship before we are entitled to go to the next one; for it is a reasonable proposition that the sense of responsibility, required for the proper exercise of the political institutions of the West, can be acquired by an Eastern people through practical training and experiment only. To admit this is not to express any agreement with those who usually oppose all attempts at reform on the plea that the people are not ready for it. . . . While, therefore, we are prepared to allow that an advance towards our goal may be only by reasonably cautious steps, what we emphatically insist on is that the resources of the country should be primarily devoted to the work of qualifying the people by means of education and in other ways, for such advance. Even the most bigoted champion of the existing system of administration will not pretend that this is in any degree the case at present. Our net revenue is about 44 millions sterling. Of this very nearly one-half is now eaten up by the Army. The Home Charges, exclusive of their military portion absorb nearly one-third. These two, between them, account for about 34 millions out of 44. Then over 3 millions are paid to European officials in civil employment. This leaves only about 7 millions at the disposal of the Government to be applied to other purposes. Can anyone, who realises what this means, wonder that the Government spends only a miserable three-quarters of a million out of State funds on the education of the people – primary, secondary and higher, all put together! Japan came under the influence of Western ideas only forty years ago, and yet already she is in a line with the most advanced nations of the West in matters of mass education, the State finding funds for the education of every child of school-going age. We have now been a hundred years under England's rule, and yet today four villages out of every five are without a school house and seven children out of eight are allowed to grow up in ignorance and in darkness! Militarism, Service interests and the interest of the English capitalists, – all take precedence today of the true interest of the Indian people in the administration of the country. Things cannot be otherwise, for it is the Government of the people of one country by the people of another, and this as Mill points out, is bound to produce great evils. Now the Congress wants that all this should change and that India should be governed, first and foremost, in the interests of the Indians themselves. This result will be achieved only in proportion as we obtain more and more voice in the government of our country. . . .

Report of the 21st Indian National Congress, 1905, pp 8–15; Reproduced in C. H. Philips (ed.), *Select Documents on the History of India and Pakistan*, [*The Evolution of India and Pakistan*], vol. iv, pp 158–9

25. SIR S. BANERJEA ON MODERATES AND EXTREMISTS, 1918

[Sir Surendranath Banerjea (1848–1925) was a prominent and highly-respected leader of the early nationalist movement in India; he was twice President of the Indian National Congress]

In the meantime a storm was brewing that was destined to cause a serious split in the ranks of Indian politicians. On July 8, 1918, the Montagu-Chelmsford Report was published. It was the signal of war. There was an angry outcry from the Extremist organs. Even Mrs Besant, who now takes the view of the Moderate party in regard to the Scheme, denounced it in her own eloquent and emphatic style. 'The scheme is unworthy to be offered by England or to be accepted by India' so thundered forth Mrs Besant in her organ, *New India*, on the very day the Scheme was published. Curiously enough, on the selfsame day a manifesto issued by fifteen gentlemen of Madras condemned the Scheme in terms equally emphatic. 'It is so radically wrong', said they, 'alike in principle and in detail that it is impossible to modify or improve it'. The late Mr Tilak said the same thing in his simple and straightforward fashion. 'The Montagu Scheme', observed Mr Tilak, 'is entirely unacceptable.'

In the midst of all this excitement and ferment, a special session of the Congress was called to consider the Report, and we who did not profess the same extreme views had to decide what we should do. Should we attend the Congress or not? We decided to abstain. We felt that these hasty and extreme views would dominate the deliberations of the Congress, and that we should not lend them the weight of our support by our presence. We accordingly held a conference of the Moderate party in Bombay on November 1, 1918. I was elected

President. It was the first of the Moderate Conferences, which are now held from year to year. Some of our friends, the Rt Hon. Mr Shastri and the Hon. Sir Narasingha Sarma among others, continued to attend the Congress, in the hope of making their influence felt. But it was a vain hope. The Congress has become more Extremist than ever, and they have since discontinued their attendance. We have parted company – it is difficult to say for how long.

The schism indeed did not take place without a strenuous attempt on our part to arrive at a compromise. Our divisions have been the fruitful source of our weakness, and we tried to prevent a fresh one. Fully three weeks before the meeting of the Congress I wired to the Joint Secretary and to Mrs Besant, asking them to postpone the Special Session of the Congress for a short time, for an interchange of views which might help to bring about an understanding. The request was not complied with, and at the last moment, just twenty-four hours before the sitting of the Congress, when a final effort was made, it was far too late – the psychological moment had passed by.

Our decision to abstain from the Congress was, as events have shown, a wise one, and I claim that we of the Moderate party saved the scheme. The combination against it was formidable. The European Associations in India, now so earnest for the success of the Reforms, were severe in their criticisms; Lord Sydenham condemned it in the Press and from his place in the House of Lords, strangely enough quoting Mr Tilak in support of his views. The *Manchester Guardian* complained that the Indian Extremists were playing into the hands of Lord Sydenham and his party. In the midst of this formidable body of opposition, the only real and consistent support came from the Moderate party in India. If they had remained within the Congress fold, they would have been overwhelmed, their voice would have been that of a minority of little or no account. The British democracy would have said, in view of the practically unanimous opposition offered to the Scheme: 'Well, if you don't want it, let us drop it altogether.' And, there being no other scheme to take its place, the prospects of responsible government would thus have been indefinitely postponed. Our difficulties were aggravated by the non-committal attitude of the British Government, whose Indian policy would necessarily be largely inspired by Lord Curzon, who was then a member of the Cabinet. Our anxieties were deepened by the proposal to appoint a Joint Committee of both Houses to deal with the recommendations of the Bill before its introduction. At such a time and amid these accumulating difficulties a decisive policy in support of the scheme was called for, if it was to be saved from wreckage; and the Moderate party resolved upon such a policy, even though separation from the Congress would be necessary. It was a heavy price to pay, but it had to be paid if the prospect of the speedy inauguration of the beginnings of responsible government were to be realized. We counted the cost and we made up our minds to incur it. To many of us, and to me in a special sense, separation from the Congress was a painful wrench. We had contributed to build up the great National Institution with our life-blood. We had raised it up from infancy to adolescence, from adolescence to maturity, and now, in full view of the crowning reward of our lifelong labours, we found the sacred temple of national unity swayed by divided counsels, resounding with the voice of conflict and controversy, and divorced from the healing accents of moderation and prudence. We could not but secede; for the difference between those who had captured the machinery of the Congress and ourselves was fundamental, and that upon a matter equally fundamental, namely, the question of self-government for India. The Congress, however great an organization, was after all a means to an end. That end was self-government. We decided to sacrifice the means for the end. That was the raison d'être of the Moderate or Liberal party as a separate entity in the public life of India.

This was the parting of the ways, Extremists and Moderates following their line of work, with something of the bitter reminiscences familiar to the members of a Hindu joint family broken up under the pressure of internecine strife. The Extremists were the loudest in their denunciations of the Moderates, who in this as in other matters did not forget the cardinal principle of their creed, moderation in all things. The Moderates were classed by their political opponents as allies of the bureaucracy, and bracketed with them in their denunciations; nor were their meetings safe from invasion. Noisy demonstrations and rowdyism were often the features of meetings called by them, to discuss public questions in which there were differences of opinion between them and the Extremists. At these demonstrations non-violent Non-Co-operations often developed into pugilistic encounters, in which the rattle of sticks harmonized musically with the shouts that were raised and the blows that were dealt. Never in the whole course of my public life, now extending over nearly half a century, have I in our public meetings witnessed scenes so disgraceful as those which have met my eyes in the course of the last four or five years. The words 'traitor' and 'shame' have become familiar terms in the vocabulary of the Swarajist wing of Non-

Co-operation which seeks to secure its triumph by soul-force. There was more of brute-force than soul-force in all these exhibitions; and what is most regrettable is that the young are dragged into these questionable proceedings with all their attendant demoralization. The ancient spirit of tolerance that has been the heritage of our people has disappeared and practices have been encouraged that are disastrous to the best interests of youth of the provinces.

However that may be, let us not forget that Extremism is of recent origin in Bengal. Our fathers, the first-fruits of English education, were violently pro-British. They could see no flaw in the civilization or the culture of the West. They were charmed by its novelty and its strangeness. The enfranchisement of the individual, the substitution of the right of private judgment in place of traditional authority, the exaltation of duty over custom, all came with the force and suddenness of a revelation to an Oriental people who knew no more binding obligation than the mandate of immemorial usage and of venerable tradition. The story is told in a biography, the authority of which has not been challenged, of one of the most brilliant representatives of early English culture in Bengal, the late Rev. Krishma Mohan Banerjee, throwing the refuse of a meal of forbidden food, on which he had fed himself, into the house of a neighbouring Brahmin. Everything English was good – even the drinking of brandy was a virtue; everything not English was to be viewed with suspicion. It was obvious that this was a passing phase of the youthful mind of Bengal; and that this temperament had concealed in it the seeds of its own decay and eventual extinction. In due time came the reaction, and with a sudden rush. And from the adoration of all things Western, we are now in the whirlpool of a movement that would recall us back to our ancient civilization, and our time-honoured ways and customs untempered by the impact of the ages that have rolled by and the forces of modern life, now so supremely operative in shaping the destinies of mankind. Will this movement succeed? I have grave doubts; for such a movement is against the eternal verities of things and that divine law of progress which the Unseen Hand of an Invisible Power had inscribed on every page of human history. But, whether the movement succeeds or not, the reaction against pro-British tendencies was partly the creation of the British Government itself, for no British Government can be wholly un-British in its traditions. In India, it has given pledges and promises, generous and beneficent, and has founded institutions with great potentialities of self-rule. In 1833, the Charter Act removed all disqualifications as regards the eligibility of Indians to high office.

But the Charter Act remained practically a dead letter. In 1858, the Queen's Proclamation made merit the sole test of qualification. Here again the pledges and promises made remained substantially un-redeemed. Local Self-government was conceded in 1882; but the restrictions imposed, about which Lord Morley as Secretary of State complained, largely nullified the boon. Then came Lord Curzon and his unpopular measures, the Official Secrets Act, the Universities Act, and, last but not least, the Partition of Bengal. All these created a strong revulsion of feeling. The methods of government followed in the new province intensified the growing sentiment and the culminating point was reached by the dispersal of the Barisal Conference in 1906. If I were asked to point to a single occasion as marking the genesis of modern Extremism in Bengal with its further developments, I should say it was the chapter of events that took place at Barisal in 1906, in connexion with the break-up of the Bengal Provincial Conference. There was then an upheaval among the leading men of Bengal assembled at Barisal, the like of which I have not witnessed. Even a man like Mr Bhupendra Nath Basu, lately a member of the Executive Council, a public man so sedate and calculating, used language which neither he nor I would care to repeat. It was a time of intense excitement; and our faith in the efficacy of constitutional agitation was shaken. If that was the temper of tried politicians, the attitude of the younger generation, who mustered strong at Barisal, may be imagined. This was in 1906. The Alipore Conspiracy Case was discovered in 1908. I returned home from Barisal full of indignation, with my unshakable optimism sensibly impaired; and one of the first things that I did was to sever what remained of my connexion with the Government. For the moment, I became a Non-Co-operator, one of the earliest apostles of that cult and resigned my office as Presidency Magistrate of Calcutta and Honorary Magistrate of Barrackpore. The resignations were a protest against the action of the Barisal authorities, and did not represent my acceptance of a definite policy or principle. I did the same thing when in 1899 I resigned my office as a Municipal Commissioner of Calcutta along with twenty-seven members of the Corporation. There are occasions when we must 'non-co-operate' and follow it up as a protest. But I altogether repudiate a persistent policy of non-co-operation, especially at a time when the Government is prepared to move along progressive lines, though the pace may not be as rapid as we should like it to be. . . .

Sir S. Banerjea, *A Nation in the Making*, pp 282–7

26. THE IMPACT OF MAHATMA GANDHI,
1919-20

... Gandhi was swept to the top in 1919-20 because he had caught the imagination of the country. The leaders were trying hard to keep pace with the rank and file whom Gandhi's speeches and writings had filled with a new energy and enthusiasm. The president of the Nagpur Congress, which put the seal of final approval on the non-co-operation movement in December 1920, rightly summed up the session as one in which instead of the President and the leaders driving the people, the people drove him and the leaders.

Gandhi was now the Mahatma, the great soul; with his voluntary poverty, simplicity, humility and saintliness he seemed a Rishi (sage) of old who had stepped from the pages of an ancient epic to bring about the liberation of his country. Nay, to millions he was the incarnation of God. In the course of a tour of Bihar when the tyre of his car burst he saw an old woman standing on the roadside. She was stated to be 104 years old and had waited in rain and without food and water for the whole day. 'For whom are you waiting?' somebody asked her. 'My son, who is Mahatma Gandhi?' she queried. 'Why do you want to see him?' asked Gandhi who now stood next to her. 'He is an *Avtara*' (incarnation of God) replied the woman. For the next quarter of a century, it was not only for his message that people came to him, but for the merit of seeing him. The sacred sight of the Mahatma, his *darshan*, was almost equivalent to a pilgrimage to holy Benares. The unthinking adoration of the multitude sometimes made him feel sick. 'The woes of Mahatmas', he wrote, 'are known only to Mahatmas'. But this adoration was the mainspring from which was drawn the immense influence he exercised over Indian public life. He inspired old and young alike. In his auto-biography, Jawaharlal Nehru has graphically related the story of the boy in his teens who was arrested during the non-co-operation movement, stripped and tied to a whipping post and flogged; as each stripe fell on him and cut into his flesh, he shouted, 'Victory to Mahatma Gandhi', until he fainted.

Gandhi had struck some of the inner chords of Indian humanity; his appeal for courage and sacrifice evoked a ready response because he was himself the epitome of these qualities. It was because he was, to use Churchill's epithet, a 'naked fakir', because his life was one of austerity and self-sacrifice that a great emotional bond grew between him and the Indian people. . . .

B. R. Nanda, *Mahatma Gandhi, A Biography*, pp 212–3

27. ANNIE BESANT ON THE AWAKENING OF INDIA, 1926

[Mrs Besant was a prominent American member of the Theosophical Society who lived for many years in India. She had a deep regard for Hindu culture and identified herself with the nationalist cause through the Indian National Congress. She was President of the thirty-second Congress, held in 1917, a remarkable tribute to her campaigning zeal]

. . . The Russo-Japanese war, a war between East and West as it was felt to be, was another element, this time from outside which helped to awaken India, and was, from one point of view, her salvation. For Indian Ideals were in peril for the first time in her history, and Indian Ideals were essentially the Ideals of the East. The peril lay in the fact that she had assimilated all other invaders and had re-made them into Indians, but the British were denationalising her by forcing on her their ways, their methods, their civilization, and were teaching her western-educated class to copy them and to regard their own as inferior. They could never be assimilated, for they were birds of passage, not settlers in the country; they carried 'home' their gains from Indian cheap labour and their pensions for having governed India inefficiently. So incessant was their insistence on their stay there as foreigners, that some Indians caught the ridiculous habit of saying, 'I am going home this year', when they were going to pay a visit to England. The defeat of the great Russian Power by little Japan sent a shock of astonishment through India. What? An Eastern Nation facing a Western Nation on a field of battle? What? The white people were not then resistless? They had been met and overthrown by a coloured race, by men like themselves? A thrill of hope ran through Asia, Asia invaded, Asia troubled by white 'spheres of influence', with settlements of white people, insolent and dominant, rebelling against Eastern laws, rejecting Eastern customs with contempt, humiliating coloured Nations in their own lands and arrogating powers to which they had no right. Despair changed into hope. Asia awoke, and with Asia, India.

A. Besant, *India. Bond or Free?*, pp 159–60

28. CIVIL DISOBEDIENCE IN INDIA, 1930

[A Pledge taken on 'Independence Day', 26 January 1930]

We believe that it is the inalienable right of the Indian people, as of any other people, to have freedom and to enjoy the fruits of their toil and have the necessities of life, so that they may have full opportunities of growth. We believe also that if any government deprives a people of these rights and oppresses them, the people have a further right to alter it or to abolish it. The British Government in India has not only deprived the Indian people of their freedom but has based itself on the exploitation of the masses, and has ruined India economically, politically, culturally and spiritually. We believe therefore that India must sever the British connection and attain Purna Swaraj or Complete Independence.

India has been ruined economically. The revenue derived from our people is out of all proportion to our income. Our average income is seven pice (less than two pence) per day and of the heavy taxes we pay 20 per cent are raised from the land revenue derived from the peasantry and 3 per cent from the salt tax, which falls most heavily on the poor.

Village industries, such as hand-spinning have been destroyed, leaving the peasantry idle for at least four months in the year, and dulling their intellect for want of handicrafts, and nothing has been substituted, as in other countries, for the crafts thus destroyed.

Customs and currency have been so manipulated as to heap further burdens on the peasantry, British manufactured goods constitute the bulk of our imports. Customs duties betray clear partiality for the British manufactures, and revenue from them is used not to lessen the burden on the masses, but for sustaining a highly extravagant administration. Still more arbitrary has been the manipulation of the exchange ratio, which has resulted in millions being drained away from the country.

Politically, India's status has never been so reduced as under the British regime. No reforms have given real political power to the people. The tallest of us have to bend before foreign authority. The rights of free expression of opinion and free association have been denied to us, and many of our countrymen are compelled to live in exile abroad and cannot return to their homes. All administrative talent is killed, and the masses have to be satisfied with petty village offices and clerkships.

Culturally, the system of education has torn us from our moorings, and our training has made us hug the very chains that bind us.

Spiritually, compulsory disarmament has made us unmanly and the presence of an alien army of occupation, employed with deadly effect to crush in us the spirit of resistance, has made us think that we cannot look after ourselves or put up a defence against foreign aggression, or even defend our homes and families from the attacks of thieves, robbers and miscreants.

We hold it to be a crime against man and God to submit any longer to a rule that has caused this fourfold disaster to our country. We recognise, however, that the most effective way of gaining our freedom is not through violence. We will therefore prepare ourselves by withdrawing, so far as we can, all voluntary association from the British Government, and will prepare for civil disobedience, including non-payment of taxes. We are convinced that if we can but withdraw our voluntary help and stop payment of taxes without doing violence, even under provocation, the end of this inhuman rule is assured. We therefore hereby solemnly resolve to carry out the Congress instructions issued from time to time for the purpose of establishing Purna Swaraj.

J. Nehru, *An Autobiography*, Appendix A, pp 612–13

29. SIR JOHN KOTELAWALA OF CEYLON ON ASPECTS OF COLONIALISM, *c.* 1930

My first contacts with colonialism at its worst were when, as an agriculturist, landowner, and business-man, I came up against the attitude of by no means effortless superiority adopted by the British planters towards Ceylonese of every class. They thought our country belonged to them, and was theirs alone to exploit, while the richer natives should be kept in their place and enjoy none of the privileges exclusively reserved for the ruling race.

Social status, sportsmanship, a university education, and physical prowess counted for nothing if you were a son of the soil. The fact that your family prospered was merely due to the tolerance of a kindly Government whose main job it was to civilize the natives and make use of them as coolies or clerks.

I am not saying that all the British officials, planters, and merchants adopted this arrogant attitude towards the people of the country. There were shining exceptions. But colonialism seemed to infect most of them with a tropical disease, of which the most familiar symptom was an ill-concealed contempt for brown, black and yellow men as such. The ancient civilization of Ceylon meant nothing to them, unless they were scholars interested in history.

The laws of the land had to be framed primarily for the benefit of British interests. Good roads, hospitals, and schools were a necessity only in the estate areas, and were apparently a luxury to which villagers and peasants were not entitled. First-class railway carriages were not meant for third-class natives even if they were Kandyan chiefs or Tamil knights.

No doubt the British planters, with the aid of Indian labour and of a Government that looked after the interest of foreign investors very well, had done a lot for the development of industries that increased the country's revenue. But was that a good reason for neglecting the basic needs of the permanent population, for resenting the claims and thwarting the aspirations of Ceylonese, and for insulting and humiliating them in their own country?

The cruder eruptions of colonialism used to enrage me in my impetuous youth. I was always a fighter, who believed in hitting hard and well above the belt. It was therefore not surprising that I came to be involved in many escapades in which I invariably felt that my might was right, and that the other fellow's wrong thinking was his weakness. I would stand no nonsense or impudence from anyone. This, I think, was the reaction to colonialism among all young men of my time with any spirit and with resources to back them; but many of them were more cautious and prudent than I could ever be. It was my belief that I was thrice armed if I got my blow in first.

Two incidents that illustrate the slave mentality that colonialism breeds and the tendency in rural Ceylon to regard British officials as demigods linger vividly in my memory.

On one occasion I was present, as M.P. for the district, at a conference at which a Government Agent was explaining in a lordly way how he administered his province. Among those present were some Rate-mahatmayas who were called upon to elaborate some of the points made by the Big White Chief. What astounded and infuriated me in the demeanour of these men was that every time they mentioned the G.A. in their well-rehearsed recitals they rose respectfully a few inches from their seats, as though they were naming a divine being. I stood it as long as I could, and then I interrupted by asking the G.A. why they did this. Had he given the impression that he was a God?

He replied that it was the usual custom in his province. 'If that is so,' I exclaimed indignantly, 'let the custom be stopped. I find it disgusting.'

The second incident was at a luncheon party when an Acting Governor was the chief guest at a Ratemahatmaya's house. I was surprised to find Village Tribunal Presidents in their best clothes acting as waiters. So unaccustomed were they to this task that one of them nearly poured soup on the back of my neck. This arrangement was supposed to be a tribute to a distinguished representative of the ruling race, in whose august presence ordinary servants had to fade out of the picture. I was more amused than enraged by this aspect of subservience to colonialism.

But I was never blind to the fact that there was something good in this form of colonialism, in spite of all the evils it engendered and the fundamentally wrong bias it gave to the country's economy.

Its advantage was that the colonizing Power was essentially democratic. There was a sincere intention to grant the people some measure of self-government. Although this was done in painfully slow stages, it gradually gave us a voice in the administration of our own affairs. We were free to criticize the Government and all its works as strongly as we liked. Public opinion could thus be educated on important issues, and the constant agitation for political reforms could become an irresistible clamour. Given national unity and wise leadership, we could make the best use of the democratic way of escape from the disabilities of the old colonialism. Can this be said of what I condemned at Bandung as the new colonialism? The answer is obvious. Totalitarian tyranny would be infinitely worse than the most ruthless imperialism known in the past.

Sir John Kotelawala, *An Asian Prime Minister's Story*, pp 20–3

30. CORRESPONDENCE BETWEEN J. NEHRU AND M. A. JINNAH, DECEMBER 1939

To M. A. Jinnah   *Bombay,*
                                                              December 14, 1939

My dear Jinnah,

Thank you for your letter of the 13th December which was delivered to me in the forenoon today on my arrival here. I sent you my last letter from Allahabad after reading and giving full thought to your statement about the celebration of 'a day of deliverance and thanksgiving' by the Muslims. This statement had distressed me greatly as it made me realise that the gulf that separated us in our approach to public problems was very great. In view of this fundamental difference, I wondered what common ground there was for discussion and I put my difficulty before you. That difficulty remains.

In your letter you have emphasized two other preliminary conditions before any common ground for discussion can arise. The first is that the Congress must treat the Muslim League as the authoritative and representative organisation of the Mussalmans of India. The Congress has always considered the League as a very important and influential organisation of the Muslims and it is because of this that we have been eager to settle any differences that may exist between us. But presumably what you suggest is something more and involves some kind of repudiation by us of our dissociation from other Muslims who are not in the League. There are, as you know, a large number of Muslims in the Congress, who have been and are our closest colleagues. There are Muslim organisations like the Jamiat-ul-Ulema, the All India Shia Conference, the Majlis-e-Ahrar, the All India Momin Conference, etc., apart from trade unions and peasant unions which have many Muslims as their members. As a general rule, many of these organisations and individuals have adopted the same political platform as we have done in the Congress. We cannot possibly dissociate ourselves from them or disown them in any way.

You have rightly pointed out on many occasions that the Congress does not represent everybody in India. Of course not. It does not represent those who disagree with it, whether they are Muslims or Hindus. In the ultimate analysis it represents its members and sympathisers. So also the Muslim League, as any other organisation, represents its own members and sympathisers. But there is this vital difference that while the Congress by its constitution has its membership open to all who subscribe to its objective and methods, the Muslim League is only open to Muslims. Thus the Congress constitutionally has a national basis and it cannot give that up without putting an end to its existence. There are many Hindus, as you know, in the Hindu Mahasabha who oppose the idea of the Congress representing the Hindus as such. Then there are the Sikhs and others who claim that they should be heard when communal matters are considered.

I am afraid therefore that if your desire is that we should consider the League as the sole organisation representing the Muslims to the exclusion of all others, we are wholly unable to accede to it. It would be equally at variance with facts if we made a similar claim for the Congress, in spite of the vastness of the Congress organisation. But I would venture to say that such questions do not arise when two organisations deal with each other and consider problems of mutual interest.

Your second point is that the Muslim League cannot endorse the Congress demand for a declaration from the British Government. I regret to learn this for this means that, apart from communal questions, we differ entirely on purely political grounds. The Congress demand is essentially for a declaration of war aims and more especially for a declaration of Indian independence and the right of the Indian people to frame their own constitution without external interference. If the Muslim League does not agree to this, this means that our political objectives are wholly dissimilar. The Congress demand is not new. It is inherent in article one of the Congress and all our policy for many years past has been based on it. It is inconceivable to me how the Congress can give it up or even vary it. Personally I would be entirely opposed to any attempt at variation. But this is not a personal matter. There is a resolution of the All India Congress Committee, endorsed by a thousand meetings all over India, and I am powerless to ignore it.

It thus seems that politically we have no common ground and that our objectives are different. That in itself makes discussion difficult and fruitless. What led me to write my last letter to you also remains – the prospect of a celebration of a day of deliverance by the Muslims, as suggested by you. That raises very vital and far-reaching issues, into which I need not go now, but which must influence all of us. That approach to the communal problem cannot be reconciled with an attempt to solve it.

I feel therefore that it will serve little purpose for us to meet at this stage and under these conditions with this background. I should like to assure you however that we are always prepared to have free and frank discussions of the communal or other problems as between the Congress and the League.

I note what you say about the Bijnor incident. It has been our misfortune that charges are made in a one-sided way and they are never inquired into or disposed of. You will appreciate that it is very easy to make complaints and very unsafe to rely upon them without due inquiry.

Yours sincerely,

JAWAHARLAL NEHRU

J. Nehru Esqr.,
Bombay
From M. A. Jinnah   *Bombay,*
                                                 December 15, 1939

Dear Jawahar,

I am in receipt of your letter of the 14th December 1939, and I am sorry to say that you have not appreciated my position with regard to the second point. I did not say that Muslim League cannot endorse the Congress demand for a declaration from the British Government. What I have said was that we cannot endorse the Congress demand for *the* declaration as *laid down* in the resolution of the Working Committee and confirmed by the All India Congress Committee of the 10th October 1939 for the reasons I have already specified in my letter.

If this resolution of the Congress cannot be modified in any way and as you say that personally you would be entirely opposed to any attempt at variation of it and as you make it clear that you are wholly unable to treat with the Muslim League as the authoritative and representative organisation of the Mussalmans of India, may I know in these circumstances what do you expect or wish me to do.

                               Yours sincerely,

                                              M. A. JINNAH
                    J. Nehru, *A Bundle of Old Letters,* pp 415–18

31. MOHAMMED ALI JINNAH ON THE POLITICAL FUTURE OF INDIA, 1940

What is the political future of India? The declared aim of the British Government is that India should enjoy Dominion Status in accordance with the Statute of Westminster in the shortest practicable time. In order that this end should be brought about, the British government, very naturally, would like to see in India the form of democratic constitution it knows best, under which the Government of the country is entrusted to one or other political Party in accordance with the turn of the elections.

Such, however, is the ignorance about Indian conditions among even the members of the British Parliament that, in spite of all experience of the past, it is even yet not realised that this form of government is totally unsuited to India. Democratic systems based on the concept of a homogeneous nation such as England are very definitely not applicable to heterogeneous countries such as India, and this simple fact is the root cause of India's constitutional ills. . . .

India is inhabited by many races – often as distinct from one another in origin, tradition and manner of life as are the nations of Europe. Two-thirds of its inhabitants profess Hinduism in one form or another as their religion, over 77 million are followers of Islam, and the difference between the two is not only of religion in the stricter sense but also of law and culture. They may be said, indeed, to represent two distinct and separate civilizations. Hinduism is distinguished by the phenomenon of its caste, which is the basis of its religious and social system, and, save in a very restricted field, remains unaffected by contact with the philosophies of the West; the religion of Islam, on the other hand, is based upon the conception of the equality of man. . . .

The British people, being Christians, sometimes forget the religious wars of their own history and today consider religion as a private and personal matter between man and God. This can never be the case in Hinduism and Islam, for both these religions are definite social codes which govern not so much man's relations with his God, as man's relations with his neighbour. They govern not only his law and culture but every aspect of his social life, and such religions, essentially exclusive, completely preclude that merging of identity and unity of thought on which Western democracy is based. . . .

H. Bolitho, *Jinnah*, pp 126–7, quoting from an article in *Time and Tide*, March 9, 1940

32. THE TRANSFER OF HINDUS FROM BAHAWALPUR CITY, 1947

[An eye-witness account of the human upheaval which accompanied Partition in India]

Next morning I was up early to supervise the transport of refugees from the camp to the railway station. This did not go at all well. When the first lorries arrived, there were no refugees ready to get into them. Though the jail camp was not an alluring spot, there appeared to be a general reluctance to forsake it for the unknown hazards of a railway journey. I began to doubt whether more than a handful of refugees would be induced to take the plunge and go by the first train. Then presently, after about twenty minutes of seemingly fruitless persuasion, there was a sudden rush and a mad scramble to obtain seats. Nur Mohammad and I tried vainly to impose some kind of order. It was utterly useless and we gave it up. Some of the lorries were not really designed for passengers and were not easy to get into. Men, women and children crowded round them, shouting, yelling and weeping, pushing and jostling and banging one another with their luggage without distinction of age or sex. In this confusion parents got into lorries without their children or their luggage, or luggage and children were thrown in first and the owners were unable to scramble up after them. It took ages then to sort this out and send a lorry off without some vital person or package missing. Consequently the lorries made very few trips and we were able to transport barely 1,000 people to the station before the train left.

We had reserved the whole train for refugees. The number that we succeeded in bringing to the station filled but did not crowd it. Muslims in general and the station staff in particular considered that the Hindus were being sent off (at the expense of the Bahawalpur Government) in far too much luxury and comfort. They wanted them to be packed like sardines, to the exclusion, if need be, of all luggage. After the first day their wish on the first point was gratified. With the use of tongas and improved arrangements for loading the lorries we were able to transport two or three thousand refugees daily to the station in time for the train. This usually consisted of seven coaches; but after the first two days we had to agree to the last coach being kept for ordinary passengers and cram the refugees into the remainder. This meant that there was no more luxury travel for them! Many had to cling like locusts to the outside or sit on the roof in the broiling sun or on the buffers. Since the journey to Hindumalkot took the whole day, it must have been terribly uncomfortable and exhausting. But those who travelled in the first train escaped these hardships.

Among these there was a prominent Hindu named Professor Mehta. With a view to allaying the general anxiety the Hindu leaders had arranged with him that he should accompany those going by the first train and come back and report how things went. He left with every profession that he would be seeing us all again the next day. However, having once got safely through to India, he never returned.

While this train was being sent off, the few Hindus still remaining in the city were being evacuated to the jail camp. I went back there direct from the station and spoke to the Hindu leaders about the need to control their people so that in future there would not be such a mad rush for the lorries in the morning. They said that they were themselves ashamed at what had occurred and were determined that the embarkation should be more orderly in future. They soon effected quite a marked improvement.

Not unnaturally they were at this time very querulous and unhappy, and it was impossible to remove all their complaints or to offer them much consolation in their misery. Several of those in the camp had some close relative in some other part of the State and wanted him or her to join them before they entrained for India. A few of these, in what appeared to be especially deserving cases, were fetched in my car and such other private cars as we could muster, but it was not possible to collect them all, still less to scour the countryside for cousins, aunts and yet more distant relations, as we were repeatedly pressed to do. There were also numerous requests for being escorted back to the city in search of some treasured possession that had been forgotten. Since such requests had ordinarily to be refused, a method was soon devised of obtaining an escort on false pretences. Knowing that we were short of grain, individual Hindus would come forward and say that they had several bags of grain stored in their houses and that they offered these to the camp 'as a free gift' though they were by now hardly theirs to give. We would then depute escorts to take them to the city so that they could point out their houses and the bags of grain. A few of the early offers were genuine; but a large number were found to be bogus. When the house was reached there would be no sign of any bags of grain; the donor would say that they must have been looted and immediately begin to search for other of his belongings. We soon had to refuse all such offers. . . .

Penderel Moon, *Divide and Quit*, pp 209–11

33. AN INTERVIEW WITH JAWAHARLAL NEHRU, 1956

He began, somewhat self-consciously, by referring to the special position he occupied at the outset of his career by virtue of his father's prominence and Gandhi's fondness for the young man. 'At the time I didn't think much about myself', he continued. 'We were so involved in the struggle, so wrapped up in what we were doing that I had little time or inclination to give thought to my own growth.' His words exuded warmth, sincerity and humility. They were simple words, gentle words, gently spoken in an honest portrait of his past.

Certain landmarks are deeply rooted in Nehru's memory. The first to be mentioned was Jallianwalla Bagh – the Amritsar Tragedy in 1919 – the effect of which has been feelingly described in his autobiography. Along with this, 'my visit to the villages' – his discovery of the peasant in 1920 – and 'my first close contact with Gandhi'. In 1920–1, 'I lived my intensest', he continued, referring to the first civil disobedience campaign. Then came prison 'a period with no peaks of experience'. Despite the sharp change from a life of activity and fulfilment, 'I adjusted very well. I have that capacity, you know. I was much less agitated than my colleagues by events outside; there was nothing I could do about it so why get involved. I was interested, of course, but I adjusted very well to the changes which prison brought.' Later, he returned to his prison experience. As he talked freely, he conveyed more poignantly than anything he has written the lasting effects of the nine years of enforced isolation from the outside world. 'I did a lot of reading and writing,' he remarked casually. He also learned the art of self-discipline and used his time to think through the next phase of the struggle for Indian freedom. There was no hint in his words of anger at his captors, nothing to suggest that his experience had produced resentment. A Gandhian spirit of forgiveness seemed to permeate his attitude as he reflected on the lonely days and nights behind the walls. But he has not forgotten them.

M. Brecher, *Nehru, A Political Biography*, pp 28–9

South-East Asia

34. ATTITUDES TO THE FILIPINO REVOLUTION OF 1898-1902

Three centuries of Spanish rule familiarized the Filipinos with Western forms of government and permitted a few Filipinos to gain practical experience in local administration. Though corrupt in practice, in theory and profession the colonial system of Spain was fine and up-lifting. Spaniards and Filipinos may have failed always to maintain high standards, but those standards were ever before them in the laws and precepts of both the state and the church. There could be no better evidence that these standards did make an impression upon the Filipino mind than the rebellion of the Filipinos against Spanish rule. The Filipinos fought and died for political ideas they had learned from the West, although the Spaniards had not put into practice what they taught the Filipinos. The leaders of the revolution were not a band of armed peasants; they were cultivated and able men with wealth and influential connections. Given protection against outside aggression, it is quite possible that they would have provided the Philippines with a workable government.

Among Filipinos the story of the revolutionary struggle is very much in the foreground of attention today, a story rich and varied enough to provide material for many an analysis. During the period of American colonial rule Rizal, the peaceful reformer, was honored as the out-standing national hero despite strong clerical opposition to the many anticlerical ideas in his works. Filipinos feel that the Americans over-emphasized Rizal because he did not advocate violent revolution, and by the same token neglected the activists. Today special attention is devoted to Bonifacio, the active leader of the Katipunan in the armed revolt against Spain, especially by the historical revisionists who seem-ingly wish to build up the image of a 'proletarian' leader who understood and organized the 'masses'. Aguinaldo is strangely underplayed by the revisionists. And those Filipinos who collaborated with the Americans in the campaigns of 1899-1902 are now described as a 'dark blot in the annals of Filipino nationalism'. Filipino nationalists draw what they need from this one great revolutionary period, which, in consequence looms so importantly in Philippine and United States relations.

G. E. Taylor, *The Philippines and the United States*, pp 48–9

35. BURMESE NATIONALISM, 1919–21

Nationalism of the modern type was a late development in Burma, not for lack of national sentiment but from ignorance of the modern world. As elsewhere in the Tropical Far East its source of inspiration was the victory of Japan over Russia, which taught the East that it might use western science to defeat the West. The stir of a new spirit was first evident in the enthusiasm aroused by the sermons and publications of a Buddhist monk who conducted a revivalist movement throughout the country from 1906 onwards, and in the foundation of numerous Young Men's Buddhist Associations (Y.M.B.A.). One outcome of the movement was a revival of interest in the past of Burma, and a society then founded to study art, science and literature in relation to Burma and the neighbouring countries attracted a considerable Burman membership. That some Burmans were beginning to look towards Japan was manifested by the visit to Japan in 1910 of a young monk, U Ottama, who subsequently played a leading part in Burmese politics, and by the publication of an account of the Russo-Japanese War, and of an illustrated description of Japan. But it was to India rather than Japan that Burmans looked for their ideas, and their current political literature came largely from India. The Y.M.B.A. movement soon developed political activities, and Government servants were warned against taking part in them. One feature of this new development was a protest against the use of footwear in the precincts of pagodas and monasteries; this protest gained such general support that Europeans had to comply with it.

Yet in 1919 the Government still regarded the political ferment as an alien importation due to 'consistent efforts by Indian agitators to capture Burman opinion'. But national sentiment had never lain far below the surface, and when Burmans studied the Indian press, or sometimes listened to Indian agitators, it was only because they hoped by copying their methods to convert national sentiment into an effective political force. In 1920, when the proposals for a reformed constitution in Burma seemed less advanced than those proposed for India, the Y.M.B.A., 'which had become the principal political organization in the country' began to advocate the Indian device of non-co-operation with the Government. When the Y.M.B.A. was succeeded in 1921 by the General Council of Buddhist Associations (G.C.B.A.), the aim of Nationalist policy was formulated as Home Rule, some favouring complete independence, and non-co-operation was adopted as the most effective line of action. On the publication of the Reform scheme the more moderate members of the association decided to co-operate with Government, so far as this did not prejudice the speedy attainment of Home Rule, and formed a separate party, known from the number of those who signed its programme as the Twenty-one Party. This marked a definite stage in the progress of nationalism: the severance, if only formal, of politics from religion. Hitherto Nationalists had been linked together, nominally at least, on the basis of their common Buddhism, but the manifesto of the Twenty-one Party was Nationalist, not Buddhist; political, not religious. In the more extreme nationalist party some Buddhist monks were prominent; there remained a close tie between Nationalism and Religion, and Nationalism still drew much of its strength from Buddhist sentiment; but the new policy made a wider appeal, potentially embracing all peoples in the country instead of only Buddhists. Since then there has been no division of principle between the various groups of Nationalists; all have been agreed on Home Rule, which has ordinarily been identified with independence from foreign control, and, apart from personal rivalries, they have differed only as to the method by which it may soonest be attained.

J. S. Furnivall, *Colonial Policy and Practice*, pp 142–4

36. HO CHI MINH ON 'THE PATH WHICH LED ME TO LENINISM', *c.* 1919–21

After World War I, I made my living in Paris, now as a retoucher at a photographer's, now as painter of 'Chinese antiquities' (made in France!). I would distribute leaflets denouncing the crimes committed by the French colonialists in Vietnam.

At that time, I supported the October Revolution only instinctively not yet grasping all its historic importance. I loved and admired Lenin because he was a great patriot who liberated his compatriots; until then, I had read none of his books.

The reason for my joining the French Socialist Party was that these 'ladies and gentlemen' – as I called my comrades at that moment – had shown their sympathy towards me, toward the struggle of the oppressed peoples. But I understood neither what was a party, a trade-union, nor what was Socialism nor Communism.

Heated discussions were then taking place in the branches of the Socialist Party, about the question whether the Socialist Party should remain in the Second International, should a Second-and-a-half International be founded or should the Socialist Party join Lenin's Third International? I attended the meetings regularly, twice or three times a week and attentively listened to the discussion. First, I could not understand thoroughly. Why were the discussions so heated? Either with the Second, Second-and-a-half or Third International, the revolution could be waged. What was the use of arguing then? As for the First International what had become of it?

What I wanted most to know – and this precisely was not debated in the meetings – was: which International sides with the peoples of colonial countries?

I raised this question – the most important in my opinion – in a meeting. Some comrades answered: It is the Third, not the Second International. And a comrade gave me Lenin's 'Thesis on the national and colonial questions' published by *L'Humanité* to read.

There were political terms difficult to understand in this thesis. But by dint of reading it again and again, finally I could grasp the main part of it. What emotion, enthusiasm, clear-sightedness, and confidence it instilled in me! I was overjoyed to tears. Though sitting alone in my room, I shouted aloud as if addressing large crowds: 'Dear martyrs, compatriots! This is what we need, this is the path to our liberation!'

After that, I had entire confidence in Lenin, in the Third International.

Formerly, during the meetings of the Party branch, I had only listened to the discussion; I had a vague belief that all were logical and could not differentiate as to who were right and who were wrong. But from then on, I also plunged into the debates and discussed with fervor. Though I was still lacking French words to express all my thoughts, I smashed the allegations attacking Lenin and the Third International with no less vigor. My only argument was: 'If you do not condemn colonialism, if you do not side with the colonial people, what kind of revolution are you waging?'

Not only did I take part in the meetings of my own Party branch, but I also went to other Party branches to lay down 'my opinion'. Now I must tell again that Comrades Marcel Cachin, Vaillant Couturier Monmousseau, and many others helped me to broaden my knowledge. Finally, at the Tours Congress, I voted with them for our joining the Third International.

At first, patriotism, not yet Communism, led me to have confidence in Lenin, in the Third International. Step by step, along the struggle, by studying Marxism – Leninism parallel with participation in practical activities, I gradually came upon the fact that only Socialism and Communism can liberate the oppressed nations and the working people throughout the world from slavery.

There is a legend, in our country as well as in China, on the miraculous 'Book of the Wise'. When facing great difficulties, one opens it and finds a way out. Leninism is not only a miraculous 'Book of the Wise', a compass for us Vietnamese revolutionaries and people; it is also the radiant sun illuminating our path to final victory, to Socialism and Communism.

M. E. Gettleman (ed.), *Vietnam*, pp 37–9

37. TUNKU ABDUL RAHMAN AND MALAY UNITY, 1926-7

[Tunku Abdul Rahman became Prime Minister of the newly independent Federation of Malaya in 1957, and of the new Federation of Malaysia in 1963. In the 1920s, and later, he was a student in Britain. In the following passage a small but significant episode of his earlier student days is recalled.]

... There was a serious side to his life. With remarkable perception, he had put his finger on one of the most regrettable aspects of Malay life in Malaya; there was no unity among the Malays. They lived and worked within the fastnesses of their State boundaries, their eyes turned inward, their daily life revolving round their own tiny microcosm – charming, courteous people who were satisfied if they had enough food for themselves and their family for the next twenty-four hours, who prayed to Allah as the Koran instructed, and who looked upon Malays from other areas as friendly intruders. There was no feeling that they all belonged to the same proud race whether they were fishermen in Trengganu, paddy-planters in Kedah and Malacca, Government clerks in Perak or budding administrators in Kuala Lumpur.

This lack of unity became an obsession with Abdul Rahman and he used to divert political conversations to the question, 'How can we Malays unite?' There clearly was no answer then. Politics and political thought had not troubled the luscious serenity of life in Malaya. . . .

To Abdul Rahman, living among people who were utterly immersed in outpourings from the House of Commons, and listening and talking to them in London pubs, the unity of Londoners, Yorkshiremen, Lancastrians and the Scots and the Welsh, welded into one nation under a single flag, was the kind of national consummation to be desired for Malaya.

Even in London very few Malay students were getting together. He thought there should be some form of unity among them, particularly as they were so far from home. At his inspiration many met in London one day and formed the 'Malay Society of Great Britain'. At the inaugural meeting, Tunku Abdul Rahman of Negri Sembilan, was elected its first president and Tunku Abdul Rahman of Kedah, its first honorary secretary. It was indicative of Abdul Rahman's determination to inculcate a pride in things Malay that it became a rule that when members were together they should speak Malay only – 'Remember you have a national language of your own. Use it when you are together, otherwise you will forget most of it while you are in England', he said. . . .

H. Miller, *Prince and Premier*, pp 46–7

38. THE CHINESE AS A MINORITY PROBLEM IN THAILAND, 1910–39

Thailand has the largest number of Overseas Chinese of any country of Southeast Asia; they number 3,000,000, or about 10 per cent of the total population. It is estimated that nearly half the inhabitants of Bangkok are Chinese or of Chinese origin, and as in most neighboring countries, the Chinese control the commerce of the capital while the indigenous population controls the government and the civil service. Until 1910, when King Chulalongkorn died, the government followed a policy of rapidly assimilating the Chinese immigrants who streamed into

Thailand from the southern part of China, and there were few problems. In 1910, however, nationalistic manifestations on both sides broke the tranquility; from then until today the Chinese minority has been intimately linked to Thailand's security and is therefore a factor in its foreign policy.

In 1910, a few months before King Wachirawut ascended the throne, the Chinese secret societies in Bangkok organized a general strike. The local Chinese had been strongly influenced by the growing nationalism fostered by the Manchu dynasty during its last years, while the Siamese were becoming more nationalistic in the wake of the country's defeat by France a few years earlier. The people were also aroused by Siamese students returning from Europe with ideas of Western nationalism. By 1910 Siam was ripe for racial disturbances. Although the Chinese general strike was decisively dealt with by Siamese authorities and was a failure, it dramatized for the first time the economic power of the Chinese community as well as the potential threat of a mass Chinese uprising against the government. King Wachirawut, who was plainly concerned about the danger, embarked on an avowedly anti-Chinese campaign, which likened the Chinese to the Jews of Europe. This campaign intensified after the Chinese Revolution of 1911, which increased the nationalist sentiments among the Chinese in Siam; and the King warned that the government would tolerate no further disorders. In 1913 the first Nationality Act was promulgated: it was directed against the Chinese community.

When Pibun Songkhram became Prime Minister in 1938, the Chinese community posed a problem because it was strongly anti-Japanese and also openly supported the Nationalist Chinese Government's war effort. As Pibun's policy was to accommodate the rising power of Japan, he could not tolerate a large Chinese opposition. Also, he had a general antipathy toward the large Chinese minority. In 1939 Pibun launched a series of sweeping anti-Chinese measures which greatly reduced the Chinese community's economic influence and also forced it to forgo much of its cultural separateness. Thai business firms were formed, assisted by government subsidy, in order to force Chinese companies to close; new taxes imposed on businessmen were designed to limit the profits of the Chinese; Chinese schools were closed; and most Chinese newspapers were forced to cease publication. So drastic were these measures that the Nationalist government of China protested, and the colonial governments in Southeast Asia also became aroused because of the impact on their own Chinese communities. Later in 1939 Pibun moderated his policy somewhat, but he publicly advised the Thai people to avoid mixed marriages with the Chinese.

D. E. Neuchterlein, *Thailand and the Struggle for Southeast Asia*, pp 97–9

39. SŒTAN SJAHRIR ON EAST AND WEST, 1935

[The author was an Indonesian who had studied law at Leyden and married a Dutch wife. He wrote the following while a political prisoner of the Dutch, in New Guinea.]

Am I perhaps estranged from my people? Why am I vexed by the things that fill their lives, and to which they are so attached? Why are the things that contain beauty for them and arouse their gentler emotions only senseless and displeasing for me? In reality, the spiritual gap between my people and me is certainly no greater than that between an intellectual in Holland and, for example, a Drents farmer, or even between the intellectual and the undeveloped people of Holland in general. The difference is rather, I think, that the intellectual in Holland does not feel this gap because there is a portion – even a fairly large portion – of his own people on approximately the same intellectual level as himself. And that portion is, moreover, precisely what constitutes the cultural life of Holland; namely, the intellectuals, the scientists, the artists, the writers.

That is what we lack here. Not only is the number of intellectuals in this country smaller in proportion to the total population – in fact, very much smaller – but in addition, the few who are here do not constitute any single entity in spiritual outlook, or in any spiritual life or single culture whatsoever. From the point of view of culture they are still unconscious, and are only beginning to seek a form and a unity. It is for them so much more difficult than for the intellectuals in Holland. In Holland they build – both consciously and unconsciously – on what is already there. They stand on and push forward from their past and their tradition; and even if they oppose it, they do so as a method of application or as a starting point.

In our country this is not the case. Here there has been no spiritual or cultural life, and no intellectual progress for centuries. There are the much-praised Eastern art forms, but what are these except bare rudiments from a feudal culture that cannot possibly provide a dynamic fulcrum for people of the twentieth century? What can the puppet and other simple and mystical symbols offer us in a broad and intellectual sense? They are only parallels of the outdated allegories and wisdom of medieval Europe. Our spiritual needs are needs of the twentieth century; our problems and our views are of the twentieth century. Our inclination is no longer toward the mystical, but toward reality, clarity, and objectivity.

In substance, we can never accept the essential difference between the East and the West, because for our spiritual needs we are in general dependent on the West, not only scientifically but culturally.

We intellectuals here are much closer to Europe or America than we are to the Boroboedoer or Mahabharata or to the primitive Islamic culture of Java and Sumatra. Which is our basis: the West, or the rudiments of feudal culture that are still to be found in our Eastern society?

So, it seems the problem stands in principle. It is seldom put forth by us in this light, and instead most of us search unconsciously for a synthesis that will leave us internally tranquil. We want to have both Western science and Eastern philosophy, the Eastern 'spirit', in the culture. But what is this Eastern spirit? It is, they say, the sense of the higher, of spirituality, of the eternal and religious, as opposed to the materialism of the West. I have heard this countless times, but it has never convinced me. Did not Hitler also say that the Aryan *Geist* was the sense of the higher, the spiritual, the moral, the religious? And is this spirituality actually such a pre-eminently Eastern attribute and ideal? It seems to me definitely inaccurate. It is possible that climatic and racial factors have had an influence on the present differences in development between the East and the West. However, it is no longer possible to determine the direction or magnitude of that influence because of the more direct and apparent expression of the influence of economic and sociological factors.

If one looks at world history *as a whole* and endeavours to understand its total development, then the perennial so-called 'essential' differences between the spiritualism of the East and the materialism of the West disappear; and instead the emphasis centers upon feudal culture with its spiritualism and universalism, on the one hand, and the bourgeois-capitalistic culture with its bourgeois ideology, its materialism, and its modern objectivity on the other.

Meanwhile, this remains the problem of the so-called 'awakening Easterner.' Turkey and China orient themselves principally and consciously toward the West, whereas India – with Gandhi and Tagore – seeks a 'national, Eastern form of life' and resists, as it were, westernization, or modernization. Gandhi places the greatest emphasis on what is 'eastern,' on the spiritual, the moral, and the religious. Tagore, on the other hand, wants Western science and modernism, but in a new Indian form that will be steeped in the 'Eastern wisdom of life' (*levenswijsheid*). In point of fact the whole thing is hardly clear.

This latter approach of Tagore cannot be the answer to the problem either, for in the East everything is more deeply rooted than in the West. This must be taken into consideration particularly if one is to understand the psychology and the spiritual position of the Eastern intelligentsia. They feel no foundation whatsoever under them. In Indonesia, for the most part, they go along unknowingly perhaps, but in Turkey, in China, and in India they are consciously searching for some secure foundation.

S. Sjahrir, Out of Exile, pp 66–8

40. JAPANESE OFFICIAL ADVICE TO TROOPS ON THE EVE OF WAR IN SOUTH-EAST ASIA, 1941

[An excerpt, in translation, from a pamphlet issued to Japanese troops prior to the invasion of Malaya in 1941.]

1. *Obeying the Emperor's august will for peace in the Far East*

The 1868 Restoration, by the abolition of feudal clans and the establishment of prefectures, returned Japan to its ancient system of beneficent government by His Majesty the Emperor, and thereby rescued the country from grave peril for the black ships of the foreigners which had come to Nagasaki and Uraga were ready to annex Japan on the slightest pretext. The New Restoration of the thirties has come about in response to the Imperial desire for peace in the Far East. Its task is the rescue of Asia from white aggression, the restoration of Asia to the Asians, and when peace in Asia has been won – the firm establishment of peace throughout the whole world.

The wire-pullers giving aid to Chiang Kai-shek and moving him to make war on Japan are the British and the Americans. The rise of Japan being to these people like a sore spot on the eye, they have tried by every means in their power to obstruct our development, and they are inciting the regime at Chungking, the French Indo-Chinese, and the Dutch East Indians to regard Japan as their enemy. Their great hope is for the destruction of the Asian peoples by mutual strife, and their greatest fear is that, with the help of a powerful Japan, the peoples of Asia will work together for independence. If the peoples of Asia representing more than half of the world's population, were to make a united stand it would indeed be a sore blow to British, Americans, French and Dutch alike, who for centuries have battened and waxed fat on the blood of Asians.

Already Japan, the pioneer in this movement in the Far East, has rescued Manchuria from the ambitions of the Soviets, and set China free from the extortions of the Anglo-Americans. Her next great mission is to assist towards the independence of the Thais, the Annamese, and the Filipinos, and to bring the blessing of freedom to the natives of South Asia and the Indian people. In this we shall be fulfilling the essential spirit of 'one world to the eight corners of the earth'.

The aim of the present war is the realization, first in the Far East, of His Majesty's august will and ideal that the peoples of the world should each be granted possession of their rightful homelands. To this end the countries of the Far East must plan a great coalition of East Asia, uniting their military resources, administering economically to each other's wants on the principle of co-existence to the common good, and mutually respecting each other's political independence. Through the combined strength of such a coalition we shall liberate East Asia from white invasion and oppression.

The significance of the present struggle, as we have shown, is immense, and the peril which Japan has drawn upon herself as the central and leading force in this movement is greater than anything she has ever faced since the foundation of the country. The peoples of South Asia deeply respect the Japanese and place high hopes upon our success. It is vital, above all, that we should not betray this respect and these hopes....

M. Tsuji, Singapore, The Japanese Version, pp 304–5

41. THAKIN NU (U NU) ON THE JAPANESE INVASION OF BURMA, 1942

Everyone in Burma who had any interest in politics knew all about the Japanese. They knew that in Japan a handful of war-lords oppressed millions of the people; they knew that in China the Japanese were committing murder and robbery and rape; they knew that Tanaka and his followers were planning to conquer the whole world. Yet apart from a very few men like Didok U Ba Cho, Thakin So and Than Tun, they refused really to believe all these things. This can easily be explained.

From the first arrival of the Portuguese in India the lack of unity among Asiatic peoples enabled Europeans with their greater scientific knowledge to dominate all the countries of the East. At that time Oriental peoples saw very few Europeans; they were overawed by their western science, their discipline and practical ability, and took them for superior beings. But gradually western prestige declined. From the opening of the Suez Canal many more westerners came to the East, and the people came to know more about them. In 1905 an eastern people, the Japanese, defeated a western people, the Russians. In the first World War Asians fought shoulder to shoulder with Europeans and proved themselves as good. And a study of Asian history revealed the glories of the past and showed that at one time Asians had been victorious in Europe.

These things made us impatient of western rule and all we wanted was a leader. The Japanese seemed to be the only eastern people that could hold its own against the West, and we came to look confidently to Japan for leadership. So people made excuses for the Japanese. 'There was probably some reason for what they did; the various charges might not be true, and in any case it was only to Japan that we could look for freedom from western rule.' So Burmans were very reluctant to believe anti-Japanese propaganda. They told U Ba Cho to stop preaching when he insisted on the evils of Japanese fascism, and they laughed at Thakin So and Than Tun as unpractical, academic. And, as it was the westerners who were most active in exposing Japanese fascism, many people believed that these men had been bribed by western imperialists and capitalists whose real object was to prevent eastern lands from obtaining independence.

In 1941 when the war spread to Asia many of our nationalist leaders were in jail. Thakin So, Thakin Kyaw Sein, Thakin Ba Hein, Thakin

Mya Thwin and I were in the Mandalay Central Jail, and along with us were many leaders of all parties, Thakin, Dama and Wunthanu. The whole jail was agog for war news. Many nationalists were rejoicing in the idea that the sooner the English had to quit the sooner we should be out of jail. But every day the jail fluttered with all kinds of disquieting rumours and gossip. 'In Tharrawaddy Jail all the political prisoners have been blown to bits with bombs.' 'In Prome Jail they've all been machine gunned.' Some of us believed these stories and were badly frightened. Others wondered if the English would take all the nationalist leaders with them when they cleared out to India. Others were glad to think that they would be all right with the Japanese who would welcome us as allies. And some were glad merely because they would soon be rid of British rule. Meanwhile Thakin So and his group were trying to spread the idea that if the fascists were to win, men would lose their manhood, and they were urging everyone to help the democratic side without reserve. But it was like a lone voice crying out from the depth of a thick jungle, and some people who could not grasp Thakin So's idea accused him of being a British agent. . . .

At that time Burmans had such faith in the Japanese that when the Japanese bombers came they would not take cover in the shelters. Some tore off their shirts and waved a welcome; they sang and danced and clapped their hands, and shouted and turned somersaults as if they did not care a curse what happened. It was not merely bad hats and old lags who went on like this, but even many nationalist leaders behaved in the same manner. I tried to make them see sense. 'It's all very well, friend,' I said, 'but even supposing you are right in thinking that your pals the Japanese won't bomb you, the English bombers may say "See how keen these people are for the Japs to come; let them have it". And when they drop their bombs you will all be killed for nothing. Don't be so rash.' But when I preached like this they jeered at me for being so timid while claiming to be a nationalist leader. The prisoners, too, from the jails in Insein, Rangoon and other parts of Lower Burma backed them up, because they had seen lots of Japanese planes already. 'They don't bomb Burmans,' they said. 'Why, every day they kept on flying over Insein Jail. Don't be so frightened, man.' And they took the other side against us.

The hottest day of all was the 8th of April when the Japanese bombed Mandalay for the third time. With a huge black cloud of smoke rising to the sky all round, you might have thought the whole large city was covered by a big black umbrella. Although it was only ten o'clock in the

o

morning, the smoke was so thick that not a single ray of sunshine could pierce through, and everywhere in the town it was as dark as night. Meanwhile quite close to the jail one building after another was crashing down. The continual bombing all round was enough to strike terror into any ordinary mortal, but the Burmans in the jail who placed so much faith in the Japanese went on laughing, and clapping their hands, and waving a welcome with their shirts.

I dare say we others might have followed their example. But our group from Rangoon, even before leaving Insein Jail had been drilled in communist catchwords day and night by dear old Thakin So. He exorcized those who were possessed with such ideas and we learned to do just what he told us. So, when the Japanese bombers came, we went down with Thakin So to the shelters and took refuge. Otherwise we might well have been found among the shirt-waving crowd.

Thakin Nu, *Burma under the Japanese*, pp 1–3, 3–5

42. ACHMED SUKARNO ON NATIONALISM IN ASIA, 1956

Our struggle towards national fulfilment has been eased by the assistance given by people of other countries and continents. The wheels of history have been oiled for us by understanding and sympathy. We have taken courage from the example and the burning words of others and the night has been made radiant by the truth and high ideals so often expressed and so sincerely struggled for.

In truth this is one world and the actions of all have an effect upon all. A little time ago, I picked up, quite casually, a history book used in schools of my country. It was a book for children of 10 to 12 years old and is also used widely by adults who have, in their maturity, learned the art of reading.

That history book contained stories from all over the world of national heroes who had fought for the freedom of their country. It told of Washington and of Jefferson, of Garibaldi and of Mazzini, of Cromwell and of Ireton. Furthermore, it told of others in other countries. It spoke of names familiar to us and beloved by us, but perhaps strange to you – of those in Egypt, in Turkey, in Morocco, in India, in Burma, in Japan and in China. All of those great men struggled that their nations might be free. Many died before that ideal could be realised but the lamp they lit has never been, and will never be, extinguished. And all of those men were related one to the other by bonds of common action and common faith.

For what did they struggle? Yes, for their nations. But what is a nation? Many great thinkers have applied their minds to this. Many answers have been given, often conflicting and usually confusing. One of the truest and most moving descriptions I know was contained in a short essay by a little-known professor of Ohio University. About 40 years ago, Professor Taylor wrote:

'Where and what is the nation? Is there such a thing? You would answer that the nation exists only in the minds and hearts of men. It is an idea. It is therefore more real than its courts or armies; more real than its cities, its railroads, its mines, its cattle; more real than you and I are, for it existed in our fathers and will exist in our children. It is an idea, it is an imagination, it is a spirit, it is human art. Who will deny that the nation lives?'

Yes, who will deny, who can deny that the nation lives, even if all the political scientists fail to define it?

We of Asia are told that the troubles of our continent are due to nationalism. This is as wrong as saying that the world's troubles are due to atomic energy. It is true that there is turbulence in Asia, but that turbulence is the result and aftermath of colonialism and is not due to the liberating effects of nationalism. I say 'the liberating effects of nationalism'. I do not mean only that nations are again free of colonial bonds, but I mean that men feel themselves free. You who have never known colonialism can never appreciate what it does to man. . . .

. . . This I know: We of Indonesia and the citizens of many countries of Asia and Africa have seen our dearest and best suffer and die, struggle and fail, and rise again to struggle and fail again – and again be resurrected from the very earth and finally achieve their goal. Something burned in them; something inspired them. They called it nationalism. We who have followed and have seen what they built, but what they destroyed themselves in building – we, too, call their inspiration and our inspiration, nationalism. For us, there is nothing ignoble in that word. On the contrary, it contains for us all that is best in mankind and all that is noblest.

L. Snyder, *The Dynamics of Nationalism*, pp 335–7

Western Asia

43. BEN GURION'S ARRIVAL IN PALESTINE, 1906

[*Note:* David Ben Gurion's earlier name was David Green]

Ben Gurion's arrival in Palestine was equally without ceremony. He was young, alone and without responsibility except to his own ideals. In 1906 the 'port of Jerusalem', Jaffa, had about fifty thousand inhabitants – thirty thousand Moslems, ten thousand Christians and ten thousand Jews. Apart from its exports and imports, the town was also the centre of the tourist trade, of proselytising societies and benevolent institutions. A German sect, the Templars, who believed it their task to regenerate Christendom from the Promised Land, had set up colonies, including Sarona, in the neighbourhood of Jaffa. An English hospital, an American orphanage, a Franciscan convent, an Italian school, a Jewish hospital, the Sh'arei Zion, and a Jewish secondary school satisfied some of the needs of a cosmopolitan community, living either in poverty or on the charity of the pious. In other respects, Jaffa with its minarets was a typical provincial city of the Ottoman Empire, neglected and run down, its limited amenities provided by foreigners. The hotels were owned by Germans – 'bargaining necessary', Baedeker warns.

'The air smelt of charity and *bakshish*', Green wrote to his father. It wasn't what he wanted. He'd had enough of ghetto towns and saw no future in Palestine on the basis of the dole.

'I couldn't resist an overpowering urge,' he wrote eleven years later, 'to see a Jewish village.' And so, like many another pious visitor who arrived in Jaffa with hope and left in distaste, David Green, on the very afternoon of his arrival in the ancient town, made his way on foot to Petach Tikvah, a settlement founded in 1878, one of about twenty Jewish villages known as *Moshavot*.

That night [he wrote] my first night on homeland soil, is forever engraved on my heart with the exultation of achievement. I lay awake – who could sleep through his first night in the Land? The spirit of my childhood and my dreams had triumphed and was joyous! I was in the

Land of Israel, in a Jewish village there, and its name was Petach Tikvah – Gate of Hope!

Far from Plonsk, in a place exotic yet familiar in his dreams, he felt that he had returned home. 'The howling of jackals in the vineyard, the braying of donkeys in the stables, the croaking of frogs in the ponds, the scent of blossoming acacia, the murmur of the distant sea, the darkening shadows of the groves, the enchantment of the stars in the deep blue, the faraway skies, drowsily bright – everything intoxicated me. I was rapturously happy – yet all was strange and bewildering, as though I were errant in a legendary kingdom. Could it be?'

The dream had become a reality. He stretched out his hand, and what he touched was solid.

My soul was in tumult, one emotion drowned my very being: Lo, I am in the Land of Israel! And the Land of Israel was here, wherever I turned or trod. . . . I trod its earth, above my head were skies and stars I had never seen before. . . . All night long I sat and communed with my new heaven. . . .

For him as for thousands more who arrived in the Second Aliyah, the wave of emigration that accompanied and followed the pogroms, the sun, the air, the contact with the soil, the sense of inner glory and dedication to an ideal, the communion of free men with their comrades and equals, had produced an unforgettable exaltation.

Throwing off the Polish–Jewish Green, Ben Gurion, as he was soon to call himself after one of the heroes of the revolt against the Romans, wrote:

Beautiful are the days in our land, days flushed with light and full of lustre, rich in vistas of sea and hill. . . . But infinitely more splendid are the nights; nights deep with secrets and wrapt in mystery.

The drops of burning gold, twinkling in the soft blue dome of the sky, the dim-lit purity of the mountains, the lucid crystal of the transparent mountain air – all is steeped in yearning, in half-felt longings, in secret undertones. You are moved by urgings not of this world. . . . In the silence you listen to the echoes of childhood; legends of ancient days and visions of the last days take shape here, quietly, flooding the soul and refreshing the anguished heart with the dew of hope and longing.

Even now, a stranger waking in the silent night in Galilee feels that here is a place for revelations and miracles where a mysterious dialogue may take place between man and God. He listens in the soft darkness and waits for a voice. For Ben Gurion, the voice was a call to physical labour which he happily answered with the hundreds of young men from the Rabbinical schools, the *yeshivot*, and high schools and universities who flocked from the Pale of Settlement, from Lithuania and from the cities of Russia where a privileged number lived, to redeem the land by labour. Some came from ghettos, others from middle-class homes; all came in search of a new life, to liberate the essential Jew from his millennial degradation. Ben Gurion's first year in Palestine was as a labourer on the land.

For a year [he says] I sweated in the Judaean colonies, but for me there was more malaria and hunger than work. But all three – work, hunger and malaria – were new and full of interest. Was it not for this that I had come to the Land? The fever would grip me every fortnight with mathematical precision, harass me for five or six days, and then disappear. Hunger, too, was a regular visitor. It would come to lodge with me for weeks at a time, sometimes for months on end. During the day I could dismiss it in all sorts of ways, or at least stop thinking about it. But in the nights – the long wracked vigils – the pangs would grow fiercer, wringing the heart, darkening the mind, sucking the very marrow from my bones, demanding and torturing – and departing only with the dawn. Shattered and broken, I would drop off to sleep at last.

M. Edelman, *Ben Gurion, A Political Biography*, pp 36–8

44. T. E. LAWRENCE ON THE EFFECTS OF THE TURKISH REVOLUTION OF 1908 ON ARAB NATIONALISM, 1926

... Arab civilizations had been of an abstract nature, moral and intellectual rather than applied; and their lack of public spirit made their excellent private qualities futile. They were fortunate in their epoch, Europe had fallen barbarous; and the memory of Greek and Latin learning was fading from men's minds. By contrast, the imitative exercise of the Arabs seemed cultured, their mental activity progressive, their state prosperous. They had performed real service in preserving something of a classical past for a medieval future.

With the coming of the Turks this happiness became a dream. By stages, the Semites of Asia passed under their yolk, and found it a slow death. Their goods were stripped from them; and their spirits shrivelled in the numbing breath of a military government. Turkish rule was gendarme rule, and the Turkish political theory as crude as its practice. The Turks taught the Arabs that the interests of a sect were higher than those of patriotism; that the petty concerns of the province were more than nationality. They led them by subtle dissensions to distrust one another. Even the Arabic language was banished from courts and offices, from the Government service, and from superior schools. Arabs might only serve the state by sacrifice of their racial characteristics. Semitic tenacity showed itself in the many rebellions of Syria, Mesopotamia and Arabia against the grosser forms of Turkish penetration; and resistance was also made to the more insidious attempts at absorption. The Arabs would not give up their rich and flexible tongue for crude Turkish; instead, they filled Turkish with Arabic words, and held to the treasures of their own literature.

Then came the Turkish Revolution, the fall of Abdul Hamid, and the supremacy of the Young Turks. The horizon momentarily broadened for the Arabs. The Young-Turk movement was a revolt against the hierarchic conception of Islam and the pan-Islamic theories of the old Sultan, who had aspired, by making himself spiritual director of the Moslem world to be also (beyond appeal) its director in temporal affairs. These young politicians rebelled and threw him into prison, under the impulse of constitutional theories of a sovereign state. So, at a time when Western Europe was just beginning to climb out of nationality into internationality, and to rumble with wars far removed from problems of race, Western Asia began to climb out of catholicism into nationalist politics, and to dream of wars for self-government and self-sovereignty, instead of for faith or dogma. This tendency had broken out first and most strongly in the Near East, in the little Balkan States, and had sustained them through an almost unparalleled martyr-dom to their goal of separation from Turkey. Later there had been nationalist movements in Egypt, in India, in Persia, and finally in Constantinople, where they were fortified and made pointed by the new American ideas in education; ideas which when released in the old high Oriental atmosphere, made an explosive mixture. The American schools, teaching by the method of inquiry, encouraged scientific detachment and free exchange of views. Quite without intention they taught revolution, since it was impossible for an individual to be modern in Turkey and at the same time loyal, if he had been born one of the subject races – Greeks, Arabs, Kurds, Armenians or Albanians – over whom the Turks were so long helped to keep dominion.

The Young Turks, in the confidence of their first success, were carried away by the logic of their principles, and as protest against pan-Islam preached Ottoman brotherhood. The gullible subject races – far more numerous than the Turks themselves – believed that they were called upon to co-operate in building a new East. Rushing to the task (full of Herbert Spencer and Alexander Hamilton) they laid down platforms of sweeping ideas and hailed the Turks as partners. The Turks, terrified at the forces they had let loose, drew the fires as suddenly as they had stoked them. Turkey made Turkish for the Turks – *Yeni Turan* – became the cry. Later on, this policy would turn them towards the rescue of their irredenti – the Turkish populations subject to Russia in Central Asia, but, first of all, they must purge their Empire of such irritating subject races as resisted the ruling stamp. The Arabs, the largest alien component of Turkey, must first be dealt with. Accordingly, the Arab deputies were scattered, the Arab societies forbidden, the Arab notables proscribed. Arabic manifestations and the Arabic language were suppressed by Enver Pasha more sternly than by Abdul Hamid before him.

However, the Arabs had tasted freedom; they could not change their ideas as quickly as their conduct; and the stiffer spirits among them were not easily to be put down. They read the Turkish papers, putting 'Arab' for 'Turk' in the patriotic exhortations. Suppression charged them with unhealthy violence. Deprived of constitutional outlets, they became revolutionary. The Arab societies went underground, and changed from liberal clubs into conspiracies. The Akhua, the Arab mother society, was publicly dissolved. It was replaced in Mesopotamia by the dangerous Ahad, a very secret brotherhood, limited almost entirely to Arab officers in the Turkish Army, who swore to acquire the military knowledge of their masters, and to turn it against them, in the service of the Arab people, when the moment of rebellion came. . . .

T. E. Lawrence, *Seven Pillars of Wisdom*, pp 42–4

45. THE ARAB GOVERNMENT OF THE HEJAZ ON ARAB NATIONAL RIGHTS, 1917

[A Memorandum by the Foreign Office of the Arab government of the Hejaz to the Secretary of State, United States of America]

Your Excellency,

For generations now, the Arab nation has been suffering under the Turkish Yoke. History has not recorded an instance of a people who have suffered the kind of enslavement and torture which this nation has endured, though it is guilty only of constituting the majority in the

Ottoman Empire. The Turks have, in consequence, looked upon it as a danger to the dominance of their race, and have treated it like a dangerous enemy. After the loss of some European provinces, they even began to intensify this treatment, since the fact that Arabs were in the majority became a fact beyond discussion. Thus, the Arab element, deprived of its rights and subjected to tyranny and atrocity, came to decrease in significance and to be enfeebled in its own country, compelled to seek in other Arab countries the life which the Turks were denying it. When the European war was declared, foreign control disappeared from the Turkish Empire, and the Turks gave full rein to their hatred and anger; they began to implement an orderly plan to annihilate the Arabs. No sentiment stood in their way, no law prevented them. To this end, they made lawful every divinely prohibited means; they used hanging, exile, prison, torture, dispersal of families, confiscations, verdicts *in absentia* and similar persecutions.

His Majesty the King, my master, tried his utmost to persuade the Turkish government to revert to the path of truth and justice, but his efforts proved vain. He therefore overthrew the yoke of tyranny and proclaimed the independence of the Arabs, in his capacity as head of the House of Quraish, that house from which have issued all the houses which sat on the throne in the Arab countries, from the Umayyads to the Abbasids and the Fatimids. His Arab people followed him, and only a few months elapsed before he founded an army, set up an administration, and expelled and annihilated all that was Turkish in the Hijaz. Medina, however, the religious standing of which absolutely prevents its bombardment and forcible conquest, he was content to blockade. His armies today are stationed in Syrian territories where they engage in operations which are all victorious and successful.

The new Kingdom has struggled for two years past to rescue a race worthy of respect, owing to its glorious history and its beneficent influence on European civilization. It cannot but expect sympathy and friendship from the great American nation. It hopes that the government of the great Republic will grant it the same recognition granted by the Allied Powers, especially now that the United States has joined the war on the Allied side. His Majesty, my master, attaches great importance to this recognition, which will be the first practical example of the principle of national liberation which President Wilson has endorsed, and which your country has joined the war to realise.

S. G. Haim (ed.), *Arab Nationalism*, pp 94-5

46. MUSTAFA KEMAL AND FORMS OF
DRESS IN TURKEY, 1925

On his journey through the region of Kastamonu Kemal struck at another such outward and visible symbol. Its disappearance was to uproot a habit deeply engrained in every male individual in Turkey. For it involved what he wore each day of his life on his head. This was the fez.

Costume, in the Islamic religion, had a deep symbolic significance. The fez itself, so it happened, was a mere century old as a form of Moslem headgear. Ironically it was a Greek Christian fashion, prevalent in the islands and initially derived from the Barbary corsairs. Manufactured for the Ottoman market in Austria, its introduction was the climax of a sartorial revolution aimed, early in the nineteenth century, at the ultra-conservative turban, and had led to riots in many parts of the Empire. But the fez in its turn soon became a symbol of Ottoman and Islamic orthodoxy as the turban had been, and as such was fiercely defended and as fiercely attacked.

Kemal's plan to replace this symbol with that of the hat was thus a daring revolutionary gesture. It was one which had been quietly simmering in his mind since the days of his youth, when he had been humiliated abroad by the stigma of inferiority conferred by his national headgear. Now at Chankaya in the evenings he had been discussing the change with his friends, consulting those who had travelled abroad as to which form of hat was most suitable.

In his own costume he had been making experiments. He was photographed on a tractor on his model farm wearing a Panama – without a black ribbon. An old friend came upon him one day in a train wearing a cloth cap with his brown tweed suit. 'Does this become me?' Kemal asked, as though seeking assurance. He revealed that in recent months he had three times dreamed of the fez. 'And whenever I did so Ismet knocked at my door in the morning to report a reactionary movement somewhere in the country.' The idea of a reform was unobtrusively canvassed in the press, but still no newspaper dared use the ugly word shapka, or hat. They preferred such euphemisms as 'civilized headgear', 'protector from sunshine', or 'head-cover with a brim'.

Kemal deliberately chose, for the disclosure of these various religious reforms, a province known for its reactionary sentiments. Boldly he was striking at the enemy at a strong point where, if his shock tactics succeeded, their impact would be twice as effective as elsewhere.

Shrewdly calculating the effect of his public image, he explained to Falih Rifki that in such a city as Izmir, where he was already known, the people would look not at him but at the hat. In Kastamonu they would be seeing him for the first time, and would see him 'as a whole, hat and all'. Kastamonu moreover, for all its backwardness, was in a sense a symbol of the Revolution itself. Bestriding as it did the direct line of the army supply route from Istanbul, through Inebolu, the Black Sea port, to Ankara, it had played a loyal part in the War of Independence, and its loyalty should survive the jolts which it was now to receive.

Nevertheless Kemal, in that distaste for the darker forces of religion which had haunted him since youth, approached his tour with unusual nervousness, asking for water when he first spoke and finding that his hands, as he raised it to his lips, were trembling. He had left Ankara bareheaded, in an open car. The people, swarming down to the main road from their mountain villages, hardly knew what to expect from this first sight of their national hero. In one village an artist had drawn on a wall an imaginative portrait of the Gazi, the slayer of infidels, as a formidable warrior with sweeping moustaches and a sword seven feet long. The villagers had spread carpets on the streets for him to walk on. One of them, a young student, recalled the scene years later:

When the President walked slowly down the street, greeting the crowds, there was not a sound. The clean-shaven Gazi was wearing a white, European-style summer suit, a sports shirt open at the neck, and a Panama hat. The few officials applauded frantically, urging on those near them, but a flutter of hand-clapping was all they would muster, so great had been the shock.

For the conqueror was wearing the costume of the infidel.

But the shock was slowly absorbed. Outside Kastamonu itself the Gazi got out of his car and walked into the town ahead of his entourage, first carrying the Panama hat in his hand, then putting it on his head. His aides did the same. Had they done so a generation earlier, they might well have been stoned or manhandled by the crowd. But now they were greeted merely with silent curiosity. Throughout his tour Kemal's interest in costume and especially headgear was made evident to all. Sometimes he remained hatless, in which case a few people out of politeness removed their own fezes. Inspecting a military detachment, he took off the cap of each soldier and examined it with attention. A few months earlier a narrow peak had been added to it ostensibly for the protection of the soldier's eyes against the sun. For had not the Prophet enjoined his followers always to fight with their faces towards it?

His approach to the sartorial question was practical. At one meeting he turned to a tailor in the audience and asked him, pointing to a man in baggy Turkish trousers and a robe, which was the cheaper – this outfit or the modern, international type of suit. The tailor replied, 'The international kind.' Pointing the moral, Kemal said to the audience, 'There, you see? Out of every costume such as this man is wearing you could make an extra suit.'

All this was a mere foretaste of what was to come – an open declaration of national policy in which civilization was equated with costume. For this he chose the port of Inebolu itself. To symbolize their part in the War of Independence, its townspeople had decorated and placed in the square a boat and an ox-cart of the type that had carried the munitions. Kemal was pelted with flowers as he drove into the town, which was bedecked with flags and branches. Later, wearing his Panama, he walked through the streets while the people crowded around to kiss his hands and his garments. He conversed with all sections of the population questioning them personally on their problems and enlightening them on his plans for their future.

For two days he took part in organized festivities. Sheep were sacrificed in his honour in barbarous fashion, but out of his sight at his request – a scruple which they ascribed to his deep devotion to animals. Bushels of apples were heaped upon him, products of the annual harvest. Schoolchildren processed before him, singing the march he had sung on the road from Samsun and crying, 'Long live our Father!' Boatmen organized a regatta for his entertainment, danced their traditional dances and sang their traditional songs. All these compliments he returned with appropriate speeches of praise to the inhabitants for the richness of their province and the enlightenment of its people.

The climax was reached on the third day, when he delivered a long oration to a dazed and respectful audience, variously clad, in the clubroom of the Turkish Hearth.

Gentlemen [he said] the Turkish people, who founded the Turkish Republic, are civilized; they are civilized in history and reality. But I tell you . . . that the people of the Turkish Republic, who claim to be civilized must prove that they are civilized, by their ideas and their mentality, by their family life and their way of living. . . . They must prove in fact that they are civilized and advanced persons in their outward aspect also. . . . I shall put my explanation to you in the form of a question.

Is our dress national? [Cries of 'no!']
Is it civilized and international? [Cries of 'no, no!']

I agree with you. This grotesque mixture of styles is neither national nor international. ... A civilized international dress is worthy and appropriate for our nation, and we will wear it. Boots or shoes on our feet, trousers on our legs, shirt and tie, jacket and waistcoat and of course to complete these, a cover with a brim on our heads. I want to make this clear. This head covering is called 'hat'.

The word was out. There was to be an end to all euphemisms. This and his other pronouncements were relayed by the news agencies to all parts of Turkey.

Lord Kinross, *Ataturk*, pp. 412–15

47. ROBERT MONTAGNE ON ARAB NATIONALISM, 1933

In 1933 Robert Montagne, at that time director of the French Institute in Damascus, noted among the Arabs of the Middle East 'a profound unity of aspiration and direction and a close interdependence between groups'.

The Arab countries [he went on in an article published under the pseudonym of Louis Jovelet] are confusedly striving for unity, for the realization of an 'Arab nation'. ... The solidarity of the various states of Arabia, which has its limits and does not exclude serious domestic quarrels, is demonstrated by a glance at the local press in the Middle East, which spreads its net wide. It is also to be seen in a ceaseless coming and going and the ease with which people settle in one country or another; above all it finds expression in a common ideology which seeks ... everywhere to arouse identical reactions in political, cultural or religious affairs. Thus an 'Arab imperialism' is being born which seeks its inspiration in the past ... or tries to link in the present ... all the national movements which have arisen separately in the various countries of the Middle East.

Having given this pertinent survey of the facts he outlined with exceptional insight the philosophy of this Arab design for living which, though still vague, was borne along by high ambitions.

While with us the idea of a nation, however complex, takes comparatively precise geographical, ethnic, political and economic forms ... in the Middle East the same concept is essentially diffused and nebulous and can be used to cover either very small groups or vast conglomerations. At the centre of the 'nebula' is local loyalty, a feeling of belonging to a district like Lebanon or to one of the great provinces of Islam

(Iraq, Syria in the larger sense of the word, the Hedjaz). In a less distinct form it appears as a belief in the unity of the race — the race which is one day to people the whole of the Arabian peninsula. Again, it is reflected in a faith in the historic and cultural unity of the peoples of Arab tongue and dialect from the Persian Gulf to the Atlantic, and finally it produces the vision of political unity throughout the vast extent of the Moslem world which, having adopted the religion of the Prophet, uses the 'sacred language of God' (even if only for liturgical purposes). . . . When a Middle Easterner speaks of nationalism . . . it is almost always impossible to know which of the four aspects of the 'nebula' he has in mind at the moment. . . . His 'Arab fatherland' has at one time 5 million inhabitants (Syria, Palestine) and at another 15 million (Arabia). It can grow to 66 million when all the Arabic speaking peoples are included and to 300 or 400 million to embrace the whole of Islam.

> P. Rondot (trans. Mary Dilke), *The Changing Patterns of the
> Middle East, 1919–1958*, pp 97–9

48. ARAB NATIONALISM AND ZIONISM:
A VIEWPOINT, 1942-4

Of all the factors which have stimulated the sense of Arab unity in the past twenty years, the most important has been the struggle of the Palestinian Arabs against Zionism. In a previous chapter something has been said about the early history of Zionism. It is necessary here to sketch its nature and its relationship with the Arabs.

The roots of Zionism are in many ways similar to those of Arab nationalism. Although an off-shoot of the age-old Messianism of the Jews, in its modern form it arose from the sense of lostness, of exclusion and of humiliation which haunts the incompletely assimilated Jews of the Dispersion. A few exceptionally gifted or fortunately-placed individuals can escape from this sense and the conflicts to which it gives rise by merging themselves in the surrounding Gentile world; but for the Jewish community as a whole, the Zionists argue, assimilation is neither possible, since if carried out on too large a scale it tends to provoke anti-Semitism, nor desirable, since it would involve the disappearance of the Jews as such and of all which their tradition contains of value to themselves or to the world. For the Zionist, the solution is not for the individual Jew to acquire the characteristics of the individual Gentile, but for the Jewish community to take on the characteristics of a national community: a normal economic and social structure, a national consciousness, a territorial home and political independence.

Zionism emerged at approximately the same time as Arab nationalism. Both movements were stimulated, although not created, by repression: the former by the Russian pogroms, the latter by the policy of the Young Turks. To both, the war of 1914–1918 was the time of crisis and opportunity. The adherents of both believed that they had been promised Palestine by the Allies: the Arabs by the McMahon letters, the Jews by the Balfour Declaration. For that and for other deeper reasons both regarded themselves as possessing rights over or at least in the country. Thus after 1918 two movements, each in its dynamic stage and each believing itself to be in the right, found themselves facing one another in a single land.

The history of Palestine since 1918 has been dominated by the struggle between them. The Jewish community has been growing in size, in wealth and in self-confidence; it now numbers over half a million, that is, roughly one-third of the population of Palestine. It has developed distinctive social forms such as the collective farms, and has created cultural institutions, an elaborate system of internal self-government and a highly organized trade-union movement. On the whole, too, as the wave of European anti-Semitism has gathered strength the claims of the Jews have increased; the old 'cultural' Zionism, which desired to create a religious and cultural centre for Jews throughout the world, has largely been swept aside by a political Zionism which aims at the establishment of a Jewish nation possessing all the political attributes of a nation and self-reliant no less in political than in other matters.

There has been a continuous growth in the strength of Arab opposition to the policy of the Balfour Declaration. They oppose it both because it prevents the achievement of their own national aspirations and because of the danger that the Jews will dominate Palestine politically and the surrounding countries economically. This policy has already in their view retarded the political development of Palestine; the independence conceded to Iraq and a large measure to Transjordan would also, they believe, have been granted to the Palestinian Arabs but for the existence of the Jewish National Home. Moreover, the Zionists are determined that self-government shall be withheld until the Jewish community has been transformed by further immigration from a minority into an overwhelming majority capable of forming a Jewish State. Jewish rule in Palestine, if it were ever established, would cut the

Arab population off from the life of the free Arab countries all around. This would be harmful not only to the Arabs of Palestine, but to those of the surrounding regions as well, for Palestine is the geographical link between Arab Asia and Arab Africa. The Arabs fear, in addition, that the Zionists, once in control of Palestine, would be dissatisfied with its existing frontiers and would be compelled by the pressure of immigration and the need for markets to carry out a policy of expansion, of subtle economic and political penetration, and of alliance with those forces, both internal and external, which are hostile to Arab independence.

In short, the Arabs regard Zionism as a force which imperils their national future. Quite apart, however, from the possible evil consequences of the policy of the Balfour Declaration, they object to it on grounds of principle. They see no reason why they should be called upon to bear the whole burden of solving the problem of world Jewry, a problem which they have done perhaps less than other nations to create. They cannot understand by what right they can be forced to become a minority in a land which their ancestors have inhabited for innumerable centuries. Further, they are humiliated by the way in which Zionist immigration has been forced upon them without their consent being asked or given.

A. H. Hourani, *Syria and Lebanon*, pp 106–8

NURI ES-SAID AND THE CONCEPT OF AN ARAB LEAGUE BASED ON GREATER SYRIA AND IRAQ, 1943

In recalling the plan set out by His Majesty's Government in the famous White Paper of 1939, Nuri gave Casey to understand that in his view the proposals had represented a belated return to the spirit of those pledges given to King Hussein of Hejaz which were to have initiated an Arab world united in a common ideal. Under the plan, the Jews would have constituted a permanent minority of about one-third of the population of Palestine, sufficient, surely, to justify the claim that a Jewish National Home as understood in the Balfour Declaration has been fulfilled.

Writing in 1943, it was still possible for the Pasha to envisage the possibility of the 1939 plan being implemented after the war. If in addition to these hopes, Great Britain and France could, in their wisdom, work for the creation of a Unitary State embracing Syria, Lebanon, Palestine and Trans-Jordan then indeed the Middle East would be set for an era of friendship and co-operation with the West that would lead Arab and Jews out of the mire of barren hate and recrimination which had governed their mutual relationship since the First World War. He, Nuri, would not insist on a complete unification of States. If a federation or confederation was preferred it would be equally acceptable. Furthermore, the people themselves could choose whether they desired a monarchy or a republic. Within the new State, the Jews would be given semi-autonomy with the right to control their own rural and urban district administration, including schools and health. In Jerusalem, a special commission composed of representatives of the three theocratic religions would be set up to ensure freedom of worship and pilgrimage. If the Maronites of the Lebanon were to demand a regime similar to that of the Jews, such as they had previously enjoyed within the Ottoman Empire then their wishes could be met. An international guarantee could ensure the status of both Jews and Maronites in their new circumstances.

There followed the obvious conclusion, that the recreated Syria, together with her sister State in the north Iraq, would form an Arab League to which others could adhere at will.

My proposals ... are based on the close relations which already exist between Iraq and all the Arabs of historic Syria. The States of the Arabian peninsula, although so near to us in language, custom and religion, have a different economy. Egypt has a larger population than the succession States and has her own problems in the Sudan and elsewhere. I have therefore assumed that these States will not at first be inclined to join an Arab Federation or League, though if such a Union succeeded between Iraq and Syria, there is every likelihood that they would in time wish to join it. But from the beginning, I anticipate that such a League, even if limited to Iraq and Syria, would facilitate joint consultation between and action by all Arab States whether within the League or not. Many of our problems are the same; we are all part of one civilization: we generally think along the same lines and we are all animated by the same ideals of freedom of conscience, liberty of speech, equality before the law and the basic brotherhood of mankind.

In the light of subsequent events, it seems a tragedy that these sane and practical proposals were not followed up. That Nuri put them forward in the belief that they were not to be treated as mere flights of fancy, is evident from the closing paragraphs of his letter. The appropriate steps, he said, would have to be taken at the right time and in the

P

right order. The union of the various parts of historic Syria should come first. A central government would take charge of such matters as currency, defence and foreign relations, leaving each state to continue its administration of local affairs. Immediate steps would be necessary to define the Jewish enclaves and responsibilities in Jerusalem. For this purpose an ethnographical map of Palestine should be prepared showing the numbers of Jews and Arabs in each town. The implementation of the plan required some sacrifices from Arabs of vested interests and sovereignty, but similar sacrifices had been made in similar circumstances by others, and Arab leaders would have to expect some temporary penalties, if they were to win that unity of which they had dreamed ever since the gathering tide of Allied victory had held out the hopes of a living Arab renaissance.

Lord Birdwood, Nuri as-Said, pp 204–6

50. THE AIMS AND COMPOSITION OF THE LEAGUE OF ARAB STATES, 1945

[The following extract gives the first three of twenty articles in the written Pact]

Pact of the League of Arab States

His Excellency the President of the Syrian Republic;
His Royal Highness the Amir of Trans-Jordan;
His Majesty the King of Iraq;
His Majesty the King of Saudi Arabia;
His Excellency the President of the Lebanese Republic;
His Majesty the King of Egypt;
His Majesty the King of the Yemen;

Desirous of strengthening the close relations and numerous ties which link the Arab States;

And anxious to support and stabilize these ties upon a basis of respect for the independence and sovereignty of these states, and to direct their efforts toward the common good of all the Arab countries, the improvement of their status, the security of their future, the realization of their aspirations and hopes;

And responding to the wishes of Arab public opinion in all Arab lands;

Having agreed to conclude a Pact to that end and having appointed as their representatives the persons whose names are listed hereinafter, have agreed upon the following provisions:

Article 1

The League of Arab States is composed of the independent Arab States which have signed this Pact.

Any independent Arab State has the right to become a member of the League. If it desires to do so, it shall submit a request which will be deposited with the Permanent Secretariat General and submitted to the Council at the first meeting held after submission of the request.

Article 2

The League has as its purpose the strengthening of the relations between the member states; the coordination of their policies in order to achieve cooperation between them and to safeguard their independence and sovereignty; and a general concern with the affairs and interests of the Arab countries. It has also as its purpose the close cooperation of the member states, with due regard to the organization and circumstances of each state, on the following matters:

A. Economic and financial affairs, including commercial relations, customs, currency, and questions of agriculture and industry.
B. Communications; this includes railroads, roads, aviation, navigation, telegraphs, and posts.
C. Cultural affairs.
D. Nationality, passports, visas, execution of judgments, and extradition of criminals.
E. Social affairs.
F. Health problems.

Article 3

The League shall possess a Council composed of the representatives of the member states of the League; each state shall have a single vote, irrespective of the number of its representatives.

It shall be the task of the Council to achieve the realization of the objectives of the League and to supervise the execution of agreements which the member states have concluded on the questions enumerated in the preceding article, or on any other questions.

It likewise shall be the Council's task to decide upon the means by which the League is to cooperate with the international bodies to be created in the future in order to guarantee security and peace and regulate economic and social relations. . . .

R. W. MacDonald, *The League of Arab States*, pp 319–20

Biographical Notes

ABDUL RAHMAN, Tunku, b. 1903, educated Cambridge and Inner Temple, London. A son of the Malay Royal House of Kedah. Government service in Kedah, 1931–45, including the period of Japanese occupation. Entered active politics only after Second World War though nationalist ideals foreshadowed in his earlier student days in London. Chairman Kedah branch United Malays National Organisation (U.M.N.O.), 1949, National President U.M.N.O., 1951. From this time onwards, he became the main architect of Malayan independence, heading the 'Merdeka' (Freedom) movement and the Alliance Party, which was a combination of U.M.N.O., the Malayan Chinese Association (M.C.A.), and the Malayan Indian Congress (M.I.C.). Prime Minister of Malaya at the time of Independence, August 1957, and Prime Minister of Malaysia, 1963.

BEN GURION, David, b. 1896, educated privately and Istanbul University. Earlier family name, Green. Settled in Palestine, 1906, exiled by Turks as a Zionist, 1915, went to America, enrolled in Jewish Legion. Member General Council of Zionist Organisation, 1920. Secretary-General of General Federation of Jewish Labour, 1921–35. Chairman Jewish Agency for Palestine, 1935–48. Proclaimed Independence of Israel, May 1948, and became Head of the Provisional Government and Minister of Defence. Prime Minister and Minister of Defence, 1949–53, and 1955–63. Leader of Labour Party. Writings include *The Struggle* (5 vols), *Israel at War, Rebirth and Destiny of Israel, Ben Gurion Looks Back* and several other books and articles.

CHIANG KAI-SHEK, b. 1887, educated as military officer, partly in Tokyo. Friend and associate of Sun Yat-sen. Became Principal of Whampoa Military Academy, 1924. Took command of Kuomintang forces reunifying China, 1925–8. Married Mayling Soong (sister of Mme Sun Yat-sen), 1927. Led purge against Communists, 1927.

Chairman of National Government, 1928; President of National Military Council, 1932–46. Director-General of Kuomintang, 1938. Defensive war against Japan from 1937. Supreme Commander of Allied Forces, China, 1942–5. President of Republic of China, 1948. Civil war with Communists, 1946–9. Retired with rump of Nationalist forces to Formosa (Taiwan), 1949, and resumed title of President. Writings include *China's Destiny, The Collected Wartime Messages of Generalissimo Chiang Kai-shek 1937–1945, Soviet Russia in China.*

GANDHI, Mohandas Karamchand, b. western India, 1869, educated London University and Inns of Court. Practised law in India, 1891, went to South Africa, 1893, where he worked for many years in the interests of overseas Indians. Organised ambulance corps in the Boer War, 1899–1902, and the Zulu rebellion, 1906. After an extensive and lasting experience of campaigning for the human rights of Indians in South Africa, he returned to India in 1914 where his name was known only in limited circles. Associated himself with G. K. Gokhale and the Indian National Congress and introduced his idea of *Satyagraha*, or soul force, as a reply to forms of political and social injustice. Took charge of the newspaper *Young India* and became a popular leader in the nationalist upsurge in India in the years which immediately followed the First World War. Arrested, 1922, and sentenced to six years' imprisonment for sedition; released on grounds of ill-health 1924, and remained fairly quiet politically until about 1928, giving attention to the problems of village communities and the big issue of caste in Indian society. Active again in Congress, 1928–30, and initiated a civil disobedience campaign in 1930. Arrested 1930, released 1931. Talks with Lord Irwin, Viceroy, 1931 and attended Round Table Conference in England in the same year. Started civil disobedience again and arrested and imprisoned, 1932–3, and 1934. Less in the Congress movement as such from this time onwards. Had long developed a habit of ritual fasting in the interests of a cause and this challenged his health very seriously at times. Associated with Congress in its attitude of conditional support only for Britain in the early years of the Second World War and to the fore in the 'Quit India' movement of 1942. Imprisoned, 1942–4. Discussions with Jinnah, 1944. Worked to try to prevent the partition of India and to try, at village level, to lessen the effects of communalism about the time of Partition, 1946–7. Assassinated by a Hindu fanatic, 1948. The extensive bibliography on Gandhi includes an *Autobiography*, first published in 1927.

GOKHALE, Gopal Krishna, Indian 'liberal' nationalist and politician, b. 1866, educated Deccan College and Bombay (B.A.), Elphinstone College. Became schoolmaster. Secretary of the first Bombay Provincial Conference of the Indian National Congress in 1888, Gokhale increasingly gave his time and energies to political life. A 'moderate' and constitutionalist, he offered a striking contrast to B. G. Tilak who might be described as his older contemporary. Both men respected each other despite sharp differences at times. Gokhale led the moderate elements in Congress for many years. In England several times, first visit 1897. Member Supreme Legislative Council of British India, 1901. Founded The Servants of India Society, 1905, to help train Indian leaders and prepare them for public life in the national cause. Worked for social reform programmes such as the extension of education and the abolition of indentured labour. Outspoken on occasion and not lacking in courage, Gokhale held a weakened Congress together after the split of 1907. Until his death in 1915 he continued to work for home rule for India within a parliamentary setting and in the framework of the British connection. Writings include various collected works of speeches and writings.

HATTA, Mohammed, b. 1902, educated (economics) Rotterdam, where he founded the Indonesian Association. Became, 1932, Chairman of the Indonesian National Education Club in Java. Arrested along with Sjahrir and exiled, 1934. Liberated by the Japanese occupation of the Dutch East Indies. Co-operated at surface level with the Japanese in order to gain concessions for Indonesian nationalism. Appointed Vice-President of the newly-proclaimed Indonesian Republic in 1945 and continued to serve in a Vice-Presidential role, subject to the limitations of circumstances, during the struggle with the Dutch, until 1956. Led the Indonesian delegation to the Round Table Conference at The Hague, 1949. Differed with President Sukarno on matters of national policy and retired from office, 1956.

HO CHI MINH, b. 1890. Vietnamese nationalist; lived in France shortly after the First World War and became a member of the French Socialist Party. In Soviet Union, 1924. In China during revolutionary period, 1925–7, then went to Siam (Thailand). Imprisoned for political activities in Hong Kong, 1931. Led struggle for independence in Vietnam during Second World War. Declared President of the Democratic Republic of Vietnam, 1945. Refused to come to terms with France and continued to fight as guerilla leader of the Vietminh. President and Prime Minister of North Vietnam following the 1954 Armistice Agreement. Resigned as Premier, 1955, but continued as President. Writings include *Prison Diary* and other works in collected form.

JINNAH, Mohammed Ali, Indian/Pakistani nationalist and statesman, b. Karachi 1876, educated Lincoln's Inn, London, 1892–6, and practised law in Bombay. In sympathy with the moderate leaders of the Indian National Congress but also concerned to preserve the identity of the Indian Muslim. Jinnah, in his own words, aimed at becoming 'the Moslem Gokhale'. He was a member of the Indian National Congress from 1906 to 1921 and worked for Hindu–Muslim unity within what was a predominantly Hindu organisation. He also became a member of the All-India Muslim League and assisted in the creation of the Lucknow Pact, 1916, which provided for separate Muslim electorates and electoral weighting. His proposals for unity were not supported by the more conservative Muslim leaders. Jinnah saw the Muslim Khalifate movement at the end of the First World War as irrelevant and damaging to the cause of Indian nationalism and he could not respond to the appeal of Gandhian policies in the period 1920–2. Temperamentally, Jinnah and Ghandi were far apart and Jinnah saw in Ghandi's 'soul force' doctrine and asceticism elements of Hindu revivalism. Jinnah seemed to have no very strong personal following in the 1920s but he attended the first two series of the Round Table Conferences in London (1930–2) and stayed in London until 1934. In the next five years Jinnah has been politically interpreted by some observers as moving from a position of 'nationalist Muslim' to one of 'Muslim nationalist'. In this connection some influence may be attributed to Dr Mohamed Iqbal who had conceived earlier the idea of a separate Muslim state. Jinnah became an effective leader of the All-India Muslim League but he and the Congress leaders were unable to achieve a *modus vivendi* on the working of the Government of India Act of 1935. By 1940, Jinnah was virtually committed to a separate state policy for Muslims, and the imprisonment of Congress leaders during the years 1942–5 strengthened his role and that of his Association. The rest of his political career is wrapped in the story of negotiation, Partition and the inauguration of Pakistan (1947) of which he became the first Governor-General. He died, after only one year of very difficult office, in 1948.

KEMAL, Mustafa (Atatürk), b. Salonika 1881, trained as military officer in Ottoman army; lieutenant, 1902; captain, 1905. Somewhat infected by revolutionary ideas by this stage. Sent on military-diplomatic mission to Tripoli, 1908. Helped to put down the counter-revolution against the Young Turks, 1909, and began to play a part in politics, while stressing, at the same time, the need for both a strong army and a strong political party. Served in the Balkan Wars and, with great distinction, in the 1914–18 war, especially at Gallipoli. Led a movement of resistance to Allied occupations in Asia Minor after the war and resigned from the army in order to fulfil a political role. His resignation hardly pre-dated his dismissal for, by this time, he was at odds with the Sultan's government in Constantinople. By the end of 1919 he was President of a Defence of Rights Congress held in Armenia and was laying down the two principles of rights of the nation and will of the people. At this time Kemal had support only from a small part of Turkey, representing less than a quarter of the country, but he successfully defied the Sultan and campaigned for the downfall of the Cabinet. A British military occupation of Constantinople helped the nationalist cause it was intended to hinder and Kemal set up a Nationalist regime at Angora (Ankara). There followed civil war against the Sultan's forces, war against the penetrating Greeks, a great deal of diplomatic negotiation and, finally, the establishment of the Turkish Republic and the deposition of Sultan and Caliphate (1923). Kemal became the new President and from then until his death in 1938 his career and the patterns of modern Turkey are inextricably interrelated.

KOTELAWALA, Sir John, b. 1897, educated Cambridge and Colombo, Ceylon. Member State Council, Ceylon, 1931. Minister for Agriculture and Lands, 1933. Minister for Communications and Works, 1935. Minister for Transport and Works, 1947–53. Founder-member of United National Party and President of the party until 1958. Leader of the House in Ceylon Parliament, 1950–6; Prime Minister and Minister of Defence, 1953–6. Writings include *An Asian Prime Minister's Story*.

LEE KUAN YEW, b. 1923, educated Singapore and Cambridge University (law). Founder member of socialist People's Action Party, (P.A.P.) Singapore, 1954, and Secretary-General of the Party. Member Singapore Legislative Assembly, 1955. Led the P.A.P. to convincing electoral victory, 1959. First Prime Minister of Singapore, 1959. Worked for merger of Singapore with Malaya and, in due course, with Malaysia (1963) but differences of outlook and policy between the Singapore and

Malayan governments caused him to put the case for secession. Writings include *Battle for Merger*, on the negotiations for a Singapore–Malaya merger.

MAO TSE-TUNG, b. 1893, Hunan province, China, son of a farming family. Educated at schools in Hsiang Hsiang and Changsha in Hunan. Became an assistant librarian at Peking University, 1918. Founder-member Chinese Communist Party, 1921; worked for a united national-ist front with the Kuomintang party, 1923, but organised for socialist revolution based on peasant and workers' support. Final break with Kuomintang in 1927. Established areas of Communist control in Hunan and Kiangsi, 1927–34. A leader of the Long March to Shensi in west China, 1934, and organiser of political cadres and areas of com-munist control. War against Japan, 1937–45, and the growth of an uneasy truce with the Kuomintang under Chiang Kai-shek. Negotia-tions with Chiang Kai-shek, 1945, the first meeting of the two for some twenty years. Civil war against Kuomintang, 1946–9. Chairman, Central People's Government of People's Republic of China, 1949. Continued to preside over and influence revolutionary China, and his full historical role remains to be assessed. Writings include, *Selected Works of Mao Tse-tung*, *37 Poems of President Mao*.

NEHRU, Jawaharlal, Indian nationalist and statesman, b. 1889, educated Harrow, Cambridge and Inner Temple. Practised law in India. Joined Indian National Congress, 1913, met Gandhi 1916. Imprisoned during time of civil disobedience campaigns, 1921–2 and 1922–3. Member Working Committee of Congress, 1924. Attended anti-imperialist congress in Brussels, 1927; visited Moscow, 1927. General Secretary of Congress, 1928; President, 1930. Imprisoned for much of the period, 1931–5. President of Congress again, 1936. Opposed to Government of India Act of 1935 and to any trends to divide India arising from the policy of the All-India Muslim League. In favour of conditional co-operation with Britain in early years of Second World War but eventually joined the Quit India campaign of 1942. Imprisoned, 1942–5. Took part in discussions on political future of India at Simla, 1945 and 1946. President of Congress, 1946. Vice-President of Executive Council, 1946. Prime Minister of India, 1947–64; during this period his career and the contemporary history and politics of India are too closely connected to allow a brief summary. His attempts to create and main-tain a secular state in India called for great powers of leadership and statesmanship. Extensive writings include *Towards Freedom, The Discovery of India, Glimpses of World History* and many collected works.

NURI ES-SAID (Nuri as-Said), b. 1888, Iraqi military leader and states-man. Military training, Istanbul 1903–6 and 1910–12 (Staff College). Army officer on active service in Balkan War, 1912. Influenced towards Arab nationalism by new trends of Turkish nationalism, 1908–14. Joined Arab officers' secret nationalist society, *al-Ahad*, 1913. In Cairo 1915, at the time of the Hussein–McMahon correspondence, and took part with Iraqi volunteers in the Arab Revolt. At the Paris Peace Conference, 1919, and closely associated with King Faisal and with the establishment of the new State of Iraq. Chief of Staff in newly con-structed Iraq army, 1921. Minister of Defence in new Iraqi constitution, 1922. Deputy Commander-in-Chief of the Army (under the King), 1924, and from 1925–30 mainly engaged on military and defence matters. As Foreign Minister he helped negotiate the Anglo-Iraq treaty of 1930, bringing the Mandate period to an end. Prime Minister of Iraq, 1930, helped to establish friendly relations between the new independent Iraq (1932) and other States and to negotiate Iraq's entry into the League of Nations. Nuri's policies did not go unchallenged in Iraq and opponents called for revisions of the treaty with Britain. By the end of 1932 he had lost the premiership but became Foreign Minister again under Raschid Ali. After the *coup* of Bakr Sidki in 1936, Nuri had a period of exile in Egypt, returning to be Iraq's Prime Minister for the greater part of the next twenty years, but the ups and downs of his career defy a summary. He was Iraq's representative to the Arab League in Cairo, 1945. His Iraq-centred pan-Arabism brought hostility from revolutionary Egypt and his pro-British and pro-Western leanings and work for the Baghdad Pact brought him enemies at home. He was assassinated, in 1958, during a military *coup* which also had the young king, Faisal II and other members of the royal family among its victims.

SJAHRIR, Sœtan, b. 1909, educated (law) Leyden University, active member of Indonesian Association (with Hatta) in Holland. Member of Indonesian National Education Club (also with Hatta); arrested (1934) and exiled until liberated by the Japanese. Became an active underground and anti-Japanese worker for Indonesian nationalism. An intellectual and a socialist, his writings include *Our Struggle* (1945) and *Out of Exile* (written mainly during years of exile and published later). Formed a new Socialist Party, 1945, and was Prime Minister, subject to the limitations of circumstances, 1945–7. His Socialist Party remained small but influential for several years; increasingly his views and those of President Sukarno differed. Arrested, 1962; he later retired from active politics, d. 1966.

SUKARNO, Achmed, b. 1901, educated (engineering) Bandung. Indonesian nationalist, active from about 1927. A leader of the Indonesian Nationalist Party (P.N.I.) and later its President. Arrested for nationalist activities, 1929; in prison until 1932. Joined the *Partai Indonesia*, later became its President. Arrested, 1933, and exiled to island of Flores, later transferred to Sumatra and released through Japanese occupation, 1942. Worked above ground, and at the risk of collaboration, for Indonesian nationalism during the Japanese period. Proclaimed the Republic of Indonesia, August 1945. President of the Republic, 1945–9. President of the United States of Indonesia, 1949; re-named Republic, 1950. Head of State, 1963–6, and concurrently Prime Minister, 1959–66. Protagonist of 'Guided Democracy' at the centre, and head of political groupings; fall from high office linked with Army and students' attitudes and popular reaction to a pro-communist *coup* of 1965.

SUN YAT-SEN, b. 1866 near Canton, educated Anglican school, Hawaii and Queen's College, Hong Kong (medicine). Active in the 1890s in anti-Manchu revolutionary organisations, mainly outside China and particularly among Chinese in the West and in Japan. Founded the 'Revive China' society in 1895 and, about ten years later, the 'Common Alliance League'. Sun's appeal to anti-Manchu traditions in south China brought him a varied following and sparked off a number of insurrections before the final successful revolution of October 1911 which overthrew the Manchu dynasty. Sun was made President of the new Republic but power went to military leader, Yuan Shih-kai, who quickly replaced him in the presidential office. Disappointed, Sun retired to Japan for a time. He married as his second wife Soong Ching Ling, daughter of a Westernised and prospering Chinese family. In the upheavals in China which followed the death of Yuan Shih-kai (1916) and the end of the First World War, Sun could plan anew for revolutionary change and, in 1921, he set up a new government at Canton with his revived Kuomintang party (or 'national peoples party') which dated from the previous revolution. Sun remained apparently at the helm of the reunification movement in China under the Kuomintang, with

Chiang Kai-shek as his military leader, and with help from the Soviet Union and the incipient Chinese Communist Party, until his death in 1925. Since he did not live to see the final split between the Kuomintang and the Communists his legacy has been claimed by both. Writings include *Sun Yat-sen, Memoirs of A Chinese Revolutionary* and various collected writings and speeches.

TILAK, Bal Gangadhar, Indian nationalist, b. 1856, educated Deccan College and Bombay (B.A.), Elphinstone College. Helped found a private school, Poona, 1880. Set up in journalism, 1881, editing, first, the *Mahratta*, in English, then *Kesari*, in Marathi. Involved as an editor in a number of disputed cases and, in 1897, gaoled for eighteen months on charges of publishing seditious material. By the turn of the century, he had become a prominent member of the Indian National Congress seeking to direct policy along lines which were at the same time more traditional and more dynamic. He used his newspaper to lend support to his political activities and led the movement for a 'new' or 'nationalist' party within Congress, breaking, in 1907, with the 'moderates', led by G. K. Gokhale. Arrested, 1908, on charges of sedition and sentenced to six years' imprisonment, served in Mandalay gaol, Burma. Returned to Poona, 1914, rather quieter and less influential than six years earlier. Active again in a reunited Congress, 1916. In England, 1918–19, working for home rule for India, d. 1920 at Bombay. Known by the honoured title, 'Lokamanya', or 'revered by the people'. Writings include a number of books on Hindu themes and various collected works.

TOJO HIDEKI, Japanese militarist-nationalist, b. Tokyo 1884. Army officer training, Imperial Military Academy, Tokyo. Military attaché to Japanese embassy, Berlin, 1919 and various War Office posts after return to Japan. Commander of the 1st infantry regiment which took part in a mutiny of the Tokyo garrison in 1936; commander of the gendarmery headquarters, 1937 and soon afterwards, chief of staff of the army in south Manchuria. Minister of War in the Prince Konoye cabinet of July, 1940 and succeeded Konoye as Prime Minister in October, 1941. Leading protagonist of Japan's pro-Axis and 'greater East Asia' programmes; declared war on the United States of America after the Japanese attack on Pearl Harbor, December, 1941. As the war progressed, he increasingly took on a dictatorial role. Forced out of office, July 1944, through the mounting pressures of defeat. Attempted suicide after the Japanese surrender in 1945, but lived to face a war crimes trial and was executed, 1948. Tojo's career can be seen to epitomise the militarist-nationalist tendencies which gradually came to dominate Japanese politics in the decade before Pearl Harbor.

U Nu, b. 1907, educated Rangoon University: schoolmaster and nationalist politician; devout Buddhist. Imprisoned for nationalist activities at outbreak of Second World War. Released through Japanese occupation of Burma. Minister of Foreign Affairs in Burma's wartime government, 1943–4, Minister for Publicity and Propaganda, 1944–5. Vice-President, Anti-Fascist People's League at the end of the war. First Prime Minister of Burma 1948–56; resigned to reorganise political groupings. Prime Minister again, 1957–8 and, with other posts, 1960–2. Writings include *Burma under Japanese Occupation* and plays and stories.

Further Reading

(Works quoted in the Source Readings are included, together with a short selection of modern publications)

NATIONALISM

Carr, E. H. *Nationalism and After*, Macmillan, 1945

Hayes, C. J. H. *Essays on Nationalism*, New York, Macmillan, 1926
  The Historical Evolution of Modern Nationalism, New York, R. Smith, 1931

Kohn, H. *Nationalism*, Van Nostrand, 1955
  The Idea of Nationalism, New York, Macmillan, 1944

Royal Institute of International Affairs, *Nationalism*, O.U.P., 1939–63

Snyder, L. *The Dynamics of Nationalism*, Van Nostrand, 1964

Thayer, P. W. (ed.). *Nationalism and Progress in Free Asia*, Johns Hopkins, 1956

ASIA IN GENERAL

Brecher, M. *The New States of Asia*, O.U.P., 1963

Buss, C. A. *Asia in the Modern World*, Collier–Macmillan, 1964

Clyde, P. H. *The Far East: a History of the Impact of the West on Eastern Asia*, 3rd ed., Prentice Hall, 1958

Dawson, C. *The Revolt of Asia*, Sheed & Ward, 1950

Easton, S. C. *The Rise & Fall of Western Colonialism*, Praeger, 1964

Edwardes, M. *Asia in the European Age, 1498–1955*, Thames & Hudson, 1961

Harris, R. *Independence and After. Revolution in Underdeveloped Countries*, O.U.P., 1962

Jansen, G. H. *Afro-Asia and Non-Alignment*, Faber, 1966

London, K. (ed.). *New Nations in a Divided World: The International relations of the Afro-Asian States*, Praeger, 1963

Kahin, McT. G. (ed.). *Major Governments of Asia*, 2nd ed., Cornell, 1963

Michael, F. H. & Taylor, G. E. *The Far East in the Modern World*, Methuen, 1956

Pannikar, K. M. *Asia and Western Dominance*, Allen & Unwin, 1955
Pearson, J. D. *Oriental and Asian Bibliography*, Crosby Lockwood, 1966
Rose, S. (ed.). *Politics in Southern Asia*, Macmillan, 1962
Tinker, H. *Ballot Box and Bayonet*, O.U.P., 1964
   South Asia, A Short History, Pall Mall, 1966
Wint, G. *Spotlight on Asia*, Penguin, 1955/59

JAPAN

Beasley, W. G. *The Modern History of Japan*, Weidenfeld & Nicolson, 1963
Beckman, G. M. *The Modernisation of China and Japan*, Harper & Row, 1965
Blond, G. *Admiral Togo*, Jarrolds, 1961
Bush, L. *Land of the Dragonfly*, Hale, 1959
Butow, J. C. *Tojo and the Coming of War*, Princeton U.P., 1961
Chamberlin, W. H. *Japan in China*, Duckworth, 1928
Chong, Sik-Lee. *The Politics of Korean Nationalism*, California U.P., 1963
Dening, E. *Japan*, Praeger, 1961
Grew, J. C. *Ten Years in Japan*, Hammond, 1944
Hibino, Y. *Nippon Shindo Ron or The National Ideals of the Japanese People*, C.U.P., 1928
James, D. H. *The Rise and Fall of the Japanese Empire*, Allen & Unwin, 1951
Kennedy, M. *A History of Japan*, Weidenfeld & Nicolson, 1963
Latourette, K. S. *The History of Japan*, Macmillan, 1957
McCune, S. *Korea, Land of Broken Calm*, Van Nostrand, 1966
Morris, I. I. *Nationalism and the Right Wing in Japan*, O.U.P., 1960
Okakura-Kakuzo, *The Awakening of Japan*, John Murray, 1905
Rees, D. *Korea, The Limited War*, Macmillan, 1964
Reichauer, E. O. *Japan Past and Present*, 3rd ed., Duckworth, 1964
Shigemitsu, M. *Japan and Her Destiny*, Hutchinson, 1958
Storry, R. *A History of Modern Japan*, Penguin, 1961
   Japan, O.U.P., 1965
Tiedemann, A. *Modern Japan*, Van Nostrand, 1955
Ward, R. E. and Dankwart, A. R. *Political Modernisation in Japan and Turkey*, Princeton U.P., 1964

CHINA

Beckman, G. M. *The Modernisation of China and Japan*, Harper & Row, 1965

Bland, J. C. P. and Backhouse, E. *China under the Empress Dowager*, Heinemann, 1911

Brandt, C. Schwartz, B. and Fairbank, J. K. *A Documentary History of Chinese Communism*, Allen & Unwin, 1952

Chen, J. *Mao and the Chinese Revolution*, O.U.P., 1965

Chiang Kai-shek. *Soviet Russia in China*, Harrap, 1957

Clubb, O. E. *20th-Century China*, Columbia U.P., 1964

Cohen, A. A. *The Communism of Mao Tse-tung*, Chicago U.P., 1964

Fitzgerald, C. P. *The Chinese View of their place in the world*, O.U.P., 1964
The Birth of Communist China, Penguin, 1964
A Concise History of East Asia, Heinemann, 1966

Hughes, E. R. *The Invasion of China by the Western World*, A. & C. Black, 1937

Johnson, C. A. *Peasant Nationalism and Communist Power (1937–1945)*, Stanford U.P., 1963

Kuo Ping-chia. *China, New Age and Outlook*, Penguin, 1956/60

Lamb, Alistair, *The China–India Border*, O.U.P., 1964

Latourette, K. S. *The Chinese, Their History and Culture*, 3rd ed., Macmillan, 1956
A History of modern China, Penguin, 1954

Mende, T. *The Chinese Revolution*, Thames and Hudson, 1961

Payne, R. *Portrait of a Revolutionary: Mao Tse-tung*, Abelard Schumann, 1961

Purcell, V. *The Boxer Uprising, 1900*, C.U.P., 1963
China, Benn, 1962

Lewis, J. W. *Leadership in Communist China*, Cornell U.P., 1963

Schram, S. R. *The Political Thought of Mao Tse-tung*, Pall Mall, 1963
Mao Tse-tung, Penguin, 1966

Snow, E. *Red Star over China*, Gollancz, 1937

Wang, Y. C. *Chinese Intellectuals and the West, 1872–1949*, O.U.P., 1966

Watson, F. *The Frontiers of China*, Chatto & Windus, 1966

Wint, G. *Communist China's Crusade*, Pall Mall, 1965

THE INDIAN SUBCONTINENT

Banerjea, Sir S. *A Nation in the Making*, O.U.P., 1925/63

Q

Bhattacharyya, S. N. *Mahatma Gandhi the Journalist*, Asia Publishing House, 1965

Besant, A. *India Bond or Free?* G. P. Putnam's, 1926

Bolitho, H. *Jinnah*, John Murray, 1954

Brecher, M. *Nehru, a Political Biography*, O.U.P., 1959

Edwardes, M. *The Last Years of British India*, Cassell, 1963

Gopal, R. *British Rule in India, An Assessment*, Asia Publishing House, 1963

  Lokamanya Tilak, a Biography, Asia Publishing House, 1956/65

Heimsath, C. H. *Indian Nationalism and Hindu Social Reform*, Princeton U.P., 1964

Jeffries, Sir S. *Ceylon. The Path to Independence*, Pall Mall, 1962

Kotelawala, Sir J. *An Asian Prime Minister's Story*, Harrap, 1956

Ludowyk, E. F. C. *The Modern History of Ceylon*, Weidenfeld & Nicolson, 1966

Malik, H. *Moslem Nationalism in India and Pakistan*, Public Affairs Press, 1963

Menon, V. P. *The Transfer of Power in India*, Longmans, 1957

Misra, B. B. *The Indian Middle Classes: their Growth in Modern Times*, O.U.P., 1961

Moon, P. *Divide and Quit*, Chatto & Windus, 1961

Morris-Jones, W. H. *The Government and Politics of India*, Hutchinson, 1964

Nanda, B. R. *Mahatma Gandhi*, Allen & Unwin, 1958

Nehru, J. *An Autobiography*, Bodley Head, 1936/53

  A Bundle of Old Letters, Asia Publishing House, 1958

Philips, C. H. (ed.). *The Evolution of India and Pakistan*, O.U.P., 1962

  (ed.). *Politics and Society in India*, Allen & Unwin, 1963

Segal, R. *The Crisis of India*, Penguin, 1965

Smith, D. G. *India as a Secular State*, Princeton U.P., 1963

Spear, P. *The Oxford History of Modern India*, O.U.P., 1965

Stephens, I. *Pakistan*, Benn, 1963

Tinker, H. *India and Pakistan: a Short Political Guide*, Pall Mall, 1962

Wolpert, S. A. *Tilak and Gokhale*, California U.P., 1962

SOUTH-EAST ASIA

Brackman, A. C. *Indonesian Communism, a History*, Praeger, 1963

Busch, N. F. *Thailand: an introduction to Modern Siam*, 2nd ed., Van Nostrand, 1964

Butwell, R. *U Nu of Burma*, Stanford, U.P., 1963

Crozier, B. *South-east Asia in Turmoil*, Penguin, 1966

Fall, B. *The Two Viet-Nams*, Pall Mall, 1963
  Vietnam Witness, 1953–1966, Pall Mall, 1966

Grant, B. *Indonesia*, C.U.P., 1964

Fitzgerald, C. P. *The Third China,The Chinese Communities in South-East Asia*, Angus & Robertson, 1965

Furnivall, J. S. *Colonial policy and Practice*, New York, C.U.P., 1948/56

Gettlemann, M. E. (ed.). *Vietnam*, Penguin, 1965

Gullick, J. M. *Malaya*, Benn, 1963

Hall, D. G. E. *A History of South-East Asia*, 2nd ed., Macmillan, 1964

Harrison, B. *A Short History of South-East Asia*, 3rd ed., Macmillan, 1966

Kennedy, J. *A History of Malaya, A.D. 1400–1959*, Macmillan, 1962/7

Lancaster, D. *The Emancipation of French Indo-China*, O.U.P., 1961

Miller, H. *Prince and Premier*, Faber, 1959
  The Story of Malaysia, Faber, 1965

Nu, Thakin (U Nu). *Burma Under the Japanese*, Macmillan, 1954

Neuchterlein, D. E. *Thailand and the Struggle for South-East Asia*, Cornell, 1965

Palmier, L. *Indonesia and the Dutch*, O.U.P., 1962

Purcell, V. *The Chinese in Southeast Asia*, 2nd ed., O.U.P., 1965
  The Revolution in Southeast Asia, Thames & Hudson, 1962

Ratnam, K. J. *Communalism and the Political Process in Malaya*, University of Malaya Press, 1965

Sjahrir, S. *Out of Exile*, John Day, 1947

Smith, T. E. *The Background to Malaysia*, Kuala Lumpur, O.U.P., 1963/5

Taylor, G. E. *The Philippines and the United States: Problems of Partnership*, Praeger, 1964

Tinker, H. *The Union of Burma*, O.U.P., 1961

Tsuji, H. *Singapore, The Japanese Version*, Constable, 1962

Woodman, D. *The Making of Burma*, Cresset, 1962
  The Republic of Indonesia, Cresset, 1956

WESTERN ASIA

Afifi, M. El-Hadi. *The Arabs and the United Nations*, Longmans, 1964

Ben Gurion, D. *The Jews in Their Land*, Longmans, 1964, Aldus Books, 1966

Bentwich, N. *Israel Resurgent*, Benn, 1960

Birdwood, Lord, *Nuri as-Said*, Cassell, 1959

Edelman, M. *Ben Gurion, a Political Biography*, Hodder & Stoughton, 1964

Elston, D. R. *Israel, The Making of a Nation*, O.U.P., 1963

Kirk, G. E. *A Short History of the Middle East*, Methuen, 1948/64

Harari, M. *Government and Politics of the Middle East*, Prentice Hall, 1962

Haim, S. G. (ed.). *Arab Nationalism*, California U.P., 1962

Hourani, A. H. *Syria and Lebanon, a Political Essay*, O.U.P./R.I.I.A., 1946

Khadduri, M. *Independent Iraq, 1932–1958*, 2nd ed., O.U.P., 1960

Kinross, Lord, *Ataturk*, Weidenfeld & Nicolson, 1964

Laqueur, W. Z. *Communism and Nationalism in the Middle-East*, Routledge, 1956

Lawrence, T. E. *Seven Pillars of Wisdom*, Penguin, 1962 (originally 1926)

Lewis, B. *The Middle East and the West*, Weidenfeld & Nicolson, 1964

Lewis, G. *Turkey*, Benn, 1955/9

MacDonald, R. W. *The League of Arab States*, Princeton U.P., 1965

Monroe, E. *Britain's Moment in the Middle East, 1914–56*, Chatto & Windus, 1963

Mousa, S. *T. E. Lawrence, An Arab View*, O.U.P., 1966

Rondot, P. (trans. Mary Dilke). *The Changing Patterns of the Middle East, 1919–1958*, Chatto & Windus, 1961

Royal Institute of International Affairs. *The Middle East, A Political and Economic Survey*, O.U.P., 1950

Tutsch, H. E. *From Ankara to Marrakesh: Turks and Arabs in a Changing World*, Allen & Unwin, 1964

Ward, R. E. and Dankwart, A. R. *Political Modernisation in Japan and Turkey*, Princeton U.P., 1964

Yale, W. *The Near East. A Modern History*, Ann Arbor, 1958.

PERIODICALS

(A short selection from a wide range)

Foreign Affairs, Council of Foreign Relations Inc.

International Affairs, Chatham House

Journal of Asian Studies, The Association of Asian Studies Inc.

Journal of South-East Asian History, University of Malaya/Singapore
Modern Asian Studies, Cambridge
Pacific Affairs, Institute of Pacific Relations
St Antony's Papers, Middle Eastern Affairs, Far Eastern Affairs, Chatto
    & Windus
The World Today, Chatham House
World Politics, Princeton

Index